LIVING HISTORY CHRONICLES

GWILYM JONES, MM

Published by

GENERAL STORE
GSPH PUBLISHING HOUSE

Box 28, 1694B Burnstown, Ontario, Canada K0J 1G0
Telephone (613) 432-7697 or 1-800-465-6072

ISBN 1-894263-50-2
Printed and bound in Canada

Cover Art by Joe Evans
Cover and Layout by Derek McEwen

General Store Publishing House
Burnstown, Ontario, Canada

National Library of Canada Cataloguing in Publication Data

Jones, Gwilym (Gwilym Thomas), 1920-
Living history chronicles

ISBN 1-894263-50-2

1. World War, 1939-1945–Personal narratives, Canadian.
2. Korean War, 1950-1953–Personal narratives, Canadian.
I. Title.

D811.A2J66 2001 940.54'8171 C2001-902865-2

Contents

Foreword

This book is the work of Gwilym Jones, who has devoted considerable effort to assembling the accounts of Canadian, British and Polish veterans of the three services through the wars of World War II and Korea—the latter being "the forgotten war," in which some 27,000 Canadians served through 1950–54.

It is particularly interesting that Gwilym chronicled the experiences of more than the combatants; he included some of the army's essential support: the Signals, Service Corps and Electrical & Mechanical Engineers, whose collective support was essential to the army's combat effectiveness.

The presence of the WRNS, CWAC and RCAF (WD) stories will surely bring forth many cherished memories and expand the knowledge of non-veterans on the essential work achieved by these pioneering women in uniform in the navy, army and air force.

The paratrooper writings will undoubtedly enlighten the readers on these innovators of air-landed warfare and one can look to the SAS for that rare specialty of trouble-shooters. The Polish Army inclusion is a good reminder of the two Polish Armies that fought alongside our soldiers in the Italian and Northwest Europe Campaigns.

Veterans' memories often focus on the hilarious, and the readers will enjoy these moments, notwithstanding the gruesome facts of war. The recollections of lost friends in combat is always there, a reminder of the 40,000 fatal casualties of WW II lying mostly in Commonwealth war graves wherever the troops "fought and stayed."

Gwilym's "Ode to Wally" is especially touching and brings to mind the deep feelings of our war history and our passage through time, just as McRae felt when he wrote "In Flanders' Fields."

As a veteran of the Korean War, I can readily empathize with the infantrymen whose chronicles appear here. I was a tank troop leader, privileged to fight from a Sherman M4AE28, but I did get my rest in a bunker just like my patrolling and trench-warfare friends. It was my honour to visit the Commonealth Cemetery in Pusan and deliver a eulogy over the majority of our 516 fatal casualties of the Korean War who are buried there.

May you all enjoy, relive and learn from these recollections of wartime veterans.

J.P. Robert LaRose
Major General (ret)
Past Colonel Commandant RCAC

Acknowledgements

I wish to express my deep appreciation to Judy Felce for her invaluable assistance in the preparation of the manuscript for this book; also to John Payne for making copies of the photographs contained herein. The branch murals portrayed in this book were painted by RCL Branch 258 branch artist Joe Evans; photographs courtesy of the author. The 1998 group photograph was taken by Alan Miller. Thanks also to Major General (ret) Bob LaRose, past colonel commandant of the Royal Canadian Armoured Corps, for his efforts in obtaining permission for me to use some of the military maps and photographs reproduced in this book, courtesy of the *RCAC Illustrated History* (Marteinson and McNorgan), the Canadian War Museum and the National Archives.

My special thanks go to the thirty-three veterans who shared some of their wartime memories to make this book possible. I also owe a special debt of gratitude to Bob Stone, secretary of the Living History Speakers Bureau RCL Branch 258, not only for his editorial contributions but also for providing willing assistance whenever called upon; I am most grateful for his counsel.

I also wish to thank designer Derek McEwen, editor Jane Karchmar, publicist Rosemary Kenopic, and publisher Tim Gordon of General Store Publishing House for putting it all together.

Also, thanks to my many friends and colleagues who gave me moral support and inspiration to help ensure in some small way that our efforts during wartime are not forgotten. Oral accounts of our experiences die with us, but the written word lasts forever.

Group photograph of members of Living History Speakers Bureau RCL Branch 258 (1988).

INTRODUCTION

These are the stories of a group of World War II and Korean War veterans who are affiliated with the Royal Canadian Legion Branch 258, Highland Creek, Ontario, in the Greater Toronto area. It is a compilation of the most memorable wartime experiences of thirty-three veterans of those wars. They are members of the Living History Speakers Bureau RCL Branch 258, an organization whose primary objective is to ensure that today's history students become aware of, and take pride in, their Canadian heritage through the anecdotal presentations of those terrible events.

Members' wartime experiences include serving in the navy, air force, army (including paratroopers, infantry, signals, artillery, armoured corps, service corps, and other support units), the WRNS, and the Women's Division RCAF. There are also former prisoners of war, London Blitz evacuees, an armed forces CWAC entertainer, and members of the Polish Army, which was an integral part of the Canadian campaigns in northwest Europe.

The Living History Speakers Bureau is composed chiefly of active service veterans of RCL Branch 258 plus women members with wartime experience. Membership, however, is not restricted to RCL Branch members but is open to any wartime veteran regardless of affiliation. The bureau services all areas of Greater Toronto and speakers are available throughout the school year, not just for the November observances. These veterans also appear by request at other community functions, including citizenship ceremonies conducted by the Federal Citizenship Court. Participation in the Citizenship Court ceremonies this year involved some 900 new citizens from twenty-five different countries.

Since October 1998, presentations have been made at some 150 local schools involving approximately 15,000 students plus over 1,000 adults in attendance. Response by teachers, students, and interested others to these appearances has been invariably positive.

This book has grown out of a desire by members to further these efforts. Each chapter is devoted to an individual veteran and includes a brief biographical sketch along with his or her story. By reading books like this one, future generations may acquire a better understanding of what Dad, Mom, Grandma and Grandpa experienced during the Great Depression and the devastating conflicts that followed, and will simultaneously gain a new respect for what it means to be Canadian.

For those who took part, in uniform or on the home front, their lives were changed forever. For those who made the supreme sacrifice and whose stories may never be told:

They shall grow not old as we who are left grow old
Age shall not weary them nor the years condemn
At the going down of the sun and in the morning
WE WILL REMEMBER THEM.

Lawrence Binyon 1869–1943

Gwilym Jones

Members of Living History in attendance at Federal Citizenship Court ceremonies with Federal Citizenship Judge Sigmund Reisor, OC (2000).

Montage depicting memorabilia and branch murals on display at RCL Branch 258, Highland Creek.

MARGARET (CROSS) ACKROYD CWAC

MARG was born and raised near Edmonton in Ardrossan, Alberta, and moved to Lethbridge in 1933. She became a "war wife" in June 1942 shortly after her new husband joined the service. They lived in Lethbridge, Calgary, Edmonton, Kingston, Halifax and Windsor, Nova Scotia before her husband was shipped overseas. She then did some stand-up comic routines for a while around army camps, on radio, and the Stage Door Canteen in Halifax. In January 1944 she enlisted in the CWAC (Canadian Women's Army Corps) and took basic training in Kitchener, Ontario, after which she was stationed in Trinity Barracks, Toronto. She auditioned for and was accepted in the Canadian Army Show, Unit No. 6, and thus began an army career as an entertainer. The unit toured camps across Canada and Marg was featured in a skit known as "Three Jacks and a CWAC," before shipping off to England in 1944. She then was featured in another skit, "Fun Fatigues," in England; then on to Belgium, Holland and Germany. She returned to Canada in 1946, enrolled in Lorne Greene's Academy of Radio Arts in Toronto, and subsequently worked as a comedienne for twenty-three years.

Among the highlights of her entertainment career in the Army Show was performing in Ottawa before the governor general, Lord Athlone, Princess Alice and Prime Minister MacKenzie King. Later, in England, she was proud to share billing with Dame Vera Lynn and Lawrence Olivier at London's Stage Door Canteen.

As an entertainer, Marg's travels have taken her across Canada over twenty-seven times and to England, Scotland, and many parts of Europe. In 1954 she toured Japan and the Korean Front to entertain the troops. Later she performed with Mart Kenny's band, and also with The Happy Gang, a well-known group of performers in the 1950s.

Margaret (Cross) Ackroyd – CWAC

Following her retirement from the stage, Marg Ackroyd has appeared as a volunteer in many community functions. These have included the Seniors Jubilee Concerts at Roy Thomson Hall in Toronto, the Unionville Heritage Centre Seniors Extravaganza, as a speaker at the Varley Art Gallery on *Women at War,* TV interviews on intergenerational issues, and various other appearances in her army uniform before school children as well as senior citizens. Among the latter was the Markham Annual 1st July Festivities, where she was the first female veteran to raise the flag for veterans' activities.

Marg is a member of Royal Canadian Legion Branch 459 in Stouffville, lives in Markham, Ontario, and is a valued member of the Living History Speakers Bureau RCL Branch 258. In 1995 she attended the fiftieth anniversary of the Liberation of Holland celebrations and was doubly impressed with the gratitude the Dutch people still show towards Canadians.

A True Story of a "War Wife"

You have heard of "war brides" during World War II. Well, I was a "war wife." My husband, Bill Cross, and I were married in June of 1942. He was called up with the twenty-year-olds in July 1942 and joined up in Lethbridge, Alberta. He was sent to Calgary, where he enlisted and stayed in Currie Barracks.

I went up to Calgary by bus and went to stay with friends. We were only in that area for a short while but I got a job at Kresges. I had worked in the Lethbridge Kresges, so they made me welcome. The assistant manager happened to have been the stockman in Lethbridge.

From Calgary, one month later on September 27th, my husband was sent to Edmonton. Well, a repeat story—I went by bus to Edmonton, stayed with relatives and looked for a job in *that* Kresges. Surprisingly, Mr. Alberts had been promoted again and sent to Edmonton, so I got a job wrapping gifts, as it was near Christmas.

We spent a lot of my husband's free time visiting my relatives. I was born in Ardrossan, now almost a suburb of Edmonton, and I still had a lot of relatives there.

A month went by quickly, and on November 30th Bill was sent to Barriefield Barracks in Kingston, Ontario. I didn't immediately go to Kingston; instead I went to Lethbridge and spent Christmas with my mother and dad. Shortly after, I headed by train for Kingston. I was able to find a housekeeping room on Princess Street, where I had a toaster and a few dishes. I usually had cereal and toast but could concoct cold meals when Bill was allowed to "visit" me. We spent the winter in Kingston. Kresges didn't need anybody but the Ladies Self-Serve store did, so I had a job again—this time selling ladies' clothes. We would fraternize with other military people and go to shows (saw lots of movies) and dances, and restaurants when we could afford a hot meal for a change.

In the spring, Bill was given a leave and we went by train to Lethbridge. It wasn't too long before he was sent, on May 27th, to Halifax, Nova Scotia. I followed him down in August. Over the summer, my mother and I went by train to visit my sister, Gwen Lewis, her hubby, Jack, and two sons. I got a job in Lethbridge slicing meat in a Safeway store.

My brother was in the navy on a corvette (*Baddeck*). He was married to a girl from Halifax, so I was able to stay at her mother's house on Henry Street. It was only a few days later that Bill was sent to Windsor, Nova Scotia. He found me a place and I went down there on a bus—no seat, so I stood all the way. The people I stayed with were named Smith, relatives of a Lethbridge girlfriend named Jean Reagh.

I was with my husband in Windsor only from August 16th until the 26th, when he was shipped out. I waved goodbye as the train pulled out from Halifax. I couldn't see him among the many heads and shoulders leaning out of the train, but I waved anyway, as I knew this could be the last goodbye.

I didn't have the money to go home to Alberta, but my brother's wife's family made me feel welcome in their house in Halifax. I got a job at Eaton's. I also began doing shows for servicemen in the Stage Door Canteen and with a group organized by "Uncle Mel," a Halifax radio man. Over the next month or so, I did shows with his group at Purcells Cove. I did some "bits" at radio station CHNS, canteens, army camps, etc. The Navy Show came to town and I began to think . . . *Maybe? Am I good enough?* It must be wonderful to train and do shows and be with the same group of people all the time.

On December 16, 1943, I went to the Navy Recruiting Office, but they didn't want any recruits at the time—not until February. My brother John was home on leave, and took his wife and me to have dinner on his ship, the corvette *Baddeck*, with a tour after dinner.

On January 8th, I went to the CWAC. Got medical tests and an IQ test—got 152. Four doctors said I was "suitable." My first actual day in the army was January 17, 1944. I was bunked in Room 27 at Kennedy Barracks, where I had a Wasserman test, dental inspection, etc. I left for basic training in Kitchener on Thursday, January 27th. Colonel Dover was our inspector and she made us turn our rings in so that we wouldn't scratch anyone when machining.

One night, we all had needles and had to stay in. We had an amateur contest and I won, reciting and singing the "Sow Song." Some officers from the Army Show were in the audience. They were talent scouts and had me audition. They said, "Do you sing?" "No." "Do you dance?" "No." "Do you play a musical instrument?" "No." "Well what *do* you do?" I said, "Recite!" Just imagine how hard up for talent they were—*I* got chosen for Unit No. 6 of the Army Show. I did graduate into singing Gracie Fields numbers and ones by Betty Hutton that didn't need much singing—just jumping around and making faces!

When I was stationed at Trinity Barracks in Toronto, we went to the Victoria Theatre, where they said I didn't need an audition. I was "in." Hooray!

We did two shows in Simcoe and we had to ride in the back of cold trucks to get there. My first Army Show performance was on March 14, 1944. Red Reid and Jack Kelly and I wrote skits for the new show. I was a fortuneteller, complete with costume, and they came to me to see their future. The first setting would be Italy: the curtains would open up and the girls would be wearing Italian costumes in front of Italian scenery. Then we would show up. We did the same thing for Russia (I was Natasha Sarova, the beautiful sniper), Africa, and so on.

Captain Romney Brent (Hollywood actor) coached us and Bob Farnon from the Happy Gang was our orchestra leader. He wrote me a comic song about Natasha Sarova: "And I'm Just a Gypsy, a Wispy Tipsy Gypsy."

We toured camps and did a show in Ottawa for the Earl of Athlone, Princess Alice, and Mackenzie King. We toured all the way out west to Vancouver and Victoria, where we took a ship up the coast and played at every army, air force and navy station. It was a beautiful trip, with the band playing at night for dances and singsongs. We also did shows at the prison camps across Canada, but we didn't see the prisoners. Our audiences were World War I vets, who were guards at the camps.

In the fall of 1944 we were told we would be going overseas. One of the girls in the show was from Detroit, so she and I hitchhiked down there on leave to see her parents. The army called us to cut short our leave and go back to Toronto to check out if we were pregnant. Tsk! Tsk! Tsk! No, we weren't!

Before going to the Continent in 1944, I toured England with three men—Doug Romaine, Nelse Hagen (piano) and Orv Wainman, pop singer. The show was called "Three Jacks and a CWAC." We visited hospitals, going from ward to ward with a portable piano. Then I got into another show, "Fun Fatigues," and went to Holland, Belgium, and, after May 8th, to Germany.

I saw my husband, Bill Cross, at a show in Germany. I knew he was overseas and he knew that I was, but we couldn't say so in letters. One night there was a commotion in the theatre in Oldenberg where we were doing a special show for General Foulkes, who was going home. The noise was from two MPs bringing Bill up to the stage. They didn't believe that Bill's wife was up on the stage. What a reunion! He caught up with me again in Almelo, Holland, where I was staying with some civilians. They allowed him to stay, too. Bette Milner did a movie called *Where the Boys Are*. In it her husband showed up backstage when she was performing overseas. I said, "They must have read my diary!"

The story has a sad ending. I did not get home until 1946. The Army Show was delegated to play for the "repats," the boys who didn't get home even a year after the war ended, and needed cheering up. I got back in March of 1946 and got my discharge at Currie Barracks in Calgary. Bill was home months ahead of me and stayed with his folks.

When I returned, we stayed alternately with his family or mine. We were offered a two-room house with no water, next door to Bill's parents. It would have meant carrying water from his parents' place and using their bathroom facilities. I must admit I was the one who didn't want to do that. Another reason for not moving in was that the DVA offered me a course at Lorne Greene's Academy of Radio Arts in Toronto. Army Show friends wrote that there were lots of opportunities in Toronto. Apparently they had singers, dancers, musicians, and comedians, but a comedienne would really be a novelty and I would be sure to get lots of work there. Well, I did—twenty-three years of it.

I left my husband in 1947 and went to Toronto. I admit it was my fault and I feel that if we could have had a family and not been separated by the war, then we would have been happy. We were very much in love, and if there had been no war—which changed us both—we would probably still be together.

There is a sequel to this. In 1995, fifty years later, I went back to Holland for the huge reception that the Dutch people extended to veterans of the war. After the very long parade, which lasted nearly five hours, a man touched me on the shoulder and said: "Do you know me?" For a moment I thought "no," and then when I looked at the identity card, which we all wore, I read "Bill Cross"!

Well, the years slipped away and we hugged and kissed and couldn't get enough words in; all sorts of questions were asked and answered. We both had married again and had five children. He still lived in Alberta—in Hanna—and I lived in Toronto. The years and the miles had separated us, but we appreciated the reunion.

Later, I wrote and sent all the pictures of him that I had (except for wedding pictures) and returned jewellery of his mother's. I received a thank-you letter, and so now that really was the end.

* * *

One of the episodes that I remember vividly about my life in the army was a combination of surprise, fright, frustration and then later a calmness about it all.

The Army Show was playing in Nijmegen, Holland, and instead of the usual Nissen huts, or rough stages out in the open air, or even the tailgate of a truck, we were actually in a theatre. It was old—at least, some bombing had left it with a leaky roof and rain-soaked floors making it appear old—but it *was* a theatre.

It had been used for plays or concerts, not movies, and still had remnants of its past glory days. I went snooping around to see what I could see and climbed a stairway to an upper floor. There was an open doorway and in I went.

Well, there was a huge square open space in the floor overlooking the stage. There were old scenery pieces, furniture, and so on, and apparently the theatre's show people would lower or raise the props by ropes through this trap door and store unused items in the room.

What I saw there, just as curious as I was, kneeling and watching, was a German SS soldier in his blue-grey uniform! He was staring down through the hole. We both were surprised. Our eyes met and I couldn't help but notice the pale blue Aryan eyes, blond hair and pink cheeks.

I don't know what his feelings were but we both must have had some fear. I know I did! I was sort of transfixed, staring at him. And then I knew I had to run, and I did, back down those stairs and into our group, who were setting up changing quarters, hanging costumes, setting up the band, etc. Of course, I wasn't quiet then, I was hollering about this German soldier upstairs. Well, Sergeant Major Jack Madden and a few of the orchestra boys ran back up and found nothing—no man, and no evidence of one—only a cluttered storage room with a littered floor.

Well, don't think I didn't get ribbed about this! "Oh, Marg, you're seeing things. Oh, Marg, you've got a great imagination. Oh, Marg, you just want some attention. You're going bonkers . . . " I was so frustrated that I couldn't get them to believe me!

We continued to play our show in that theatre for two days more. It rained, and that wet floor was even wetter. The orchestra boys had their feet up on the stools where they were sitting. They made a bit of an umbrella over their music so the notes wouldn't run during the show.

Whenever I—and some of my closer pals—had a chance, we looked again around the upstairs, but nope, no evidence of any habitation. We went on with our tour and wherever there were Canadian troops, the Army Show performed.

By this time the war was over, it was May, and in our audiences there were many boys getting anxious to get home again. I'm sure we all tried harder to give them a good show and, in my case, a laugh or two.

The day that the war actually ended, we were in Arnhem and the girls in the show—well we *were* "girls" then—were sleeping in a bombed-out school. One of the classrooms had less damage than the others, but a leaky roof was preferable to sleeping in a tent. In the middle of the night we heard guns going off, blasts of some kind, hollering, shouting and such an ungodly racket that we thought we were being invaded. Soon one of the men came from the tent camp and told us that the war was over, they had heard the news on the tent camp radio. It was certainly exciting for all of us, too. Our husbands, boyfriends, family, all seemed closer in our minds, and we cheered as much as the Dutch people did.

We started repeating some of our show places and sure enough I enquired when we got back to Nijmegen about the man in the theatre attic. I'm sure glad I did, because we found out that there had been *two* SS men up in that attic. They had been hiding in the big ventilators in the theatre's air fans. They removed the big grille on one end. Inside they had a P38, and a Luger and ammunition, as well as food. The local people had continued our search and found them. Apparently at night they would go out foraging for food, and had been up in that theatre for who knows how long. They had escaped from a truck carrying prisoners of war, but the driver couldn't chase after them or he would have lost all of them.

At least I was vindicated. My "story" was finally believed. I had been so frustrated trying to make them believe that I had actually seen a German soldier in the theatre. I wonder if they watched the show! I wonder what they thought of my loud, grunty "Sow Song"? (Those crazy Canucks!) We'll never know.

Well, that was the closest I had ever come to the enemy in Europe. When I sang in Japan and Korea, I had a little "close call." The ladies in our show were being brought back to camp in jeeps to our "hooches," a tent top over a bottom wooden floor with about a three-foot-high wooden wall around the floor. They made much better shelters than just the tents and camp cots we had on the Continent. En route home, the North Korean border was close by, and they started shooting at us. We sure hightailed it home!

I was spared, but one of the Red Cross nurses with us in the jeep wasn't so lucky. She was shot in her shoulder. We couldn't keep in touch but when I was entertaining at a hospital, I heard from the staff that she had recovered.

In my almost three years of service, I was most fortunate to escape being wounded.

We had one "hospital" unit in England. We travelled in a small ambulance from one military hospital to another. We had our own little mini-piano that we pushed from ward to ward. We did have a good tour, and at Christmas in 1944 we were asked to perform at the Stage Door Canteen in London. We augmented a show of professional entertainers with "Three Jacks and a CWAC."

Laurence Olivier did his speech, "Once more unto the breach" from his *Henry V* movie. Another artist was a beautiful lady singer who had the most charming manner and her voice was just magnificent. I had never heard of her, but when she sang "White Cliffs of Dover" I felt so proud to have appeared on the same show. I never forgot her name once I had heard it—as you can guess, it was Vera Lynn. She is still doing shows today and looks as charming and sings as well as she did on that day so long ago.

While we were on our hospital tour, we worked at Bransome hospital. I am not sure if it was an older civilian hospital, but at that time it was a military hospital situated on the grounds of Lady Astor's estate. She had kindly asked us over for "tea" and we had gone there, knowing that *she* was famous. We didn't know that her other guest was going to be *extremely* famous, and neither did she. This was the summer of 1945. VE day had gone by and VJ day was coming up when General Doolittle dropped his bombs on Hiroshima. We sure remember *his* name now!

AL ARMSTRONG

ARMOURED CORPS (8TH RECCE REGIMENT)

AL was born in 1925 in Toronto and enlisted in the army in 1943 at age eighteen. He took his armoured corps training at Dundurn, Saskatchewan, prior to being shipped overseas. He was with the 8th Recce Regiment (14th Canadian Hussars), 2nd Canadian Division, in France from D-Day +30, going into action near Carpiquet. His squadron spearheaded the campaign sweeps through Caen, Falaise, Elbeuf, Dieppe and Dunkirk in France, then through Belgium into Flanders to north of Antwerp in Holland. His regiment then led the way in clearing out the area north of the Scheldt Estuary in October 1944, where the combat operations at Bergen op Zoom against fierce enemy resistance resulted in many casualties. Al remained with his regiment through to the end of hostilities in Europe and was discharged from the army in 1946.

Al returned to civilian life and was employed by Loblaws until he retired as a store manager in 1994 after fifty-three years of service. He joined the Royal Canadian Legion in 1964 and was a founding member (Sergeant-at-Arms) of the RCL Branch 258 Colour Guard in 1966, becoming captain of the guard in 1977. During his twenty-three-year tenure, the Colour Guard has been awarded many trophies. Al is particularly proud of winning first or second place on over a dozen occasions at the annual Warriors Day Parade in Toronto. In 1997 he was awarded the Meritorious Service Medal (MSM) by the Legion for services rendered.

Al has been an active member of his Legion branch for over thirty-six years and is highly regarded as an executive member of the Living History Speakers Bureau RCL Branch 258. Al is also an avid military history buff, and has an enviable collection of wartime artifacts and memorabilia. Some of his fondest memories are of the enthusiastic receptions by the Dutch people he received during his participation in the 1972 and 1975 celebrations of the liberation of Holland.

ONE TROOPER'S STORY

One day, while on a routine reconnaissance patrol in Belgium, our scout cars were stopped by mines in the road as we entered a village. I was in the assault troop. We were working out of half-tracks, and were called to assist in trying to clear the road ahead. On arrival we were fired on from a civilian graveyard at the side of the road. We dismounted, ran for the graveyard, and returned fire with light machine guns and rifles, taking cover behind the gravestones. Jerry was driven back, and brought up a heavy machine gun and a mortar team. He really laid it on us, but by good luck a troop of Sherman tanks turned up to assist us.

It was just about dusk. The red and orange flashes from the tank guns were weird combined with the explosions of the mortar shells, some of which landed among the graves, throwing up bits and pieces of coffins and their contents. It was something out of a nightmarish Dante's *Inferno*. Unreal! As it got dark, Jerry pulled back, taking his wounded and equipment with him. We did the same, glad to break the action off, since no one was getting anywhere.

This incident was just one small action. It did not alter the course of the war one iota. It was simply one more example of the futility of war. We went back to our half-tracks and other vehicles to drive back the way we came.

The day seemed like one more lost cause. No one spoke or laughed.

* * *

Our regiment (the 8th Recce Regiment, 14th Canadian Hussars) led the 2nd Canadian Division to the first towns and villages liberated in Holland.

Shortly after arrival, a food break was called. Coleman stoves were handed out so we could heat our rations: hard tack, canned stew, bully beef, tea, etc.

What we were not prepared for was the innocence of war: the men, the women, the young and the old, but most of all the children—tattered, torn and hungry. As we started to eat, two or three children appeared, then more and more of them, standing silently watching every mouthful we ate. The elders stood back and called to the children to come away, but the feel of hunger was too great for them to move out of sight of food. Some of us started to feed them from our mess tins, and then our whole group became a feeding chain, all the way from the mellow of heart to the hard-nosed trooper. Others, mostly older people, stood back, too proud to take or ask for food.

When we moved on, we left what food we could at the side of the road.

After leaving Bergen op Zoom, we pursued the 15th German Army into northwest Holland, and fought the Battle of the Scheldt Estuary in late October 1944. Every now and then the enemy turned on us, causing heavy losses. Even in retreat they were good soldiers.

Our infantry regiments at this time were sometimes fighting in deep water. As we advanced, the Germans blew up the dykes, flooding the land. Men and tanks found it tough going.

Battle conditions were bad, but the state of the civilians was far worse. When the enemy retreated, they looted everything: foodstuffs, transportation (even bicycles), cattle, chickens, etc. There was not one locomotive running in all of Holland. I had soldiered through France and Belgium and seen nothing compared to this.

In November, we had to dig in. The Front became static. The winter of 1944–45 was the coldest in forty years. We did what we could for the civilians. At Christmas 1944, our mail finally caught up to us. Most of our regiment turned our parcels from home over to the children in the towns and villages close to us. Some of the kids couldn't understand why St. Nicholas left razor blades in their wooden clogs. How these people survived I don't know. I saw them digging up tulip bulbs and sugar beets buried in the fields.

In early spring 1945, word came down from HQ and our regiment went on half rations (nobody complained) to help feed the civilians. In April or May 1945, a truce was called in our sector and food was trucked in. In each truck was a Canadian driver and an enemy co-driver, both armed.

In March 1945, the balance of the Canadian army was brought up from Italy. South Holland was liberated in October-November 1944. The northern part was liberated by the 1st Canadian Army and British divisions in the spring of 1945.

Amsterdam and Rotterdam fell to us, and it all ended on May 8, 1945. Following VE day, the people of Holland at first treated us coldly, thanks to a retreating enemy who informed them that Canadian soldiers were brutal and paid murderers.

Today, a Canadian, young or old, travelling in Holland is a hero. Their gratitude has been overwhelming. Dutch children are taught about Canada's effort to liberate them, and they care for our graves. I have seen the children's decorations on our graves, and I was informed they make this an annual event every May 5th. I have been back twice to visit our burial grounds in parts of Holland.

Many of their people immigrated to Canada (mostly to Ontario) in the 1950s and 1960s.

In early summer of 1945, I took a train from Charing Cross Station to a small place in Kent to see a lady friend of mine. After getting off the train, I had a long wait for a bus to complete my journey. There being a pub close at hand, I decided a pint was in order. The pub had not been open long, as there was only an elderly couple sitting in the corner. I walked in and up to the bar and ordered a pint of Mild & Bitter. The old couple kept staring at me and the lady seemed upset. Finally, the landlord put a pint on the table and said it was from the couple in the corner, and would I join them, which I did.

As I sat down, the man said, "I see you're in the Tank Corps." I agreed, and he said their son was in the Tanks and was in the British 8th Army (desert). The lady said, "You know, you gave us quite a shock when you walked in. You strongly resemble our boy, same figure and all."

We made the usual small talk and they asked my name. I told them it was Al. The man asked what Al was short for. When I said it was short for Albert, the lady let out a short gasp, then said their son's name was Albert. I then asked if their son had come home yet. The man gave me long look and said their lad wouldn't be coming back. I was at a complete loss for words.

Finally, as I got up to leave, I put my arms around the lady, who was softly crying. I told her how very sorry I was and firmly shook hands with the old gent. Both wished me a safe journey home and God bless.

For me the war was over, but for that English couple it would be a very long time before they would know peace. Damn this war.

* * *

Al Armstrong – Armoured Corps

In our troop (Armoured Corps Training) of forty men, one half were "conscripts," one half "active service." The NCOs and W. Officers instructed us to lean on the conscripts to "go active," which we did. One in particular, fed up with this treatment just before graduating, "went active" but specified to the "brass" that, because of his religion, he would not bear arms. I was friendly with this man and found him a decent sort. After we "active types" shipped out overseas, I often wondered what had happened to him, as he did not leave with us.

In May 1946, aboard the *Ile de France*, on our way home, I was walking on the upper deck and saw a group of men talking. One of them stepped out of the group and spoke to me. It was my "conscript" friend from Saskatchewan.

On his battle dress tunic he was wearing the same campaign ribbons as I was wearing. His shoulder flashes read, "Royal Canadian Medical Corps." On one sleeve he had two wound stripes—a real fine soldier, and he looked it.

We stood talking for a while. He informed me that when he returned to his hometown in Saskatchewan, he would stand up in his church, in front of his elder or pastor, and inform them that he had never shed blood, but had seen lots of it. His weapons were a Red Cross haversack over one shoulder, and a stretcher. (In my humble opinion, the Red Cross was a good aiming mark.) The man was very sincere and had the strength of his convictions. Then he returned to his friends. I did a lot of soul searching while pacing the deck.

The words of Kipling's "Gunga Din" went through my mind: "Din, Din, Din, you're a better man than I am, Gunga Din."

* * *

In my opinion, all wars are folly; there are more losers than winners. In any given year, there are forty or fifty small wars going on. If politicians and war profiteers were to spend a few months as front line infantry soldiers, peace would not be long in coming.

HUGH R. BETTS

ROYAL CANADIAN NAVY

BORN and raised in Saskatchewan, Hugh became a member of the Air Cadets in 1939. He joined the Royal Canadian Navy at age eighteen in 1942 at HMCS *Chippewa* in Winnipeg. He was trained in naval communications before volunteering to join the Royal Navy as a signalman aboard the cruiser HMS *Kent* in Scapa Flow, Scotland. The *Kent* was a convoy flotilla leader on the Murmansk run to Russia. In June 1944 he transferred to HMS *Nabob*, engaged in the strike force against the German cruiser *Tirpitz*, sister ship to the *Bismark*. Torpedoed by Nazi U-boats, Hugh was on the bridge and badly wounded, but the *Nabob* survived, travelling over 1,000 miles through rough seas and enemy harassment back to Scapa Flow. Hugh was hospitalized in Scotland, and later spent a year in the Army Service Hospital in St. Hyacinthe, Quebec, prior to being discharged.

Following his release from the navy, Hugh enrolled at the University of Toronto to study radiography, and interned at Sunnybrook Veterans Hospital. He became a head technologist and began a lifetime career in pharmaceuticals, sales and marketing. Following retirement in 1978, he formed Mobile Health Services (Toronto Homes for the Aged).

As a member of Rotary, Hugh is currently active in raising funds for Centenary Hospital, Scarborough. He is also an active member of the GTA Task Force for Seniors, Scarborough East Area, as well as being a member of the Living History Speakers Bureau. A Royal Canadian Legion member since 1948, Hugh was instrumental in obtaining the Bofors gun placed in front of RCL Branch 258, Highland Creek.

A FATEFUL DAY IN MY NAVY CAREER—AUGUST 22, 1944

HMS *Nabob* was the first Canadian-manned aircraft carrier to survive after being torpedoed off Norway's North Cape on August 22, 1944, and was home to 852 Squadron Flying Grumman Avengers.

I was transferred to the carrier HMS *Nabob* in July 1944 from the cruiser HMS *Kent* in Scapa Flow, Scotland, when the strike on the German cruiser *Tirpitz* was being planned. On the fateful day, the *Nabob* crew had been at action stations since 1000 hours. *Nabob* and the Fifth Escort Group were detached to the west. The flight deck was being cleared of aircraft.

I was on my way to the bridge to stand watch when a torpedo struck the starboard quarter. I was thrown up against a bulkhead, crushing my left side. I was able to make my way up to the bridge to see the sturdy *Bicherton*, a British destroyer, steaming full speed between the *Nabob* and the direction from which the first torpedo came. The second torpedo struck the destroyer, sinking it. A third torpedo shot past the bow of the *Nabob*. Fortunately, this torpedo missed the *Nabob* or else it would have been sudden death for the ship.

Captain Lay was expecting the worst when he gave the order *prepare to abandon ship*. Four hundred ratings were transferred to the HMES *Algonquin* and the HMS *Kempthorne*. Below deck was a scene of furious activity as the damage control party raced about closing doors and hatches, and sealing off sections of the ship. Chief Engineer Hinchcliffe went below and received reports on the damage. He reported it was definitely worthwhile attempting to save the ship.

The *Nabob* was the first escort carrier to survive a torpedo hit. She arrived back at Scapa Flow with a skeleton crew, after travelling more than 1,000 miles in a variety of weather conditions and enemy harassment. Total casualties were eleven Royal Canadian Navy sailors killed, ten Royal Navy sailors killed and over twenty seriously wounded. I was transferred to the naval hospital at Niobe, Scotland, and then returned to Canada on the *Queen Elizabeth*, which was used as a hospital ship. I was then hospitalized at the naval hospital in Ste.-Hyacinthe, Quebec, for a year.

Hugh R. Betts – Royal Canadian Navy

The incident I have written about was the last large naval operation of World War II. It is documented in British naval reports. A number of ships were lost and the return of the *Nabob* to Scapa Flow was considered one of the most courageous naval actions of World War II. I am proud to have been a part of it.

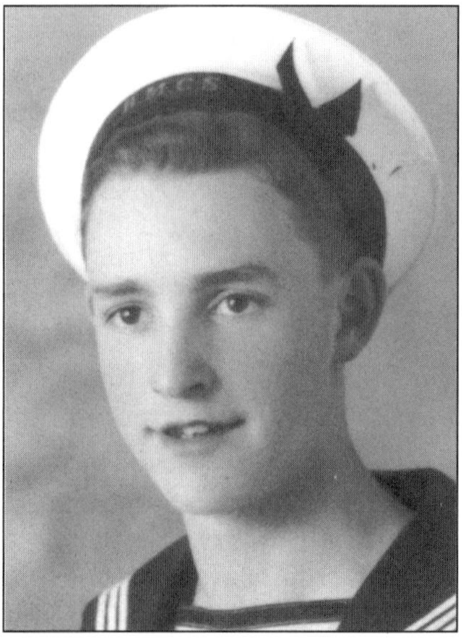

JOHN M.K. BOW, CD — CANADIAN ARMY RCEME

ORIGINALLY from Windsor, Ontario, John has lived in Scarborough since 1970. He was a member of the high school cadet corps, and as a teenager served as a Merchant Navy lake seaman. He was also a member of the Windsor Regiment, Royal Canadian Armoured Corps (Militia).

In February 1944 he was accepted at age seventeen as a recruit in the Canadian Army, following unsuccessful attempts to join the navy and air force. He was classified as unfit to serve overseas due to lack of weight (eighty-two lbs) and became a driver instructor at No. 5 CDMS in Woodstock, Ontario. During the war he trained male and female personnel on driver mechanics, wheel, track, tanks and motorcycles. At the cessation of hostilities, he re-enlisted in the regular forces and served until his discharge in 1961. He left the forces as a six-foot 186-pounder with the rank of QMS (WO2) RCEME barracks sergeant major, and was awarded the CD (Canadian Forces Decoration).

John embarked on a career in accounting and auditing, became a comptroller for several business firms, and later formed his own bookkeeping business. He is also a consultant for the Canadian Management Association (CMA) and in 1990 he retired from the Revenue Canada taxation auditing field to tend to his ailing wife, Gladys.

John first joined Royal Canadian Legion Branch 578 in 1961 after leaving the army, but later, in 1985, he, his wife (an ex-ATS ambulance driver), and their three children joined en masse the Highland Creek RCL Branch 258. He served for two years as editor of the branch newsletter (*Highlander*); was with the 258 Players; is a member of the Branch 258 Colour Guard; participates in cribbage, shuffleboard and euchre; is immediate past president of the Scarborough Veterans' Association; and is an active member of the

Living History Speakers Bureau RCL Branch 258. He was also a member of the Toastmasters' Club.

My Experiences of World War II

Prior to becoming draftable age, I tried joining the navy, army, air force and the Merchant Navy. The Armed Forces gave me a flat *no*, because of my beanpole appearance. The Merchant Navy said yes, but I could only serve on the Great Lakes aboard the S.S. *Noronic*. At the end of the season I was laid off.

Right after New Year's, I made the rounds again with the navy, air force and army. This time the army said *yes*, providing I stayed in Canada. They categorized me as a P2R, which meant I was underweight, but hopefully they could add more meat onto my bones. Can you imagine a six-footer weighing only eighty-two pounds? That was me. Frank Sinatra and I had something in common. We both were tall and skinny. He was sometimes portrayed as a microphone stand with a bow tie attached!

During this period, Canada adopted the common American and European program of conscripting everyone when they reached the age of seventeen-and-a-half. Germany conscripted as young as fifteen. You had to be nineteen to serve overseas in the line of fire. In Canada, there were some who opposed this system. Some figuratively "took to the hills" to avoid the draft. Those who did not volunteer for overseas duty stayed in Canada and were classified as "zombies." Those who were found to be medically unfit were not accepted and were classified as 4-F; they were issued with a brown discharge button to wear on their jackets.

Although I was underweight, it was felt I could put on the necessary weight so that I could go overseas. An overseas volunteer was issued a two-inch round blue badge with the letters "G S" embroidered in gold on it. This was worn on the lower part of the right arm of a soldier's tunic. Though I was one of a few who served with a bunch of zombies, I wore mine proudly.

In Toronto, the army recruiting depot, known as Manning Depot, was located in the Canadian National Exhibition grounds and the horse palace was also used for sleeping quarters.

At the outbreak of war, we did not have any tanks or rifles. We were very poorly prepared to defend ourselves from any transgressor—just like the United Kingdom. We relied upon the

United States to protect us. We used cardboard boxes to simulate trucks, broomsticks to simulate rifles. To simulate a tank we stuck a broomstick out of the front of a box to represent its cannon. To practise truck convoy manoeuvres, we used bicycles and "pony-shanks" until we had it down about perfect (this was to conserve on gasoline).

Canada was just coming out of the Great Depression and there wasn't much work to be had. If you didn't have a job, you went on welfare for assistance, but you had to do mediocre city work for it. Once the war broke out, a lot of the unemployed joined up. There now was an abundance of work for everyone. Numerous plants shot up overnight to manufacture all the needs for our armed forces. That could be rifles, Bren guns, tanks, boats, uniforms and ammunition. In Long Branch they made rifles, in Ajax, boats, in Scarborough and Windsor, Bren gun carriers, just to mention a few.

To ensure that there would be enough essential food and materials for our armed forces, the civilians were put on rations, but they were not as strict as they were overseas. Here in Canada, gasoline, butter, sugar, clothing materials, meats and poultry products, among other things, were rationed. We were all given ration books and if you lived in a boarding house, you surrendered your ration book to the landlady so that she could buy sufficient food products. Some people would trade sugar coupons for gasoline coupons if they didn't need sugar, and so on. You could buy only one suit of clothing a year, so homes would make do if someone in the house needed extra clothing for a special occasion. Swimming suit manufacturers eliminated the central part of ladies' swimming suits, thus creating the bikini.

When I finished my advanced army training at Camp Ipperwash, I was posted to No. 5 CDMS (Canadian Driving and Maintenance School) in Woodstock, Ontario, because I was mechanically inclined at that time. Here, I assisted in the training of male truck drivers on right-handed overseas style trucks, motorcycles and tracked Bren-gun carriers. The trucks didn't have any heaters or roll-up windows in them. So in the wintertime, flaps were buttoned to the doors to keep out the draft and buckets of hot coals were used to keep our feet warm for a spell. The girls had it much easier. We taught them how to drive conventional left-hand trucks on paved roads, and only during the daylight hours.

John M.K. Bow, CD – Canadian Army RCEME

All of the fighting and war activities of World War II were not contained in Europe and North Africa. We, here in Canada, had our share, too.

Some of it was done right here in our own Canadian waters, especially in and around the Halifax Harbour area. The Nazi submarines would try to sink any ship that was destined for Europe or the war fronts. Some of these U-boat skippers even had the nerve to sail exposed above the water down the St. Lawrence River, maybe as far as Trois-Rivières, and were entertained by the local residents. The Merchant Navy ships would sit on the horizon like wooden ducks in a shooting gallery at a carnival and the Nazi U-boats would pop them off, sinking them. The Axis even sank a hospital ship that was clearly marked, bound for Canada, just off our coastline, as well as the defenceless Newfoundland ferry in the middle of the Cabot Strait. The RCAF base at Mont-Joli was no exception, as it was torpedoed by the fast-moving Nazi U-boats.

German wolf pack submarines could stay out for months at a time. Their mother submarine was kept safely offshore in a neutral area. If it hadn't been for our Royal Canadian Air Force North Atlantic Squadron, the sinking of our ships by German U-boats would have continued endlessly. The airmen used to spot the subs from the air, and either sink them or mark them for corvettes to drop depth charges on them. These airmen would sometimes get seasick just watching the waves. Some were stationed in Iceland, which, in part, was pro-Nazi.

The Royal Air Force did not have enough safe air space to train their aircrews in the UK, so they sent them to Canada for training. We used Canadian-built Harvard and Avro Anson biplanes to train them. (A British airman that I knew who was sent to help with the training in Canada was not entitled to the Defence of Britain Medal as long as he remained in Canada.) Canada built many airplanes and the most common ones were the Mosquito fighter plane and the Lancaster bomber. Some of these airplanes were ferry commanded to the UK by female pilots. Parachute training was done mostly near Brandon, Manitoba.

The most successful spy training school was right here in Ontario, in Whitby, I am told. The man in charge was called "Mr. X." There was a film made about his camp, *A Man Called Intrepid*, as well as a book called *Camp X*.

German prisoners of war, mostly Luftwaffe pilots, North African fighters, and submariners, were billeted here in Ontario in such places as Kitchener, Gravenhurst, North Bay, Port Arthur (now Thunder Bay), and Bowmanville. They had it easy and were well fed, not to be compared with the way the Nazis starved their prisoners of war. If they escaped, there was no place for them to go and they could not get back to Germany. They were guarded by our Veterans' Home Guard, consisting of men who were too old to serve overseas. A well-known Canadian even dressed up in a German uniform, complete with helmet, and drove around on a motorcycle in Montreal and nobody even stopped him!

These are only some of the things that remain predominantly in my mind after all these years. My mother, like most mothers, was proud to have members of her family fighting for Canada. To indicate this to neighbours and passersby, she hung a pennant in her living room window with two stars on it—one for my brother, who was serving overseas with the RCAF Iroquois Squadron, and the other for me.

A group of us Scarborough wartime veterans formed what is called the Scarborough Veterans' Organization. Most Legion and veteran organizations use the fourth verse from a poem entitled "The Fallen," written by Laurence Bunyan. I read the whole poem and from it I extracted parts and formed our own more meaningful opening prayer. It goes like this:

"They went with songs to the battle; they were young;
Straight of limb, true of eye, steady and aglow.
They were staunch to the end against the foe.
They sit no more at familiar tables of home.
They sleep far from where they used to roam.
Age shall not weary them nor the years condemn.
At the going down of the sun and in the morning
WE *WILL* REMEMBER THEM."

John M.K. Bow, CD – Canadian Army RCEME

WWI, Army Mural – PPCL 1 Snipers, Ypres

GERARD (GERRY) BRENT RCAF

GERRY was born in Fort Erie, Ontario, and raised in Hamilton. Having survived the Depression and graduated from Collegiate—and because he had qualified as a ham radio operator—he was actively recruited by the RAF. On August 1, 1940, at age seventeen-and-a-half, he enlisted in the RCAF and was posted overseas to RAF Yatesbury for training as a radar mechanic. He was among the first group of Canadians involved in that activity, called RDF mechanics at that time.

In 1940 Gerry served on CH (chain home) and CHL (chain home low) radar stations (used to detect low-flying aircraft) in both England and Scotland. In early 1941, he was posted to Egypt during the Middle East Campaign, and served in the Western Desert Mobile Radar Unit, taking part in the great retreat code-named "Crusader." He was then posted to Takoradi on the Gold Coast, West Africa, on loan to the Royal Navy, serving as radar mech/operator on AMC *Queen of Bermuda*. He then took part in the invasion of Madagascar, later returning to the RAF station in Sierra Leone, serving the three radar stations there. At the end of 1943 he was posted back to the United Kingdom, serving four stations. He was returned to Canada at the end of 1944 to join "Tiger Force," slated for Japan. Gerry was discharged in September 1945.

Post-war, Gerry was employed by Bell Canada for thirty-five years. During this period he was on loan for two years to Western Electric, working on the DEW Line under contract with the US Air Force. He then spent four years on Mid-Canada Radar for Bell on special contract. Most of his career with Bell involved radio, microwave, and engineering projects. Following retirement from Bell he spent ten years with Ontario Hydro Communications in microwave, fibre optics engineering.

For the past eleven years, Gerry has been (and still is) a volunteer with the Scarborough General Hospital. He is now a welcome new member of the Living History Speakers Bureau RCL Branch 258.

MOST MEMORABLE TIME IN WW II

I returned to the UK for Christmas 1943 after almost three years in the Middle East and West Africa. On my fourteen days' disembarkation leave, I had a relapse of malaria and spent most of my leave in hospital. When I reported for duty in January, the wing commander at Bromley said, "You've had a pretty rough time, so I'll post you to Swingate Radar Station" (about three miles north of Dover). I was pleased with this posting, because I had served as a radar mechanic at Swingate in 1940. I found it had expanded a lot and now included an Oboe station (Pathfinder Navigator).

When I left Swingate in 1940, there had been about twenty-five WAAF and seventy RAF pilots. Now there were almost a hundred WAAF and twenty-five airmen. My first reaction after three years without women was that I'd died and gone to heaven! We had a Flt. Lieut. CO and a WAAF section officer as admin.

I was now a flight sergeant and senior NCO for operations. My first duty was to assign personnel for the four operator and four mechanic watches. I divided them up, matching ranks, skills, etc., and posted the list, no sweat. In less than half an hour of posting the list, I had tearful, angry, and overly sweet WAAFs pounding on my door wanting shift changes because of "horrid girls," "loathsome girls," "toffee-nosed girls." I was soon learning my heaven was more like hell!

The second day on site, I was inspecting the receiver block and realized an incident was taking place. An incoming target was on the screen with no IFF (identification friend or foe) from the aircraft. It was approaching dead on to our station, losing altitude and only travelling about 140 mph. At one point it looked like it was below the level of the cliffs, but it pulled up at the last minute and just missed our block, making a belly landing about 200 yards away.

I phoned the medical people for an ambulance and picked up a couple of mechanics, and we ran to the downed B17 Fortress from the USAF. The pilot—a major—was struggling to remove the Norden bombsight, but appeared to be smoking a cigar. We asked about the rest of his crew and he replied, "They're all stiffs." We removed eight bodies, but there should have been ten. We never knew whether they were blown out of the plane through the flak holes—one of which was as big as a jeep—or whether they were thrown out to lighten the load. All the machine guns were gone.

I made arrangements for motor transport to the railway station in Dover and a rail warrant for London. The major, carrying the bombsight in a fitted bag, wanted to visit American HQ in London. I now revised my watch schedule to free up two guards for the plane on a twenty-four-hour basis so the clocks, compass and radios wouldn't walk.

Unlike the RAF, the USAF had crews on site the following day, and amazed everyone by putting air bags under the wings to lift the body while they lowered the undercarriage. They installed new propellers, filled the gas tank and removed the anti-glider wires on the field. The plane was flown off the field at three p.m. that day.

I thought I was supposed to be having a rest.

The roofs of the barracks were full of patches where shrapnel from the German cross-channel guns at Cap Gris Nez, as well as our own ack-ack debris, fell.

A couple of days later in the transmitter block I found that the routine cleaning of salt sea spray from the antenna insulators was overdue. There was no rush of volunteers to climb the 360-foot towers and be lowered by breeches buoy seat to wipe off the insulators with an ether-soaked rag.

It was a sunny day, not too cold. I had often done this routine and didn't mind heights, so I grabbed a guy as ground man to control my descent in the breeches buoy chair with the rags and bottle of ether. There was a series of steel ladders leading to the top and, being young, I was soon on top and sitting in the chair. I was lowered in ten-foot intervals to meet each insulator. There was a procedure to protect oneself from radio frequencies burns, since the 900-kilowatt transmitters were energized on a twenty-four-hour basis.

The work proceeded until I reached the sixty-foot platform where the antenna system terminated. I swung over and stepped onto the platform, ready to descend the ladder to ground level and climb up the second of the four towers.

I was startled to hear the bosun's chair crash to the ground as my ground man dropped the rope and ran for cover. There was the scream of aircraft engines in a dive, together with cannon and machine-gun fire. As I turned to look, there was a Messerschmitt 109G slightly below the level of the platform throttled back from his dive, and about twenty feet away! I could see his blond, straight hair, no helmet or goggles, just a headset on his ears—a rather good-looking guy. As he shot past me, he poured on the coal, evidenced by a stream of black smoke from his exhaust pipes, and climbed parallel to the line of our towers. Here he was safe from ack-ack. If his dive had been a few minutes earlier, I'd have fallen from that 360-foot level and been smashed like an over-ripe melon. I later learned that the 109G was one of four fighters that had fired twenty-mm cannon shells at three Land Army girls, wounding one, as they worked in a field on a neighbouring farm.

Although I was shaken, pride made this Canadian sergeant round up the ground man and complete the remaining three towers. We should have been warned there was a "red alert" on, and we could have delayed the cleaning job.

All went well for a few days, and I got to play the piano in the local pub for the beers that soon lined the piano top.

Our CO was concerned that people were not following the air raid and shelling rule to immediately take shelter, and instructed me to ensure they were posted on all bulletin boards. I was also to talk to them and convince them they must comply or face disciplinary action. Two nights after the orders were posted and announcements made on the Tannoy (PA system), we received a direct hit on the WAAF (Women's Auxiliary Air Force) shelter by a one-ton, twenty-inch German shell. There were no survivors and we lost thirty-two girls.

The shelter site was bulldozed and a small cross erected. Thank God for the WAAF officer who helped me write the letters to the parents and next of kin for the CO's signature. The letters were all different, not just copies. In the days following, our watches had to be doubled to make up the loss, and several girls developed shingles and other nervous disorders. The Wing HQ took action, and all remaining WAAF were posted to various other stations.

My posting to Rye in Surrey came about a week later. My posting to Swingate for a "rest" was about the worst four weeks of my service life. (Although I had been strafed and wounded by a twenty-mm cannon shell fragment in Egypt, it happened so fast and we were fighting so hard that it never affected my emotions.) Two days after I left Swingate, an RAF Mosquito bomber, with two Canadians as crew, hit a balloon cable and crashed and burned, killing them and severely damaging the station cookhouse and dining hall. Dover was truly Hell's Corner.

WW I, Air Force Mural – Billy Bishop, V.C.

MARION CHAMBERS RCAF (WD)

MARION was born in Brockville, Ontario, in 1922 and had seven brothers and sisters. She enlisted in the Royal Canadian Air Force (Women's Division) in 1940 at age eighteen, and received her basic training in Rockcliffe, Ottawa, remaining there for one year while training as an instrument mechanic. She was then transferred to No. 1 Manning Depot in Toronto and served in an old garage on Adelaide Street, assembling and testing oxygen masks. She was in Toronto for about a year. There, she received her corporal stripes and met her future husband, Ben Griffin.

Marion was then assigned to the Eastern Air Command in Moncton, New Brunswick, where she performed tests and calibration on the navigational instruments and F24 cameras mounted on the wings of Liberators, Catalinas and Cansos aircraft.

She received her discharge in 1943, returned to Toronto, and married Ben Griffin. They settled down to work at his family-owned Rouge Valley Inn and had four children, two boys and two girls. Having rebuilt the Inn after it was destroyed by Hurricane Hazel in 1954, she and Ben divorced after twenty-two years of marriage and went their separate ways.

In 1967, Marion married Cecil Chambers and worked at a variety of jobs before retiring from the Corps of Commissionaires. She first joined the Legion in 1953, left, and rejoined in 1983. She is also a life member of the 48th Highlanders Ladies Auxiliary. At Royal Canadian Legion Branch 258, Highland Creek, she has served in several executive capacities, and also in the Ladies Auxiliary of the branch, which she joined in 1981. She is now the secretary of the Scarborough Veterans Organization and is an active member of the Living History Speakers Bureau RCL Branch 258.

MY STORY

My wartime experiences were not as traumatic as some, and I did not serve outside of Canada. From Brockville, at that time a small town in Eastern Ontario, I enlisted in the Royal Canadian Air Force (Women's Division) in Ottawa and did my basic training there. I was designated as an instrument mechanic and stayed there for a few months' extra training, which lasted about a year. With seven other girls I was then posted to No. 1 Equipment Depot in Toronto.

We worked in an old garage on Church and Adelaide Streets, assembling and inspecting oxygen masks. I really don't think the air force knew what to do with us, as they forgot to send our papers with us when they posted us to Toronto. Consequently, we did not receive any money for a couple of months. We were in trouble, as we had to find money to rent rooms, and for food and transportation. Also most of us did not know Toronto; a couple of us came from British Columbia, another couple from Nova Scotia, and of course I had never been out of Brockville. We pooled our resources and picked a couple of rooms from the newspaper. They were located near St. Clair and Yonge Streets. We could not get much money from our parents, as this was still the Depression. We borrowed from anyone we could. It did not occur to us to go to the depot and lodge a complaint.

We did not have money for transportation, so we had to walk to and from work every day. I suppose this was really good for us, but I can remember being very tired. Also we lived on cheese and crackers for days on end. I still can't eat cheese and crackers without thinking of this. If anyone asked us out for dinner, we jumped at the chance. One night we were invited to go as a group to the Rouge Valley Inn. They had good meals there and of course we all went. This was where I met my future husband. His family owned the Rouge.

While in Toronto, I was promoted to corporal. After about eight months, I was posted to a flying field in Moncton, New Brunswick, to work on aircraft instruments, which I found very interesting. We would fly in the aircraft and calibrate the instruments, and if they needed repair, the airmen would take them out of the aircraft so we could repair them in the shop. We also painted the dials with radioactive fluorescent paint. We would have to go under ultraviolet lights every day and if we glowed or sparkled too much, we were taken off that job for a while and would work on something else. We also repaired the large F24 cameras that were mounted on the wings of the aircraft.

It was quite an experience to be in barracks just a short distance from the flying field. There were only nineteen RCAF Women's Division instrument mechanics in Canada and although there were other women on the base, the discipline was very strict. We also had airmen from Norway assigned there for training.

I was also posted to Halifax for a few months to do the same assignments. We flew over the ocean and this was a bit scary, as I did see some enemy submarines off the coast, and also witnessed many aircraft accidents. This lasted until 1943 when I took my discharge, returned to Toronto, and married Ben Griffin.

JACK COTTER

Royal Canadian Regiment - Airborne

A MARITIMER, Jack was born in St. John, New Brunswick in 1933 and joined the militia at age sixteen. The following year, on August 31, 1950, he enlisted in the regular army. He did his basic training at Camp Borden, after which he joined the 1st Royal Canadian Regiment (1-RCR) in the Signal Platoon. After signal training, he attended the initial regimental level jump school at Rivers plus Camp Shilo, and earned his paratrooper wings.

His regiment arrived in Korea in March 1952 and saw action north of Seoul in battles such as Hill 187 ("The Hook"; "Bowling Alley") and Hill 355 ("Little Gibraltar" or "Old Baldy"). Jack served as corporal of Signals Platoon for the duration of hostilities, mostly maintaining communication lines between outposts and command, as well as taking part in intelligence-gathering patrols and fighting off enemy attacks on their trench lines. The commanding officer, Col. P.R. Bingham, received the DSO for their heroic stand at Hill 355. The battalion was relieved and shipped home in August 1953.

Following his discharge from the army, Jack has had several careers in business—including manufacturing and sales positions in his own and other companies—in security, and as an insurance company building coordinator, despite having suffered a heart attack in 1976. A family man, he and his wife Joan have four children and nine grandchildren.

Jack is deeply involved in community affairs and has been a member of the Royal Canadian Legion Branch 258 since 1984, where he has served on the branch Board of Management and as a zone delegate. He is also a member of the branch Colour Guard as a s/sergeant and rifle training instructor, as well as being a past chairman. He also serves as vice-president of the Korea Vets Association Unit 59 and as a zone delegate for his Legion branch.

He enjoys being an active member of Living History Speakers Bureau RCL Branch 258, where he is a former secretary and now chairman. He is currently serving as second vice-president of the branch, responsible for chairing the Board of Management and the Poppy Campaign, and as band liaison.

The War in Korea—"Old Baldy"

The brigade occupied the right sector, with our regiment holding the formidable Hill 355, also known as "Old Baldy" or "Little Gibraltar." The dugouts and bunkers were leaking, and some were caving in from heavy bombardment of artillery and mortar fire. Our spirits were not dampened, as Colonel Bingham gave a humorous shout: "Stop bitching! It appears our maid has missed us!"

During this time, Ralph (Moose) Fisher was the driver operator and bodyguard for Colonel Bingham. On the hill, Moose, Colonel Bingham and I heard the message: "Welcome to you, Colonel Bingham and your men." At this point, being somewhat surprised, I asked Colonel Bingham if he had relatives here. With a look of surprise, then with a breaking smile and mustache moving slightly, he replied, "It's possible, you know, Cotter, but quite unlikely." The colonel, a man of strength and discipline, and well suited to his command, also had a good sense of humour.

It was very clear that the enemy always knew the name of who was on all the positions at any given time, even down to the donation and delivery of Carling beer on August 11th. Yet, on August 25th, CSM McNally of "D" Company climbed to the peak of Hill 355 and placed our regimental flag on top. It is still not known why the Chinese did not shell it, although this front was a hot spot for the remainder of our time there.

During this time, our lines of communication were constantly being blown out, requiring a line crew to replace them daily, if not more frequently. (Unfortunately, the Chinese had set their mortar range about every few yards, thus the name of the road: "Bowling Alley.") Ralph (Moose) Fisher and Otto Blain, who had the job of laying these lines, were once caught in a mortar barrage. Their vehicle was overturned. Fisher and Blain were trapped in a ditch, and they had to wait for the Pioneer Platoon to dig them out.

Flag of the United Nations flying above the Imjin River, Korea, February, 1952. Photographer Paul E. Tomelin.

On my one and only attempt at this road, aware of Fisher's past experience, we made it through when the first shell hit in front, by putting the vehicle in reverse and then speeding forward. Perhaps it was only a one-man mortar team. As we drove back and immediately went forward, a mortar shell fell to our front, and then as we went forward the shell fell to the rear. Once we were moving forward, we didn't stop until we were well out of mortar range.

Shortly after, at the base of 355, Captain (Jiggs) MacDougal of the Royal Canadian Signal Corps, who was attached to the regiment, was directing a helicopter to our position using what he thought was a smoke grenade. Unfortunately, it was a phosphorus grenade, and it exploded in his hand. Fisher assisted others in putting him in a pool of water to help slow down the burning. He was then flown out by the same helicopter he had been trying to guide in.

I recall, shortly after, a message from "A" Company that Corporal Bud Cox was injured and was being sent down from 355 and Captain Taylor was requesting an NCO for Communications. The choice was between myself and Sergeant Doyle. Finally, Sergeant Gerney made the decision that I was to go, as Sergeant Doyle was married and I was single. Gerney said, "Get your butt up there. They need replacements. And keep your head and butt down."

The incoming shells and mortars were going for the entire day and there were rumours that we were getting shortfall from our own American guns. On reaching the top, having crawled most of the way and taken shelter in bunkers that were partially destroyed, I fell into a bunker where there were two signal operators, one being Corporal Drinkwater, and another whose name I don't remember. When I told him Taylor needed Signals, as Cox was hit, Drinkwater replied, "We've been running from bunker to bunker, guess no one could find us."

The shelling and mortars were still coming in, and the air was filled with burnt gunpowder and smoke. After a few minutes (which seemed like hours), we started to leave the bunker, but were turned back by mortar fire. It was as if the Chinese knew exactly where we were. About fifteen feet from the bunker, Drinkwater turned to go back, saying that he'd forgotten his .45. I grabbed him and told him to forget it, as we were needed at HQ. No sooner were the words out of my mouth than there was a direct hit on the bunker and it ended up a pile of rubble.

As we were going to enter HQ bunker, someone yelled words that apparently were the first part of the password for that period of time. Thank God Drinkwater was with me, as I had not been given the password by Gerney before leaving (or perhaps I was too damn scared to remember). I did remember to take my Sten gun and .45. Yet this was little comfort, really, as the Sten at a distance couldn't hit the broad side of a barn door, and the .45 was only good if you were close enough to make it count.

Finally inside Command bunker, Captain Taylor briefed us. Because of the heavy shelling, they had lost all communications with the outpost position, and lines had to be run to the outpost to find out what was going on. It was late at night and this was, in part, to our advantage; the only light was that of the exploding shells and enemy flares that lit the areas for moments at a time.

Our first attempt at getting a line to the outpost began quietly, excluding the noise of the mortar shells coming in with a whistling and whizzing sound over our heads. As we laid the new line, I was in front with the reel, and Drinkwater followed, ensuring the line was concealed from foot traffic. When we reached the outpost, we found that the men were okay, but their radio set was damaged from shrapnel. While connecting the line, the mortar fire was saturating the forward area, and we could see many of the enemy advancing in the flashing glare of their mortars.

We advised Capt. Taylor of the situation—the large movement of enemy troops, the advancing mortars, and the automatic weapons being fired. When we returned to HQ bunker, Taylor said he had lost communications again. As we set out again to the outpost, checking the lines on the way, we found a break in the line, which we repaired, and then continued on to the outpost. The men who had rifles had the bayonets fixed, and the automatics were fully loaded with spares beside them. Within a few yards of the outpost, I found a break in the line and when I started to repair and splice I noticed the break was smooth, requiring me to peel down to bare wire. This break was not caused by a shell explosion—it had been cut.

Moments later, now in the trench, we met the Chinese coming over the wall. We hit the dirt and fired. I emptied my Sten, double clip, and reached for my .45. They were now on us. The smell from them was like rotten vegetables. My Sten was now empty, but our advantage for the moment was that the trench was too narrow for their rifles to be swung around. Those with burp guns seemed to take off up the hill towards HQ position.

Thank God for our basic training—hand-to-hand fighting lasted for only a short period of time, but it seemed like an eternity. I think we had surprised them, for one or two had left the trench and a couple took off through the trench. We then headed back to HQ (I do believe we broke the one-mile dash record!).

Contact was still in place with the outpost. Capt. Taylor called for mortars and artillery fire walking the barrage down the forward slopes of our position, and told the outpost to pull back. I'm really not sure if the outpost got back; the fighting was fierce and the smell of burnt-off mortar shell powder, and the rattling of small arms and cracking of shells landing was like a nightmare. It appeared that the Chinese had little fear of death; they kept coming in swarms, yelling and screaming. The regiment held 355 for many days. When the shelling stopped, it was as if the skies opened up and poured in sunlight.

As the medics retrieved our casualties, I asked somebody about the guys from the forward position, in particular Bill Elliot. I was told he was just behind them, and when I asked again, he pointed to a soldier with a backpack. Bill didn't make it. What was left of him was in that backpack.

By the end of August, the heavy rains had stopped. During August and September 1952, they appeared to be throwing everything North Korea, China and Russia could supply, not only at our position but along the entire hill ranges 355-227-187, and action was even reported on the hills behind us, 166 and 152.

It was now mid-1953. Word came down that we were being shipped home. I knew it would be hard to leave our fallen comrades who now lay in the war-torn country of Korea, thousands of miles from home, and those who were in POW camps. To this day I still give thanks to God for my survival of that so-called police action, but the emotional scars and frequent nightmares still return me to Korea. We as soldiers were taught to fight and survive, but were never told how to handle the mass killings by the enemy of women and children and the elderly upon which we stumbled. The stench and crying around those mass graves are things I could not cope with. Yes, part of my nightmares.

On our return to Canada, with short stops along the way, we were treated with great fanfare, especially by the Royal Canadian

Legion branches. As we entered Ottawa, Mayor Charlotte Whitton gave us the keys to the city. However, the government paid little or no attention to us, including our prime minister, Louis St. Laurent. It took over forty years for our government to admit that the Korean theatre of operation was not a police action but a war. Then they approved military service medals—and mailed them to us.

Perhaps if those politicians had been there with us, and suffered the hardships of cold, rain, and K rations—not to mention the brutal assaults of the Chinese forces day after day—and watched their buddies shot down or wounded by enemy fire; if they had lived in bunkers with mud for a floor and half their protection blown away by enemy fire; if they'd watched mortars and shells come in and they'd had to hear the cries of the wounded, they would have declared very quickly that this was war.

As a boy of seventeen, I soon became a man. I do not regret my involvement in Korea. It was worthwhile to help those in need from savage invaders, and to help in some way to give them a chance for freedom and democracy. After all, we are Canadians.

STANLEY R. CROFT, MBE, CD Royal Air Force

BORN in Worcester, England, Stan enlisted in the Royal Air Force on January 21, 1939, prior to his eighteenth birthday. He was trained as a wireless operator/air gunner at Uxbridge, Yatesbury and Pwllheli (North Wales), and in 1939 was awarded his aircrew wing. He served with the 236 Squadron RAF, 2 Bomber Command, and 500 Squadron RAF, 16 Group, Coastal Command, and was promoted to warrant officer. His group performed anti-invasion reconnaissance, and provided cover for the Dunkirk evacuation in 1940. While with 500 Squadron flying reconnaissance operations, his Avro Anson was shot down in August 1940, crashing into the North Sea. Stan was picked up by a Dutch fishing boat, but taken prisoner upon reaching shore. He then spent five years in six different prison camps (*Dulag/Stalag*), and attempted escapes on six occasions, finally reaching freedom on April 17, 1945, after his sixth attempt.

Stan was demobilized in 1946 from active service but remained with the RAF until 1951. He moved to Canada in 1952, later joined the RCAF (Reserve) in Downsview, and retired with the rank of major in 1981, having been awarded the Canadian Forces Decoration (CD). He attended the Institute of Municipal Assessment Course for three years at Queen's University, and then joined the Ministry of Revenue Assessment Division, retiring as manager in June 1985.

Stan is a family man with three children, seven grandchildren and three great-grandchildren; his wife is an ex-WAAF. Stan is also a life member of the Royal Canadian Military Institute (RCMI), the RAF-RCAF POW Association, the Air Gunners Association, a life member of the Royal Canadian Regiment, and an active member of the Living History Speakers Bureau RCL Branch 258.

For his various exploits as a prisoner of war, Stan was appointed a Member of the Order of the British Empire (MBE). The following is an extract from the *London Gazette* dated June 28, 1946:

> The King has been graciously pleased to give orders for the following appointment to the Most Excellent Order of the British Empire: To be Additional Members in the Military Division of the said Most Excellent Order:
>
> Warrant Officer Stanley Raymond Croft (632266) RAF, No. 500 Squadron
>
> Warrant Officer Croft was rescued by Dutch fishermen after his aircraft had crashed in the North Sea in August 1940. He was taken to a small fishing village near Amsterdam where he was captured by the Germans. His first attempt to escape was from *Stalag* VIIIB in October 1941 when he exchanged identities with an army private and joined a working party at a factory near Ratibor. Warrant Officer Croft succeeded in leaving the factory but was recaptured shortly afterwards. In February 1943 while at *Stalag Luft* I, he gained admission to the hospital at Neubrandenburg on a pretext of having his tonsils removed and, disguised as a Serbian worker, made his escape. Warrant Officer Croft made his way to Stettin by train and attempted to board a ship for Sweden, but he was arrested. Although he received severe punishment for each of his attempts, Warrant Officer Croft persisted in his efforts and in August 1943 he and a companion cut the wire surrounding the camp and made their escape disguised as civilians. They reached Stralsund before being captured. Whilst serving fourteen days for this escape, he and a companion cut through the bars of the cell with hacksaw blades, but were captured as they were getting through the perimeter wire. Warrant Officer Croft took part in many tunnel-digging operations, all without success.

FREE AT LAST

Flying reconnaissance ops in an Avro Anson of 500 ("B") Squadron from Detling in Kent, our crew of four crashed into the North Sea from heavy German flak the night of August 8–9, 1940.

Two of us were picked up by Dutch fishermen and received by Germans on return to shore. We spent three days in hospital in Holland and then were taken to *Dulag Luft* for interrogation. Two days later I was transported to *Luft* I Barth as *Kriegsgefangener* No. 178.

I contemplated escape at Barth, but before any good plan could be formed, I was transferred along with forty-nine other "Kriegies" to Lamsdorf *Stalag* VIII B, which was a most despairing sight, being occupied in the main by British Army boys from Dunkirk. These conditions made it even more important to me to find an escape route. I paired up with Dickie Holmes from 10 Squadron and we changed identities with two army types and joined a work party of eighty about to leave for farm work, which we thought would give better opportunities for escape.

On arrival at the work area, we were billeted in what appeared to be an old theatre in which the seats had been removed and bunk beds installed. After roll call, we were locked in for the evening, and as soon as the guards left we proceeded to unlock ourselves out. Unfortunately, however, the guards returned when we were halfway through chopping the door down. Needless to say, they took a dim view of this and promptly let us have it with rifle butts. One guard hit me on top of the head and the lights went out. I came to in a hospital. I had my head sewn up by a German doctor who asked me what had happened, so I told him. Apparently the guard said I had fallen and cut my head on an iron bedpost.

Needless to say, we were promptly returned to VIII B and spent a month in the *Straffe Lager*. Then we made the switch back to our own identities and returned to the RAF compound. End of attempt #1.

* * *

I did do a second reconnoitre of the camp one evening. I slipped out of the RAF compound to see what other possibilities there were, but was picked up by one of the guards who led me to the *Straffe Lager* for identification and punishment. However, on finding out that the duty *Unteroffizier* was at the other end of the building, he told me to wait while he went to get him. As soon as he disappeared round the corner, I climbed the fence and made my way back to the RAF compound. An identification parade was held the next day, but the guard did not recognize me in the lineup, so the incident passed. I'll bet he's still wondering where I'd got to.

In May 1942, we were all transferred to Sagan. Our number had grown from the original fifty to about 300 by this time, and we, excluding the officers, were the first group to open up the NCO's side of *Luft* III, along with a few odd bodies who had been taken directly there from *Dulag Luft*.

Luft III did not look at all promising for escape, but I still kept thinking about it, hoping something might light the flame. It finally did when the word went out that we were all going back to *Luft* I at Barth. Apparently all the officers at Barth were being moved to Sagan to make it an all-officer camp and Barth an all-NCO camp.

We renewed acquaintances with some of the chaps we knew in 1940 and had left behind in 1941 when we moved to VIII B. But now some of the escape thoughts I had had in 1940 came back.

I, along with J. Thompson, Slim Somerville, Duggie Adams and Jack Axford, started work on some tunnelling, but got caught and spent several terms on bread and water solitary in the cooler.

After some time trying to think of an escape plan in conjunction with Tommy Thompson, who shared my enthusiasm to get back to "Blighty" as soon as possible, we heard from some POWs who had had hospital treatment of sorts for one thing or another that the convalescent camp at Neubrandenberg was fairly easy to get out of.

Tommy, who had been suffering from a hernia, and I, who had enlarged tonsils, persuaded the German medic—with the help of the British doctor—that we should be sent to Neubrandenberg for treatment. Tommy left a few days later, and I followed the day after.

When I arrived at Neubrandenberg, Tommy had already been operated on, and when I saw him the day following my arrival, he was in a sorry state—barely able to walk. We discussed the situation and decided that I should see about getting my tonsils out so that we could recuperate together and, at the same time, formulate our escape plans.

I was taken the next day to the hospital in Neubrandenberg for a tonsillectomy. However, the German doctor said he could not remove the tonsils in a swollen state and so I was taken back to the camp.

As soon as I arrived back in the camp, Tommy came over to say that one of the Polish doctors had overheard a conversation about

Tommy and myself being in Neubrandenberg, and a guard was on his way from *Luft* I to take us back.

Apparently the *Abwehr* (security) officer at *Luft* I, Hauptman Von Miller, had returned from leave, and when he heard that Tommy and I were at Neubrandenberg, he put two and two together and came up with five.

Tommy was in no condition to travel the escape route, so I decided it had to be that night—alone.

We casually walked around the compound until it was nearly dark but the perimeter lights had not come on. Seeing that the guard was approaching his furthest point away with his back towards me, I said, "I'm going over now," to Tommy. With that, I quickly scampered over the wire and into the bush outside the camp. I don't think the whole thing took more than ten seconds, but it seemed an awful long time.

I waited to see if there was any alarm, but all was quiet so I made off through the bush until I hit the main road leading towards Stettin, about 100 kilometres away.

Keeping to the edge of the highway, I made quite good progress without any interruption until about two a.m. I was walking through a very small village when suddenly, out of the shadows, stepped a member of the *Volksturm* (Home Guard), with a rifle levelled at me. He cried, "Halt!" I halted. He said, "Who are you?"

"A Serbian worker going through to work at Pasewalk," I said in German. I happened to remember that Pasewalk was the next largest town on the main road towards Stettin. He stood there for a few seconds, not saying anything. I thought, well, here goes, and I walked on past him and on down the road. He did not raise the alarm. I considered that maybe he was just as scared as I was.

After walking all night and all day, resting at intervals, I finally arrived at Pasewalk, having walked a total distance of about sixty-five kilometres from Neubrandenberg.

I made my way to the railway yards to find a Stettin-bound boxcar that I could get into for a rest, as my legs felt like they were coming off at the thighs. I located one loaded with grain, crawled in through the top hatch, and promptly fell asleep. It was five p.m. I knew the time because I could see the big clock on the platform. I woke up once, but it was pitch black outside and nothing stirred, so I went back to sleep.

When I woke up again, it was five p.m. the next day. I had slept twenty-four hours! My legs were quite stiff, but I got the blood moving again by rubbing them, and decided I had better take a look outside.

I had no sooner touched the ground than I was spotted by one of the railway porters. I ran across the tracks towards a moving goods train that happened to be pulling out of the station. I made it to a flatcar that was loaded with the fuselage and wings of an airplane. I leapt on board and was rapidly taken away from my not-so-friendly porter.

After a breather, I started to look around to see if I could find a label indicating the train's destination. I found one and, to my dismay, this train was going to Stralsund, 150 kilometres from Stettin, where I wanted to get to, and only about forty kilometres from *Luft* I.

The train did not stop until it got to Stralsund several hours later. I dropped off just outside the station in the dark and went to explore the goods trains in the yards to get one back to Stettin.

During my search, I came across a boxcar labelled Trelleborg, Sweden. I think I tried every way possible to get into it, but to no avail. Giving it a good kick, I recommenced my search for a Stettin-bound train to continue my journey.

I located an open-top truck going in the right direction, and made myself comfortable and awaited the trip. Many hours of half-awake and half-asleep travel finally got me into Stettin. Now began the search for a Swedish ship or some outside help to get to Sweden.

I made my way down to the docks and wandered around without challenge until, from the quayside, I saw a ship in the river with the Swedish flag flying. It was still light, so I decided to walk away and come back later.

Thinking that a church would be a fairly safe place to pass a couple of hours, I went into a Lutheran church nearby, which had the front door partly open. I lay down and dozed for a while and was awakened by the minister, who asked what I wanted. I told him I was in need of rest and maybe some bread and water if he could spare it. He asked me who I was and so I told him the truth. He told me he could not help me and that I should leave immediately. This I did.

After wandering about for a while, I started to make my way towards the quay where I had seen the Swedish ship. She was still there.

It was still too light to try and get to her, so I started to walk back off the quay when I was accosted by two *polizei*. Asked who I was, I told them the Serbian story again, and walked on past. However, they were not satisfied and came and took my arms and walked me to the cop shop.

There, I was greeted by the police chief, who interrogated me for identification, although I think they knew who I was.

I was taken to the military prison, where my identification was confirmed. I spent the next three days in this prison and finally a guard from *Luft* I came and, half an hour later, I was on a train back to *Luft* I and twenty-one days of bread and water and solitary confinement in the cooler. End of escape #2.

* * *

One day, Tommy Thompson and I noticed a dark spot at the perimeter wire that was, we judged, about a yard wide. It appeared that the lights' arcs did not quite meet at this particular point, so we studied the situation for several nights, timing the guard's up and down patrol, the distance from the billet to the wire, etc. Finally, we decided to hide in the cookhouse, wait till dark, and then crawl across the compound some 200 feet to the dark spot at the wire.

We prepared ourselves with food, wire cutters, notched sticks about two and a half feet in length to support the barbed wire so it would not fall on us and trap us, and maps of the general area.

A dark, foreboding sky indicated rain and a poor moon on the day we decided to go.

The boys (our escape committee) were informed of our decision, and we hid in the cookhouse while roll call took place and they covered for us. About nine o'clock we made our way out in the darkness from the cookhouse and crawled on our stomachs across the compound. We made our way to the warning wire and I lay parallel to the main wire and started cutting. As soon as the guard approached the light, we stopped, and when he passed the next light we recommenced cutting. This process was repeated again and again as he returned on his beat. Slowly but surely we edged our way through the barbed wire entanglements, supporting the ends of the cut wire with our notched sticks.

Finally, we cut the outside strands of wire and waited patiently for the guard to go past, his jackboots only about two feet away from our faces. Fortunately for us, it was a particularly dark night, but with a considerable amount of rain, and we were soaking wet. Soon the guard had passed and was well down to the end of the beat, and we crawled out and made for some small trees and scrub outside the camp.

It was an amazing feeling, standing there looking at the camp from the trees. Guards, machine-gun towers, searchlights, barbed wire—all these security measures—and yet here we were, on the outside looking in. It had taken about four hours to accomplish this feat.

We didn't stop to reflect long and made off in the dark towards Stralsund. We planned to get from there to Stettin, or directly to Sweden by postal train, if possible. I thought we might give it a try from Stralsund after my previous experience in the railway yards. Maybe we could make it this time.

After walking during the night, we stopped for a rest in the morning and to clean ourselves up a bit. We made Stralsund okay, and waited for darkness to explore the railway yard for boxcars labelled "Nach Trelleborg, Sweden." So focused were we on our search, we failed to hear the stealthy approach of two guards and three station porters. We were nabbed and taken to the local cop shop and then returned to *Luft* I. The usual fourteen days' solitary with bread and water followed in the cooler. End of escape #3.

* * *

While serving the sentence, German security decided to put up a wood-and-straw screen in front of the barred windows of the cells so that we could not see what was going on outside, or call across to our friends in the compound. I used the handle on my cell broom to knock a hole in this screen so that I could see, but the guards took exception to this and I promptly received another ten days in solitary for damaging Reich property.

Fourteen days passed, and Tommy returned to the compound, but I still had ten days to go. I was soon joined in the next cell by

Jack Axford. Jack had climbed the wire when no one was looking, but his freedom was short-lived and he was now my next-door neighbour in the cooler. All was not lost, however, as Jack had been able to bring in with him a small, short hacksaw blade that was sharp enough, we found, to cut the cell bars. By carefully cutting so as not to attract attention, Jack cut through his bars and then passed the saw to me by swinging it on a piece of string from his cell window to mine. The screen they had so diligently put up also prevented the guards on the main gate from seeing us pass things from cell to cell.

Very soon I had my bars cut through and we found, to our satisfaction, that the ersatz soap provided by the Germans matched perfectly the colour of the paint on the cell bars. This soap, pushed into the saw cut on the bars, prevented the guards from noticing anything wrong.

My ten days were running out, so we decided that at the first opportunity, out we go. Luck was with us almost immediately—a night air raid. The camp lights went out, the guards went out to their air-raid shelters, and we bent our bars wide and went out, too.

We crawled quickly round the cell block and made it across the compound to the warning wire. We listened for guards, but could not hear anything. We were just about to stand up and climb the wire when the camp lights came on and we were face to face with the business end of a rifle held not too firmly by the "Dauntless Dieter" who apparently stayed at his post and braved the air-raid warning. He called for assistance and we were marched back to the cooler.

The expression on the face of the *Unteroffizier* in charge of the cooler was worth a million. He could not believe we had just walked in the front door. He grabbed the cell door keys and rushed down the corridor and opened up the cell doors and lo and behold, there we were—gone. He probably would have killed us right there if he could. Long, dark, cold nights on the Russian front loomed ahead for him for negligence of duty.

Next morning, back for sentencing: twenty-one days in solitary. End of escape #4.

* * *

Life had been rather hectic over the past few months, so I decided to cool it a bit. And besides, the security guards were watching us "boys." If we were seen talking together for too long a time, they figured there was something afoot.

We were suddenly moved to *Luft* VI at Hydekruk almost without warning. The Lithuanian border was only about six or seven miles away, but it was German occupied and didn't appeal very much as a place to escape to anyway.

We did a bit of reconnoitring but did not come up with any real plan of attack regarding escapes.

Our stay at *Luft* VI did not last too long, and the Germans shipped us out in the hold of a ship from Memel. The Russians were apparently not too far away.

Other than a rather disturbing air raid on the docks at Stettin, where we were put in boxcars after disembarking, and a fairly hairy run of about four kilometres from the railway station to *Stalag Luft* IV at Grosse Tyschow, life was becoming monotonous—due mainly to the fact that it appeared the war was now well in our favour, and to get shot at this point for escaping would be rather foolish.

In January 1945, about 300 of us plus about 100 Russians, Poles and Ukrainians started what ended up to be a twelve-week march to freedom (not that we knew it at the time).

The march was twenty, thirty and sometimes forty kilometres a day in all kinds of weather, sleeping wherever we could. Cold, soaking wet, hungry, it became a matter of physical endurance and survival.

After about nine weeks, two of our gang were in bad shape. Tommy Thompson and Abernathy were suffering from dysentery, so Slim Somerville and I decided the four of us would leave the marching to somebody else and make our own way.

We all slipped away in the night and made a few miles before we came to a farm with a big two-storey barn. This would be ideal for a place to rest and give the invalids a chance to recuperate in some dry hay and warmth.

However, it was not to be. Our notoriety made us conspicuous, and our absence was soon noted and a search made. We were found by one young guard who had been a member of the *Hitlerjunge* and a real true-blue Nazi. A real nasty customer.

He quickly lined us up against the barnyard wall and was preparing to dispatch us with the usual German efficiency. I was so convinced we were going to be shot right there, I said to Slim, "Well, I guess we've asked for it."

Fate now took a hand. The farmer and his wife came running out, telling our Nazi boy that if he wanted to shoot us he had better find another farmyard. The farmer's wife was a kind-hearted woman and, seeing Tommy and Jimmy in bad shape, took them into her kitchen and gave them some warm food. The farmer said we were entitled to at least have a last meal. Our Nazi friend was cooled off and he ate with us and then we took off, with him guarding us, marching to catch up to the rest of the column. End of escape #5.

* * *

A few days later, one night in a barn about ten kilometres from Eulzun, Slim and I were awake and we could hear what sounded like gunfire, and it was pretty close by. I said to Slim, "How about it? Let's beat it in the early morning." So away we went. I made my way along the highway, stealing a bike from a house on the way.

I was pedalling along when, passing a farm towards a wood, I heard machine-gun fire. I literally fell off my bike into the ditch and

crawled back to the farm and hid behind a woodpile. Down the road came an armoured car, which stopped in the middle of the road some fifty yards from the farm. Not quite knowing what to make of it, I called out in German, "Who's there?"

A soldier stood up in the armoured car, and right away I recognized the black beret of the Tank Corps. I now called out in English and stood up.

The soldier shouted to his comrade, "Don't shoot!" Then to me: "Stand in the middle of the road and identify yourself," which of course I did, thinking to myself: at last I've made it!

Although the war had only another three weeks to go, as it happened, I didn't care—at last I was free again!

It was April 17, 1945.

WW I, Air Force Mural – Billy Bishop, V.C.

HERB DANTER — ROYAL CANADIAN ARTILLERY

HERBERT A. (HERB) DANTER was born on December 27, 1920, in Mimico, Ontario, the fifth of seven children of Walter and Emma Mary Danter, both of whom emigrated from England in 1911. Mr. Danter Sr. was an accountant for the Central Region of the CNR. Herb's three brothers also served in WW II, one in the RCN, one in the RCAF and another in the army. Herb's uncle had fought with the 18th Battalion (Western Ontario Regiment) in WW I.

Herb Danter joined the 2nd Battalion, Toronto Scottish Regiment (MG) in July 1940, and remained with the NPAM until re-enlisting in July 1942 in the newly recruited 117th Field Battery RCA (Canadian Army Active), to try and get the higher medical category required for overseas service. He was sent to Camp Petawawa for basic training (for the second time).

In October of that year, Herb was transferred to the 23rd Field Regiment RCA (sometimes known as "Landers Lilies" after a certain CO's keenness for whitening all cap and rank badges) in Camp Sussex, New Brunswick. The 23rd went overseas as part of the 4th Canadian Armoured Division in July 1943 and was stationed in the south of England.

Herb was attached to the Royal Artillery (for discipline and rations) and went to the Royal School of Artillery in Larkhill, where he was "fine-tuned" in gunnery and specialty training as an OP Ack and a GPO Ack. After graduating from the RA School in the "Gospel According to Larkhill," he returned to his regiment, where he practised his skills from Normandy until the war's end in Germany.

As part of 4th Canadian Armoured Division, the 23rd Field Regiment (Self-propelled [SP]) arrived in Normandy in July 1944 and relieved a field regiment of the RA of the 7th (UK) Armoured Division (The Desert Rats) at Caen. At the breakout of the British and Canadians at Caen, the 2nd Canadian Infantry Division and the 4th Canadian Armoured Division leapfrogged each other to Falaise with the intention of meeting the Americans, and thus setting a trap for the German army in France.

For the next ten months, Herb Danter was either at the OP or out on recce ahead of the fast-moving guns. The 23rd Field Regiment (SP) gave close support for the infantry units and the armoured units of the 4th Canadian Armoured Division as they fought through the rest of France, Belgium, Holland, and finally into Germany. The 23rd ended the war not far from Wilhelmshaven, Germany, on May 4, 1945. For a short time after that, Herb was employed in the orderly room near Amersfoort, Holland, processing returning homeward-bound troops until his turn came for repatriation.

In 1946, after his discharge, Herb got a job as a travelling representative for a furniture manufacturer in Toronto. Herb is married and has two daughters and a granddaughter.

He is presently enjoying being the secretary of the Toronto Artillery Ex-Sergeants Association and the co-chairman and secretary of the Limber Gunners Association. Both of these organizations are affiliated with the 7th Toronto Regiment RCA in Moss Park Armoury, Toronto.

"BAPTISM BY FIRE"

As a self-propelled field artillery regiment giving close support to the infantry regiments of the 4th Canadian Armoured Division, we landed in Normandy in July 1944. We were to relieve an artillery regiment of the 7th British Armoured Division (The Desert Rats) just south of Caen. Being a member of our battery's (36 Field Battery—Cobourg, Ontario) recce party, we were sent in as part of the advance party to arrange the transfer.

Now this particular gun position that my party was assigned to was overlooked by enemy-held territory. They (the enemy) had to know we were there to take over, because they gave us a tremendous welcome with a heavy artillery barrage. Our only spot of safety (such as it was) happened to be underneath our half-track recce vehicle. We must have looked a trifle foolish trying to dig a big enough hole by clawing away at the earth! My thoughts flashed back to the soothing words of our divisional commander, Major General George Kitching, who, when we were still in England, promised to "ease us into battle" (George should have buttoned his lip). Even the battle-hardened Desert Rats admitted that they had never encountered such a fierce barrage before. So when we returned to our regiment and our respective batteries, we were, to say the least, all shaken up and a little punchy; but after a few drams of the "elixir of the gods" we settled down and actually began to feel a little proud that we had been the first ones in the regiment to receive our "baptism by fire."

The next "flashback" of memory is during the breakout of Caen (Normandy) by the 21st Army Group, comprising British, Canadian, Polish and other sundry units under the overall command of General Bernard Montgomery. Our 4th Division, which was one of the spearheads of this exercise ("Operation Totalize"), was to leapfrog with the 2nd Canadian Infantry Division down the Caen to Falaise Highway (Route Nationale 158) to team up with the 3rd Canadian Infantry Division (the D-Day Boys) and to meet up with the Americans advancing from the south, in the hope of trapping the bulk of the German army in that pocket.

The enemy, trying to escape down this highway, was mercilessly pounded day and night by air force and artillery. The scene was one out of Hades—the road was choked with the decaying bodies of both men and horses, which the Germans used quite extensively as transport. In those hot days of August 1944—the hottest summer in Europe in twenty-five years—it didn't take long before the stench of death became apparent. It was so bad that even the pilots in low-flying planes remarked on the awful stench of putrefaction that drifted skyward when they flew over.

In this operation, our rear lines were bombed by the US Air Force on August 9th, with resulting heavy casualties to our medium artillery and headquarters groups. This was called a tragic mistake; and on the following August 14th, this same mistake was duplicated by the RAF and RCAF when their heavy bombers let loose with their bomb loads, resulting in a great many more casualties. This was one of the bad side effects that close bombing created. We were choked with clouds of dust from both of these episodes, and we still had to continue on the attack, no matter what.

There was a rather amusing incident in this dark drama. We were issued long, yellow marker flags that we were to place on top of our vehicles as aircraft recognition signals; so when the Yanks started to bomb us, we were all calling for these yellow flags. In the ensuing maelstrom caused by the exploding bombs, our poor old quartermaster was running around in the thick cloud of dust that engulfed us, trying to hand out these yellow markers. Someone screamed, "For Gawd's sake give me something yellow to wave!" and one of the chaps in my group yelled back, "Wave me, *I'm* yellow!" Humour has no bounds.

In this operation I can still remember the oppressive heat, the choking, blinding dust, and especially the stench of rotting bodies of both men and horses. No one who was there and came through it will ever forget the Caen to Falaise road in Normandy circa August 1944.

The mad dash chasing the remnants of the German army (and they were powerful remnants) through the rest of France and into Belgium came to a halt when we reached the Leopold Canal. It then became static warfare in late September 1944. There was little activity except in patrol strength attacks by both ourselves and the enemy.

Here is another location that I well remember. Since static warfare would never finish a war, plans were made to mount an attack called "Operation Switchback" to start on the nights of October 5th and 6th with a terrific artillery barrage as openers. Since I had learned how to plot barrages as part of my gunnery training, I was called back from the Forward Observation Post (OP) to help at the Battery Command Post back at the guns in preparing this action. The call came to me by wireless at around 2200 hours, so off I was sent by myself in the middle of the night.

It was one of the blackest of black nights—there were no guiding lights such as moonlight or stars to help me—so I started down a gravel pathway that led from our little observation post in the hope that I was going towards our gun position. It was eerie—the only sound was made by my walking on the gravel, otherwise it was dead quiet and dead black. I would stop every other second to listen for any movement, because I had been forewarned of heavy patrol activity on both sides. Now here is where one starts to sweat even though the night is damp and chilly!

It seemed like an eternity out there by myself—I presumed or imagined that I could hear rustling coming from the underbrush on both sides of the path, and here and there I thought I heard a twig snap. I was happy that it was so dark out, because if I couldn't see them, then they couldn't see me—although they could hear my footsteps and, let's face it, if I had bumped into one of our patrols or an enemy patrol, I don't think I would have had time to say anything.

All of a sudden the lane, with its crunchy gravel, ended. I had come to a field. Where to from here? I was completely lost. Suddenly I saw a crack of lamplight for an instant, and by this time I couldn't care less, so I headed for it not knowing who or what it was. I came upon a huge tarp covering a mound of earth—or so I thought. Then I heard the sound of voices; they sounded like Canadian voices—hurrah, they *were* Canadians! I bounded into this safe haven and not only was it an artillery command post but it was *my own* battery command post. You've gotta be lucky some of the time!

I was well received by a casual "Glad you're here now because we're going to be at this all night. By the way, what took you so long getting here?" Anyhow, to make a long story short, they gave me a few rations (Compo) and a couple of swigs from a bottle full of the "nectar of the gods," after which I was settled down enough to help out with this huge fire plan. In retrospect, I'm thankful that I even had a crunchy path to follow on such a dark night; otherwise I probably would have gone round in circles.

The last incident that I will comment on happened in Germany in early April 1945 while we were slugging it out in the mud of early spring and into the final stages of the European War. (I will not refer to any incidents in Holland. These should be in a separate document entitled "Extra Special.") Everything by this time was in a fluid state, and by this I mean, instead of our infantry being ahead of us, we were quite often in the lead with our self-propelled guns, and we were firing at targets at ranges of 500 yards or less.

This particular event occurred on the morning of April 8, 1945 while my battery (36th Field Battery from Cobourg) was breakfasting prior to another move. The location was on the edge of a small forest (*Wald*) on the outskirts of a village by the name of Sögel situated in the area of Hochwald. The fog was thick and we lingered, waiting for it to dissipate before we moved off. I went to our recce vehicle and sat inside studying our route for the day, and when the fog lifted all hell broke loose.

Apparently a squad of Nazi paratroopers had landed during the night and hidden in the woods just off our gun positions, and as soon as the fog cleared they started their attack. Our SP guns (thank God we had them) saved the day for us—the gun crews took on the role of tanks and they advanced into the woods firing their 25-pounders point blank, at the same time raking the same woods with machine-gun fire. We held the paratroopers off until nightfall when one of our infantry regiments of the 4th Division (the Lake Superior Motorized Infantry Regiment) came and finally cleaned things up.

Sadly, however, we suffered quite a few casualties, and it must have been very hard for our padre to notify the families, especially since the cease-fire was only a few weeks away.

LEST WE FORGET.

JAN DE VRIES

PARATROOPER

A NATIVE of Friesland, Jan came to Canada at age six in 1930. He attended East York Collegiate during the Depression, and then held several jobs, including working in a war plant during the early years of WW II. In February 1943, at age nineteen, he enlisted in the 1st Canadian Parachute Battalion and received basic training in Brantford, Ontario, then para training in Camp Shilo, Manitoba. The battalion shipped overseas in July 1943 and became part of the 3rd Brigade of the 6th British Airborne Division under the command of Brig. James Hill, DSO (2 Bars), MC.

Jan parachuted into Normandy with the battalion at 0030 hours on June 6, 1944, hours ahead of the D-Day landings. He was wounded by a sniper in August 1944, evacuated to England, and returned to his unit in September 1944 at its Salisbury Plains base.

His unit then participated in the Battle of the Bulge at Christmas 1944, and moved into Holland in February 1945, relieving infantry units. The battalion then jumped into Germany in the Rhine Drop on March 24, 1945, near Wesel. They then fought their way across Germany, linking up with the Russians at Wismar on the Elbe River near the Baltic Sea on May 2, 1945. Jan returned to Canada and was discharged in February 1946 at the age of twenty-two.

Post-war, Jan pursued a career in construction with Cadillac Fairview, and later with the Daniels Group Inc., retiring as construction manager in 1993. He was elected president of the 1st Canadian Parachute Battalion Association in 1995 and, in 1997, was a co-founder of the Living History Speakers Bureau RCL 258.

His duties with the Parachute Association entail extensive travel, involving many public ceremonies, but he still finds time to be an active executive member of Living History, and is one of our most valued speakers. Jan's primary interest is having the students of today learn of Canada's success in past conflicts that could otherwise have resulted in the loss of our freedom.

Jan is also a member of RCL Branch 258, Highland Creek, Ontario, and is active on its building committee. Jan is a director of the Canadian Airborne Forces Association, a director of the Canadian Airborne Museum in Petawawa, Ontario, and a director of the Canada Juno Beach Centre, a memorial/educational centre to be constructed in Normandy to commemorate Canada's contribution to victory in WW II.

MEMORIES OF A "PARA"

Canada

In late 1942, I finally convinced my mother that I would have to join the military sooner or later. I decided the air force was for me. After much testing, the eye doctor said that I was, to a degree, colour blind, so aircrew was out of the question. Ground crew did not appeal. I then went looking for the navy recruiting office.

On the way, I saw a group of parachutists and was impressed with their appearance. I knew instantly that was for me. I immediately signed up at the army recruiting office, specifying the Paras.

After six weeks of basic training and passing a review board, I was sent to the new parachute training centre at Shilo, Manitoba. I had completed only three weeks' training when I was shipped overseas with the battalion without qualifying, as the battalion was under strength. I eventually arrived in Bulford, England, and then was sent to Ringway to earn my wings.

Ringway, England

During the last week of August 1943, after much training, an instructor, four other first-time jumpers, and I were taken up 700 feet in the basket suspended below a balloon. On the words "Get ready," one at a time we sat down at the edge of a round hole in the floor of the basket with our feet hanging through. We were instructed to arch our backs so the parachute could clear the side of the hole on the order to go. The ground sure seemed a hell of a long way down! On the word "Go," I cleared the hole nicely and fortunately did not hit my nose on the far side of the hole.

Falling, falling, falling! I know I am frozen stiff! When is that 'chute going to open? One hundred and ninety feet later, there is a rustling sound and the 'chute opens. I feel relieved. The instructor's voice is heard through the megaphone from below, but I am not listening. I'm enjoying the view. In no time it is all over. I hit the ground, go into the expected roll, and then get hell from the instructor for not listening to instructions. I'm happy and grinning. I've completed my first of eight jumps to qualify for wings.

June 6, 1944, D-Day, Normandy

My jump on D-Day was not the best experience. I dropped some miles off the DZ and spent the night slowly making my way to the coast, missing the attacks in which I was supposed to take part. Arriving at our planned defence position sometime in the afternoon, I was immediately ordered to go and find the Germans. After getting back and reporting where I had located the Germans, I dug my slit trench just in time to dive for cover when we were shelled for the first time.

June 12, 1944, Normandy

After the usual morning barrage lifted, word came down to gather fighting gear and report, on the double, to Company Headquarters. About forty of our company gathered, leaving about ten men to hold our position. We were ordered to double to Brigade Headquarters where Brig. James Hill, DSO (2 bars) MC took charge. The brigadier took off, with us running behind him, in the direction of some heavy action that we had been hearing earlier on, thankful that someone else was catching hell. As we approached the area, a tremendous amount of shell bursts and bullets splitting the air enveloped us. The brigadier calmly moved along, telling us to "Move along, chaps," as we bent lower to the ground as we ran.

Fortunately, we were advancing in a depressed laneway and no one got hit. That changed when we crossed a road into a field where jeeps, ammunition, trailers and Bren gun carriers were burning and exploding. We advanced into bush. While being raked by machine-gun fire and air bursts overhead, we were told to dig in at the front edge of the bush. Two of our fellows who dropped behind an abandoned Vickers were hit before they had fired off a full belt.

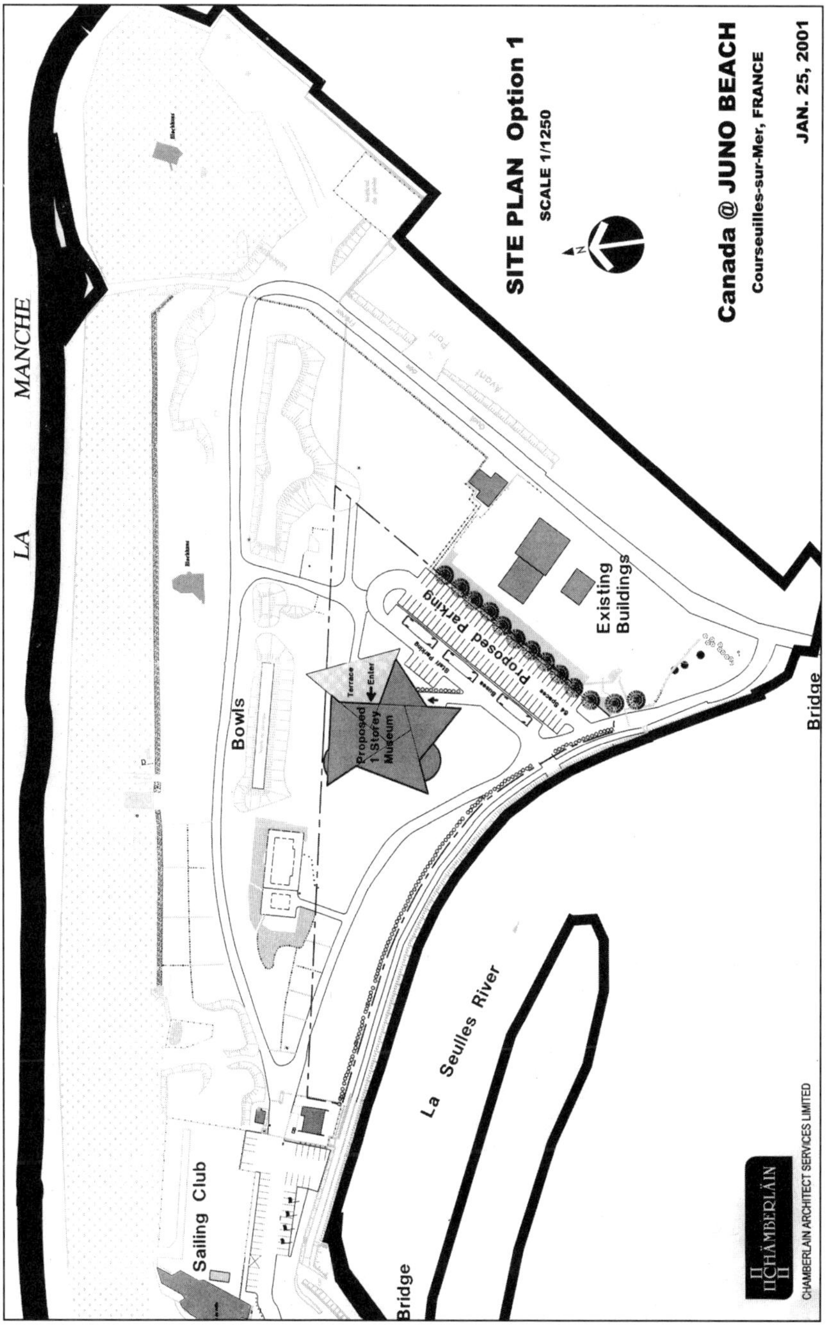

Schematic of Juno Beach Centre being constructed to commemorate the landings in Normandy, June 1944.

The ground was extremely hard about eight inches down, and little progress was made digging a slit trench. We were told to be ready to fire at will when we saw the enemy. An hour later we were still trying to dig deeper as the air bursts were taking their toll when, on our right, three Sherman tanks, one behind the other, moved forward, turned in our direction at the side of a large château nearby, and proceeded to slowly draw up to about seventy-five feet in front of my position. I was thinking how great it was to have three tanks in front of me when the lead tank was hit just as it was turning its turret in the direction from which the attack was coming. Not a minute later, the other two tanks were hit and burst into flames with some of the crew piling out. Now, in front of me I had three burning tanks lighting up the night sky, and no field of fire.

Not long after, the air was split by huge shells headed toward the enemy. Luck was with us. Navy fire was called down on the German tanks and infantry, fortunately breaking up their attack.

The next morning, the twenty or so of us that were left trudged back to our own defensive position and dove into our own slit trenches just ahead of the regular morning barrage.

Sometime Later in June 1944, Normandy

Our rear echelon was frequently attacked by German patrols sneaking through the bush between our position and the British 8th Battalion, which was on our right. Orders were to have a man move into the bush just before dark, stay out of sight, and when, in the dark, German patrols were heard coming through, get back quickly and warn the rest of the platoon to open fire.

On the night of my turn in the bush, I found a nice, solid tree to hide behind and stayed very quiet for at least a couple of hours. I felt very lonely and vulnerable, and imagined I heard Germans coming every few minutes. What I finally heard made me very apprehensive. It was the sound of mortars being fired. I had no idea whether they were ours or the enemy's. I quickly got my answer when I heard the loud siren-type noise of the "moaning minnies," the eight-barrel German mortars.

The first group dropped some way ahead of me. After that, all hell broke loose, as mortars and shell rained down in the area. I lay petrified for an unknown length of time, as there was no depression into which to crawl. Eventually, a shell burst close to the other side of the tree that I was behind. This left me blinded and deafened. The flashes of bursting shell in the dark were unnerving and the ringing in my ears was unbearable. A lull occurred and I ran as fast as I could back to my line, even though no Germans would send patrols out through their own barrage. I yelled, "They're coming!" and got into my slit trench. Even though my ears were still ringing, there was nothing wrong with my nose. In the morning light, I realized I must have run through the platoon latrine on my way to my trench!

August 7, 1944, Normandy

Our battalion moved up out of Brigade Reserve and took over the British 8th Battalion position in the Bois de Bavent. Information was given to our battalion on what to expect in the area. Our platoon was given a position along a thick, mounded hedgerow alongside a field with thick bush on the other side. It was about noon and the company cook sent word to come to where the kitchen was set up for dinner. The cook dished out the usual bully beef stew that we had been eating for weeks. I got mine down, but my stomach rebelled a bit later and I threw up. It must have been a sign of what was to come. I ate a slice of bread on the way back to the hedgerow, looked over the slit trench my partner and I would occupy, and checked our field of fire and for air burst protection. We heard a sharp whistle blast and an order was given to dive for cover. A single mortar shell hit close by. It turned out that the Germans were lobbing mortars over on an irregular schedule, and a man in a forward post would blow a whistle when he heard the mortar being fired.

My name was called and I received an order to go through the hedge into an open slit trench about thirty-five feet out into the field. I looked over and asked, "What am I supposed to be out there, a target?" Previously, the "Brits" had a man out there as a forward lookout and we were to follow suit. Being a good soldier, I ran across to the trench, jumped in, and waited. As instructed, I used the binoculars provided to scan the bush in front for Germans. As could be expected, there was nothing to be seen but leaves.

After about two hours, there was an explosion and I was thrown against the back side of the trench. Bending forward to keep my head below the top of the trench, I tried to figure out what had happened. Had I missed hearing the whistle and did a mortar shell land close by? Then I noticed blood dripping onto the trench floor and found that my shoulder was numb. Realizing that I had been hit, I called back for help. One of my buddies ran over, planted a shell dressing onto my shoulder, helped me up, and acted as a shield as we ran over to the hedgerow.

A German sniper had made his way through the bush and picked me off when he saw me in the open field. My section sniper later informed me that he had seen the German sneaking through the trees and was waiting to pick him off when the German fired at me, and then left. Had I been aware of that at the time, I would have sworn, but I realized I was lucky. The German was a lousy shot. My wound was a "blighty," an excuse to get out of battle for a while. I also heard later on that no one else was being sent out to that trench.

I had a rough ride in a Jeep to the coast as a sitting casualty, then a flight in an Anson mail plane to a civilian hospital, where I was bathed by a group of student nurses. Sadly, the next day I was transferred to a Canadian general hospital for a month before returning to the battalion.

March 1945

Outside of frozen feet in the Ardennes and diarrhea in Holland, nothing significant happened to me until March 24, 1945, at 1000 hours. I was one of the sixteen thousand soldiers that jumped over the Rhine River into German home territory. When my parachute opened, I could hear the crack of bullets close by me. Looking up, I saw a number of small holes in my 'chute and looked down to see where I was going to land. At first it looked good, and I prepared to land. Unfortunately, as sometimes happens, a ground breeze caught my 'chute and carried me over the edge of a bush. I was coming down through the branches of a tree when my 'chute caught on something above and jerked me to a stop, jamming my arms up and my helmet half over my eyes. Try as I might, I could not reach the fighting knife attached to my leg to cut myself free. There I hung, in a cold sweat, watching branches drop around me as the German machine guns swept the area.

Luck was with me! Some time later, two paras from a British battalion came along. I called for help and one boosted the other up until he could grab my feet. The additional weight pulled my 'chute free, and all three of us tumbled to the ground.

The rest of my war was comparatively easy.

PATRICK FELLOWS

ROYAL NAVY

PAT was born in Birmingham, England, and as a teenager spent several years with the British Air Training Corps (Air Cadets). In February 1943, at age eighteen, he joined the Royal Navy Fleet Air Arm, and initially, as he phrases it, was sent on courses galore, including a flying school in Canada where he scrubbed out after landing in a farmer's field. He was then placed on a deck officers' training course in England. The course was terminated after D-Day, and he was assigned to the frigate HMS *Manners*, spending most of the balance of the war on convoy duty in the North Atlantic as the ship's writer. In January 1945 his ship was torpedoed by a German U-boat off the Isle of Anglesey, and lost its stern, with much loss of life. Later he was transferred to the aircraft carrier HMS *Trouncer* headed for Japan just prior to VJ day. He was demobilized in May 1946 and immigrated to Canada in 1949.

Pat was a business writer with the *Toronto Star* for twenty-eight years, and before that with the *Telegram*. He enjoys sundry activities, including golf, going on European cruises, some freelance writing, and babysitting five grandchildren from two daughters. He still spends time with the ShareLife Roman Catholic Charity and is a member of the Toronto Press Club and the Scarborough Golf Club (Social), as well as being an active member of the Living History Speakers Bureau RCL Branch 258.

WHAT DID YOU DO IN THE WAR, DADDY?

I thought you'd never ask. But since I've been asked to write a "most memorable experience" story, pull up a chair.

I should point out that individual experiences of war vary hugely. The soldier who fought land campaigns in close combat will have a different perspective from the bomber pilot who took even greater risks in many missions over enemy territory. Or the sailor who spent monotonous months at sea hunting—and dodging—U-boats. Or the guy who landed in a prisoner-of-war camp, sometimes for several years.

My father went to France in 1914, endured four years of trench warfare and was badly wounded ten days before the Armistice of November 1918. That's how he met my mother, who was a nurse. But for Wars I and II, I wouldn't be occupying this space.

But to get back to war at sea. It can erupt suddenly, catching even the watchful, when enemy submarines choose to attack. This is the type of event that came closest to demolishing me in WW II.

I had been in the Royal Navy about sixteen months before I got to sea, the intervening time being spent on an aborted flying course and other diversions, which are topics for later.

So I will begin on D-Day, June 6, 1944. I had returned from flying school in Canada and was taking a deck officers' training course in Portsmouth (Pompey) barracks. When the invasion of Europe began, the course was scrubbed and the participants dispersed, supposedly to more vital duties.

I was left vegetating in the barracks while the huge armada left Portsmouth for the beaches of France. To my surprise, I didn't get sent into the Channel and, hating life in the barracks, I asked for a "draft"—anywhere. I had to do this a couple of times before finally receiving instructions and a rail ticket.

The slip said, "Manners, Liverpool." *Manners* was not, as I at first feared, a charm school, but a captain class frigate, built in the US and named after some RN officer who had served his country well. Once I had located the ship at Seaforth dock, I walked timidly up the gangway and saluted the quarterdeck. You don't want to be seen to be a neophyte the first day aboard.

I had taken a circuitous sixteen-month route to get here, but I did experience a real feeling of exhilaration at GETTING A SHIP. I was assigned a mess aft (the back end), underneath the depth charges, and unloaded my kitbag.

Aside from routine work, I don't recall what specific job I was assigned to, but shortly afterward, the executive officer got me appointed to ship's writer—a clerical job. I must have given the impression of being bright, because another rating was bumped to accommodate me.

There was a special branch of the navy (supply) that did this sort of thing, but only ashore and on the bigger ships. Smaller ships usually assigned a rating with office or writing experience. This office job was an elite position. It gave me control over the issuing of ration cards and travel vouchers for men going on leave. There were, of course, restrictions on both documents, but (dare I say it) not for A/B Fellows. (Shame on you, Fellows!)

Action Stations was one of the two forward three-inch guns. Nobody liked being on gun crew; it was hard on the ears and exposed to the weather. One day, the gunnery officer rigged up what must have been a primitive range calculator in the ship's office. I was assigned to operate it under instructions from the bridge. Now I could both do my "day job" *and* go to an action position insulated from the noise and the weather. Talk about privilege.

It was the summer of 1944 and the Atlantic was fairly well behaved. The worst of the submarine war was over, although, as we later found to our cost, it hadn't lost its sting. But it was very comforting to know that the German air threat had been pretty well eliminated.

Shepherding a small armada of slow ships across the ocean was tedious, but as winter drew on and the weather worsened, there was more to occupy our minds. On one trip out, a fellow escort, a corvette, had to turn back when part of her bridge was washed into the sea.

Our job was to get the convoy into North American waters and hand it over to Canadians or Yanks, who would run it to Halifax and other Eastern seaports. We would put into St. John's, Newfoundland, to provision and rest and ogle the locals. Where is Mary Le Valliant? I remember St. John's being a plentiful source of a commodity that was scarce in Britain—ketchup. A hero back in Brum was a matelot who could bring home a case of ketchup—the fish and chips were waiting!

The weather was always fine when we entered the narrows to St. John's Harbour. When we sailed out to pick up a Europe-bound convoy with men and war *materiél*, it was always into dense fog (as expected in that part of the world). We had a relatively primitive form of radar, but one of my jobs was to stand on the fo'c'sle and peer into the dense mist, ready to holler like hell if some other occupant of the area threatened our integrity.

We were no strangers to one of the perils of war—doing more damage to your own forces than the enemy's. Collisions were an ever-present danger. To foil U-boats and still protect the slowest ship in the convoy, it was the practice to sail in a zigzag pattern. On October 26, 1944, a clear night with a calm sea, a navigation error zigged or zagged us into an accompanying escort corvette, HMS *Rose*, which was manned by Norwegians.

We struck the *Rose* amidships, causing her to sink fairly quickly with, I believe, the loss of three lives. She is probably lying somewhere off Newfoundland, perhaps in the general area of the *Titanic*.

I was asleep at the time of impact and didn't feel it. I went to my action station (in the office, of course) and wasn't able to observe the rescue effort. I don't know who was at fault. Our officer of the watch, a Lieut. Collins, was court-martialed, but apparently got off with a reprimand.

Perhaps because the dock space was needed, on one occasion we left St. John's and moved down to the harbour at Bay Bulls, a typical Newfoundland outport. It was December 18th, and the captain suggested celebrating Christmas at anchor rather than on the 25th when we would be at sea. This seemed like a good idea, so a Jeep was sent to St. John's to pick up some turkeys and assorted seasonal goodies, and the cook got to work. It was a cheerful event with no submarines, no watchkeeping, no weather worries. No problems.

That was to be our last convoy call in North America before we were knocked out of the contest. A few months later, Bay Bulls was the scene of surrender of U-190, which had earlier torpedoed HMCS *Esquimalt*, one of the worst tragedies ever to hit the Royal Canadian Navy. (As things worked out, I was later to become friendly with Werner Hirschmann, the engineer officer of U-190. After release from a POW camp, he settled in Canada and helped computerize Metro Toronto's traffic control system.)

While we were flopping around in the Atlantic on rough winter nights, sipping steaming hot "ky" (thick hot chocolate you could walk on), many a matelot's thoughts turned to "goin' up the line and settlin' down." My own sympathy lay with going up the line, but all this free travel, tedious though it sometimes was, just whetted my appetite to keep on going.

The *Manners* was the kind of ship many sailors preferred—a compact escort vessel with not overly structured discipline and a co-operative workaday atmosphere. First names weren't used, but nicknames were.

The guys who occupied the two bunks below me were "Ginger" Hardy and "Grubb(y)." Both died in the action I describe below, as did "Jock" Leggatt, "Blacky" Blackwell, "Tug" Wilson, a young seaman named Banning and several others whose names escape me.

A substantial part of the navy was always ashore. If you were waiting for a sea draft, the challenge was to appear to be busy. How many times a day could you roll up your hammock (I only slept in hammocks ashore; American-built ships had bunks) or clean the mess deck? Yet you couldn't have people lolling around doing nothing IN THE NAVY.

The powers that be used to think up all sorts of half-assed things to keep those naturally lazy ratings busy. "Report here. Report there. Fall in here. Fall in there." But the ratings themselves were not without resources. One trick was to keep walking around flourishing an important-looking piece of paper. You weren't going anywhere, but looked as though you were on your way to some office or another, and if you didn't get there, the war would be lost because some stupid crusher (naval policeman) questioned your perambulations.

But back to sea. At this time, German U-boats were using a new weapon—acoustic torpedoes—in a last-ditch bid to salvage the underwater war. Acoustic torpedoes follow the sound of a ship's screws, eliminating the need for a lot of calculations.

We were brutally introduced to this new weapon on a cool morning in January 1945, in the Irish Sea. We came under the attention of U-1051 as we proceeded north to Liverpool. I was on the bridge when an explosion occurred at our rear. From a forward position, there didn't seem to be any structural damage, but it soon developed that we no longer had motive power.

We had trailed a "foxer" on a line, a device designed to set up a diversionary noise. It may have attracted a torpedo, but in the process our screws appeared to have been damaged.

Damage control crews rushed aft only to get caught in a second, much more lethal, explosion. The quarterdeck disappeared along with racks of depth charges and the canteen and mess deck below. No one in that part of the ship survived. What was "home" to me for seven months now lies on the sea bottom off the Isle of Anglesey at 53° 39' N, 5° 23' W, along with some now barnacle-encrusted personal belongings.

As the ship heeled, the upper deck amidships came under water and one seaman found himself washed over the side. Fortunately, he was able to swim back aboard as the *Manners* was righting itself.

If this event had occurred five minutes before or after, I would have been back on my mess and not here to reminisce. As it is, I remember bodies and debris flying and a huge chunk of anchor cable heading in my direction. I dodged it, need I say, as it wrapped itself around a lookout position.

The bosun's mate (if I remember his rank correctly), a fellow named Pitcher, motioned me over to the middle of the bridge and pointed up the mast to the crow's nest. "Get up there," he shouted.

Wow, I thought, if this bloody ship is hit again and keels over, I'm going for one helluva ride. All right for the post-war midway, maybe, but not right now. But orders is orders. England expects . . .

So I started up the mast. Below and behind me, dead and wounded were lying on the deck. I remember a Charlie Spencer, beside himself with grief, going around trying to comfort and help anyone who was not beyond assistance. Charlie was the right stuff that day, but to my knowledge he didn't get any medals, although he was mentioned in the captain's report (which I later scrutinized at the Public Record Office in London).

A petty officer and seaman Asdic team were given DSMs (Distinguished Service Medals) for establishing a "ping" contact with the U-boat and enabling the frigates *Aylmer*, *Bentinck* and *Calder*, which had arrived on the scene, to sink it with all hands. *Manners* was officially credited with half the "kill."

But here I was, not having any particular fondness for heights at the best of times, climbing leg over leg to this lofty, and maybe perilous, perch.

Halfway up, I heard a shout. The captain's attention had been drawn to this receding figure and he reacted immediately. "What are you doing up there? Get down here." After all, what good was a crow's nest view to a crippled ship?

We were taken in tow to Barrow-in-Furness, where the *Manners* awaited a trip to the breaker's yard. It was now what the insurance industry would call a "constructive total loss." Of about twenty men sharing the mess, I believe only two of us survived.

With the European war over, I was drafted to HMS *Trouncer*, an aircraft carrier, as it ammunitioned for an assault on Japanese positions in the Far East. The A-bomb brought a sudden halt to that war and gave us a pleasant peacetime cruise halfway around the world.

Werner Hirschmann, whom I mentioned above, was a close friend of my late neighbour, Karl Kassbaum, a career officer (*Korvettenkapiten*, or lieutenant-commander) in the *Kriegsmarine* (German Navy). We lived right across the street from each other in identical bungalows.

Our friendship was cemented by a certain amount of common experience during and after the war. Karl's ship was sent to the bottom by a British submarine (the last act of HMS *Thames*), and I had been torpedoed by a German submarine. Karl got the worst of it. He lost his ship and most of his crew, went into the water and spent some time in lifeboats.

A man who had been a destroyer commander and flotilla leader in one of the world's major navies, Karl suffered humiliation and hardship in the wake of defeat. He was forced to take a job as a farm labourer immediately after the war to support a wife and three children.

A Canadian university team in Germany triggered Karl's interest in Canada and he came here in 1950. His first jobs were wheelman on the Great Lakes and moving furniture. Subsequently he got into property management. By coincidence, my first jobs in Canada in 1949 were furniture removal and Great Lakes deckhand.

Karl died in his eighties. His wife, Inge, lingered on for a few more years. She was a smart woman with what I regard as an un-German sense of humour. She told of the time she and Karl were living on a naval base at Kiel. The surrounding area was camouflaged to look like farmland. The Brits would come over and dutifully bomb the place, but one night dropped only leaflets. The message to the Germans was, "Why don't you move those wooden cows around once in a while?"

On demob, May 10, 1946, I collected the standard suit of clothes, shoes, and a raincoat, fifty-six pounds sterling, and exited the Royal Navy. I had been in uniform three years and three months.

LIVING WITH THE WAR

I think we were one of the first families to own a radio in the late 1920s, but by 1939 the Depression had left its mark and we were "wireless-less." On September 3, 1939, I stood in the entryway between our house and the next council house listening through an open window to Neville Chamberlain's squeaky voice declaring war on Germany.

My mother was in shock. She had nursed my father back to health after he was badly wounded in France ten days before the armistice that ended the "Great War." Now she had two sons who might have to put their lives on the line. But she was spared another round of desperate anxiety. At this time she was ailing, and she died of cancer in 1940 before the verdict was in.

At war's outbreak, I was just fifteen and thought I might escape it because all the talk was that it would be over very quickly. Famous last words! My brother Peter, being four years younger, could look for a longer reprieve.

In the early weeks, a German *Blitzkrieg* smashed Poland, while in the west the inactivity became known as the "*Sitzkrieg*" (sitting war). But after the Germans occupied Norway, Chamberlain resigned as British prime minister and Winston Churchill took over. On May 10, 1940, Germany opened the battle of Western Europe, attacking Belgium, Holland and France.

The Luftwaffe battered Rotterdam and other cities, and the Brits took to the air raid shelters. British preparations for war included the distribution of thousands of corrugated steel shelters, big enough to hold the average family.

If you wanted one, you got one, and the idea was to dig a hole in the back garden, put the thing together, and build up a protective earth bank around it. Some just erected the structure on the ground and left it there, and in the post-war years it became a storage shed. I suppose there are still a few left housing lawn mowers and garden tools.

We didn't ask for a shelter—too much work setting it up, probably. And there was no guarantee you wouldn't get hit in one.

There were the inevitable cases of families being wiped out in the shelters while their homes remained intact.

When the air raid sirens sounded, we moved under the stairs. My sick mother's bed had been brought down into the living room to make the necessary moves easier. And there we waited on edge for the typical whistle of a falling bomb while the Heinkels and Dorniers went "hmm-hmm-hmm" overhead.

I think the nearest miss was at the end of the street, perhaps a couple of hundred yards away. A "stick" of three HEs (high explosives) were dropped in a line along the main road, mercifully sparing nearby shops and houses.

During one raid (I must have gone off to the war by this time, or perhaps I was out "fire-watching," or maybe on police messenger duty at the local cop shop), Peter tells how he heard the telltale whistle of a falling bomb. This was it, he decided, and took a dive under the dining room table. He said later: "I was sure it had my name on it." The intruder exploded a safe distance away. Dad looked at Pete under the table and asked nonchalantly, "What are you doing under there?" Dad probably knew that if you heard it coming, it wasn't going to hit you. That at least was the commonly accepted theory.

But small firebombs came down all over the place, though I don't recall any serious conflagrations in the nearby area. Some of these bombs didn't go off, and police and firemen were out next morning collecting them. Peter recalls that they were temporarily stored in a yard at the back of Harborne police station. He and some other kids would go over the wall, taking care that Inspector Ward wasn't watching, grab some of the little beasties, stuff them inside their jackets and take off.

They would transport this load of war *materiél* up the street and behind the church. In a corner of the pathway that skirted the church field was a rickety structure known as the "cow shed." Inside were a bench and a vice. The kids would put the bombs in the vice and unscrew the bodies from the caps. They emptied out the phosphorus and poured it onto a pile a short distance away. Then they threw matches into it. Whoosh! Seems hazardous, but there were apparently no accidents. Whatever they said about *Reichsmarshal* Herman Goering, he did provide our youth with some "light" entertainment in an era when such delights as fireworks were otherwise unobtainable, and no one had any idea that solace could be found in drugs.

I wonder where all the stuff went that fell out of the sky on these dark nights. I have one solitary tail fin from a German incendiary bomb. It sits on the bar downstairs.

Where is all the shrapnel from the anti-aircraft barrage? There was lots of it around after a raid and it caused superficial damage. Shrapnel was a particular hazard of being outside during an air raid.

There was an anti-aircraft gun on a golf course about a mile to the west of us. I never saw it, but it must have been of fair calibre. The scuttlebutt was that it was a naval gun. When it let go, it was as though an earthquake had hit the neighbourhood. I don't think it brought anything down except a few hundred slates from the roofs of houses.

A major target for the Germans in the area was the Austin works at Longbridge, which, if I recall correctly, was building warplanes. (Ironically, many years after the war the Germans became owners of the plant through BMW Motors. But it rang up large losses and they had to sell it. One of its products was the upscale Land Rover.)

I remember one night in the blackout when there was total darkness. Usually you had an outline of something, somewhere, but this was utter blackness—no moon, no stars. Zero. I groped my way to the main road, where there was some light from the shaded headlamps of cars.

Unexploded bombs were a scary hazard, especially if they were in obscure locations. The bomb squad (you want the final definition of heroes?) was kept busy. One of Peter's recollections is that one such intruder crashed through a large house in Harborne Park Road and found a lodging place in the wine cellar. The bomb squad did its usual efficient job, during the course of which (the story goes) the sergeant in charge helped himself to a bottle of wine. The homeowner reported the theft and the sergeant was reprimanded. How tough can you get with a guy whose life can be ended by pulling too hard on a pin?

The early war years saw a couple of very hard winters in England. Food and fuel were scarce. Blizzards blocked streets and there was some interruption of bread and milk supplies. Most houses were heated by coal, delivered every week or so, and burned in a fireplace. The coalman would hump the stuff in on his back in hundredweight bags and dump it in the "coal house," which was given roughly the same standing in our little council dwelling as the bathroom.

The bath and the big copper vessel for heating bath and laundry water were state-of-the-art appliances in the bathroom. The washbasin was the kitchen sink. Running hot water was not thought of when the house was built sometime in the 1920s. It was eventually provided by a gas heater, which my father installed.

But back to the coal house. Britain had plenty of the black stuff but more than once we ran out when snow stalled truck deliveries. I built a crude wagon and trudged a mile with Peter through the drifts to pick up the precious cargo.

There were actually gas fires upstairs, but they were rarely used. The gas supply was metred and required frequent replenishments of one shilling. There was a potential hazard if the fire went out when the metre ran down and the tap was left open for gas to escape when the next shilling was deposited. The downstairs coal fire was out by bedtime, and many is the time we arose next morning to the chill of a winter frost.

The church was in the charge of the Passionist Fathers and a couple of the younger priests could swing a mean bat and hurl down terrifying fastballs. I remember Father Jerome and Father Athanasius. The latter was Tyrone Power handsome and turned up one day in the uniform of a Royal Air Force chaplain. Female hearts beat faster. But how unfair—he was a priest!

Thus did the war affect us all.

ROBERT (BOB) FIRLOTTE

Paratrooper; Regular Army

BORN in 1917 at Campbellton, New Brunswick, Bob served for three years before WW II in the militia with the North Shore (NB) Regiment. He joined the active army in April 1940, and served for over two years in England with the Carleton and York Regiment, progressing from private to CSM. In June 1942, he returned to Canada for officer training and served afterwards at various training centres until volunteering for the paratroops in June 1943. He then served a year at the Parachute Training Centre at Shilo, Manitoba, finally joining the 1st Canadian Parachute Battalion in England in August 1944.

Bob participated as a platoon commander in the airborne operation over the Rhine River into Germany in March 1945, and remained in action until meeting up with the Russian army at Wismar on the Baltic as the war came to an end.

Bob remained in the army after the war, serving in nine different regimental, training and staff appointments in twelve different places, including Korea, retiring in 1966 after twenty-six years of service with the rank of major. His regiments included the Princess Patricia's Canadian Light Infantry (1945–53) and the Queen's Own Rifles of Canada (1953–66).

In civilian life, he worked in personnel administration for Dupont of Canada at Kingston, Ontario, for three years and for the Ontario Government in Toronto for seventeen years, finally retiring in 1985.

At eighty-three years of age, Bob is still very busy, working as a volunteer, most notably as an executive member of the Living History Speakers Bureau RCL 258, and the 1st Canadian Parachute Battalion Association, for which he has been issuing magazine-sized newsletters for over eighteen years.

OPERATION VARSITY

In May 1937, I joined the militia with the North Shore (NB) Regiment, mainly because I heard about a field day during the 1937 summer camp at Sussex, NB. At the field day, I placed first in four events. My prizes were four white envelopes in each of which were three dollars cash (a two-dollar bill and a one-dollar bill). This vast sum of twelve dollars in one afternoon was more than my pay for the whole period at camp! On the same day, I was promoted to "acting l/cpl without pay." It was an auspicious start to my twenty-nine years in the army.

When war broke out in September 1939, the North Shore Regiment was not mobilized as expected. I joined the active army anyway, and arrived in England in May 1940 as a reinforcement to the Carleton and York Regiment. I finally was posted overseas to the 1st Canadian Parachute Battalion in August 1944.

With no officer vacancies in the battalion at that time, I was posted to command the 3rd Parachute Brigade Defence Platoon, made up entirely of British soldiers. In this capacity, on March 24, 1945, I parachuted into Germany in the largest airborne operation of the war, and remained in action during the advance across Germany to Wismar on the Baltic Sea, where we met the Russian army on the day the war ended.

My most memorable war experience was the parachute drop into Germany east of the Rhine River on March 24, 1945. Code-named "Operation Varsity," it involved the 6th British Airborne Division and the American 17th Airborne Division. The 1st Canadian Parachute Battalion formed an integral part of 3rd Parachute Brigade, 6th Airborne Division.

In late February 1945, we were informed that a major airborne operation was being planned. Then, on March 20, 1945, at very short notice, our whole division was moved at night with as much secrecy as possible to three brigade-sized concentration areas in southeast England. Our 3rd Parachute Brigade, consisting of Brigade HQ, 8th and 9th British Parachute Battalions and 1st Canadian Parachute Battalion, moved to its concentration area based on a large mansion on a private estate some distance north of London. Army huts and other facilities were scattered around the area with a ten-foot-high fence of concertina barbed wire surrounding the whole area. Once in, there was no getting out!

The next three days were spent in detailed briefings for all ranks. We learned that at ten a.m. on March 24th, we would parachute from C-47 Dakota aircraft into Germany, two miles east of the Rhine River, in the largest airborne operation ever and remain in action afterwards until the end of the war. For our brigade, the 8th Battalion would land first, followed immediately by Brigade HQ, the Canadian Battalion and the 9th Battalion. Every man was briefed three times with the aid of maps, wall-mounted blown-up photos, and the latest intelligence reports. We had to memorize the locations of significant features on the ground, including buildings, trees, hedges, obstacles, and possible enemy positions. We wrote our last letter home, well knowing that for some, it would indeed be the "last letter."

On March 23rd, the evening before the drop, the BBC News reported that General Montgomery was preparing a major offensive, that forty miles of the front along the Rhine had been blanketed with artificial fog, and that Berlin had reported their expectations of paratroop landings east of the Rhine. This news did not particularly fill us with joy!

We were ordered to bed at eight p.m. So, off we went, no doubt with thoughts of "Ten tomorrow morning" on our minds.

During the night we got a rude awakening when a German buzz bomb landed less than 200 yards outside our concentration area. We saw in the morning that it had landed and exploded in a field, making a large crater and blowing a very big barn into a precarious position, leaning towards a nearby farmhouse. We were glad that it didn't land in the concentration area but wondered if it was an omen of worse things to come.

We were awakened at four a.m., and, after a huge steak breakfast, we were trucked to the Chipping Ongar Airport. My platoon of thirty-six men was split into six groups to fly in six different aircraft with other members of the Brigade HQ. At the airport, the young pilot of our Dak expressed amazement at the heavy loads we were carrying, and said he felt bad about having to dump us out over German positions in broad daylight, never mentioning anything about the risks he was taking himself.

We put on our parachutes, loaded ourselves with our equipment, weapons and ammunition, and made a thorough check of every man's parachute and load. Then the time came to board the aircraft.

I was number eighteen in the eighteen-man stick (group) and the last to jump. I sat right up against the pilot's compartment with my batman, Jock MacAskill, number seventeen, who sat directly opposite and facing me. At last we were rumbling down the runway in the first lift of twenty-seven planes. I looked at my watch and it was exactly 7:00 a.m. But we had hardly lifted off when the crew chief announced that they had left their wheel chocks on the edge of the runway and were turning back to get them as, after dropping us, they would be landing in France. The plane never really stopped as the crew chief jumped out at the para exit door, grabbed the chocks, threw them in, and was pulled aboard, with the pilot assuring us that we would catch up and regain our position in the flight.

The 24th of March 1945 was a beautiful, sunny day. We soon crossed over the English Channel and turned east towards Germany. Our plane bounced around at times when it hit the slipstream of other planes in front. With the jump door open, it was almost impossible to carry on a conversation. A few slept, but most stayed awake and were quiet with their thoughts. The three hours in the air passed all too slowly.

At last we were given a fifteen-minute warning. Then the red light at the door went on, giving us a five-minute warning. The jump master gave the orders: stand up, hook up, check your equipment, sound off for equipment check, close up and stand in the door. I looked down and saw a ribbon of water—the Rhine. Almost immediately, we saw puffs of smoke all around us—anti-aircraft fire. The green light went on.

Number one leapt out the door with the rest of us following very closely towards the door. As number eighteen, the last jumper, I stuck very close to Jock in front of me, when suddenly with four or five of us still on board, the plane jerked violently as a flash of fire streamed past the windows from the starboard engine. Our plane was on fire. Just as Jock got to the door, a violent jolt of the plane threw him off his feet backwards away from the door to strike hard against the inside wall. With no hesitation, he bounced off the wall and with two long strides, leapt out the door like a charging bull. I followed quickly, but the plane was so unstable I sort of bounced out the door.

We learned later that the plane crashed with no survivors. They didn't need the wheel chocks after all.

By the time I jumped, we were at a very low altitude, and I quickly sensed that there were no other paras on the ground. We were indeed the first stick to land in this area of the drop zone (DZ). I looked around, and from our briefings recognized a row of three houses at the edge of the DZ. I prepared to land and slammed into a telephone line that I had not seen. With my hands up on the risers controlling the parachute, one of the telephone wires caught my wristwatch, broke the leather strap and away went the watch with the stem of the watch gouging a small tear in my wrist, which I didn't notice until much later. I landed safely with my parachute draped over the telephone lines.

Already, bullets were cracking past us, seeming to come from all directions. The battle was on. While scrambling out of my parachute harness, I kept the three houses in view and saw, about 200 yards away, seven or eight German soldiers running from the houses to what appeared to be nearby slit trenches. They quickly opened up on us, but within seconds one of my Bren gunners was blasting away at them. Almost immediately, other troopers were dropping among us and quickly joined in the fight and the position was wiped out. But I had lost two very good men. Tupper, a platoon favourite, was killed instantly by a bullet through the forehead, and Tilshead was badly wounded in the thigh.

As soon as I could, I gathered several men and headed for our rendezvous (RV) several hundred yards away. I still remember vividly some of the events as we made our way across the open ground. We had gone only a very short distance when another of my men was wounded by a bullet in the right arm. A field dressing was applied, and he continued on with us. We came across one of our Canadian battalion members on his knees looking at his hands, which were covered with blood. He seemed dazed and had a wicked cut across the side of his face. Someone saw a medic nearby and hustled him over. The medic looked at the casualty, grimaced mightily, and then got to work. Soon after this, a mortar bomb dropped near enough to splatter the right side of my jump smock and my right hand with ground and tiny shell fragments. (The cuts on my hand got infected, took weeks to heal, and left some scars.)

We passed several troopers caught up on a power line where they had been instantly electrocuted. (We had not been warned of power lines.) We also saw two jump aircraft on fire. From one, we saw three men jump from a very low altitude. None of their parachutes opened in time to save them. They may have been crewmembers. The other aircraft went crashing into the trees in a ball of fire.

By the time we reached the RV, it had been secured, and we were surprised to see a large group of very grim-looking German prisoners sitting on the ground—all of them members of the German 7th Parachute Army. Amidst it all was Brigadier James Hill, taking stock of the situation and issuing orders.

It was only after reaching the RV that I realized Jock was hurting and missing his haversack. It is hard to believe, but it had been shot clear off his side upon landing and he had the torn web straps and a nasty bruise on his side to prove it. Jock was made of good stuff.

By now, the gliders of the Air Landing Brigade were coming in from all directions on the same DZ upon which we had landed. Some crashed on landing and some were shot up by enemy fire both in the air and on the ground. It was sheer pandemonium, with small aggressive battles still going on all around us.

Our HQ 3 Para Brigade RV was a small axe-shaped piece of woods jutting out into our main DZ. Just after my arrival there, one of the Horsa gliders came in directly towards the RV, but was too high and looked as if it were going to go over our heads or crash into the trees. At the last moment, the pilot made a sharp left-hand turn, whereupon the tip of his right wing hit the tops of the trees, which turned the glider back facing the trees and, crashing into them, it stopped within fifty feet of where we were standing. All aboard survived, although the pilot broke both of his legs. Fortunately, this glider carried the brigadier's Jeep and wireless set, which survived without damage.

Early in the afternoon, the Brigade HQ staff, with my platoon providing protection, moved from the RV a short distance through the woods, past a knocked-out German 88 battery with their dead lying around, to an old school building that the HQ staff occupied. The whole back yard had been a garden and we dug in, with the prisoners doing most of the work.

The school overlooked a broad, open piece of low ground with a narrow road and a bridge over a small stream. Just as we arrived at the school building, the enemy sent a whole platoon down this road towards our position. As they crossed the bridge, they were ambushed and wiped out by a Canadian platoon.

Late in the afternoon, a scout car was spotted approaching the bridge and was identified as belonging to the leading element of the 15th Scottish Division, which had crossed the Rhine earlier in the morning. I was sent down to the bridge to meet them and, with dead Germans lying all around, the Scots greeted us with great relief and were certainly impressed with the Airborne.

In the evening, leaving my platoon with my sergeant to guard the Brigade HQ and the prisoners, I ventured off to the DZ with my batman to see if we could find our two unaccounted-for members. We found both of them at a field dressing station in a small church at the edge of the DZ. One had a very bad leg wound, while the other was simply staying with his wounded pal and helping out.

With the help of medics and prisoners, the dead and wounded were still being brought in. The dead were lined up in long rows in the churchyard with many more German dead than ours. Not a pleasant sight!

I got back to my platoon with daylight fast fading and asked my sergeant for the location of a latrine. He pointed to a row of poplar trees at the foot of the garden and said that I would find a fine Jerry-built latrine there. There indeed was a deep trench with a stout bar between two trees as a seat. I had just started when the inconsiderate enemy began to mortar our location. The first bombs landed well off to my left. Then several fell directly behind me, with shrapnel hitting the trees over my head. At about the same time, I thought I saw in the dim light a bit of ground splash up in front of me. Was it a dud mortar bomb? At this point, I left in rather a hurry. I mentioned this to Jock, but I am sure he did not believe me. The bombing continued for a short time with no damage to our location.

We got very little sleep that night because of the constant nightlong artillery bombardment from our side to protect our flanks. Further, we had to mount sentries to guard against enemy patrols and prepare for a dawn attack by the enemy, which in fact occurred, but was repulsed with no casualties to our Brigade HQ group.

At first light in the morning, I again headed for the latrine and, to my amazement (and some satisfaction) there were the fins of a large mortar bomb sticking out of the ground less than ten feet from where I had been sitting! I alerted everyone around and reported it to a British engineering officer, who marked it and said he would have it blown as soon as we left the area. My discovery made Jock a believer! And after the events of that day I firmly believed that both he and I would survive the war.

WW II Mural, 1st Canadian Parachute Battalion, 6th June 1944, Normandy

RALPH E. FISHER 1st RCR Airborne

RALPH, nicknamed Moose, was born and raised in Toronto, and joined the 48th Highlander Cadet Corps in 1943 at age thirteen. He served in that regiment's reserve battalion from 1945 to 1950.

At age nineteen, he enlisted in the 1st Royal Canadian Regiment and was trained in signals, explosives, and as a sniper. As well, he was a member of the Airborne Unit. He served in Korea with his regiment in HQ Signal Platoon from 1952 to 1953, engaged as a wireless operator, line crew, bodyguard, and at times as Mortar Platoon support. While serving in Germany in 1955–57, as part of the British Army of the Rhine (25th Brigade in Soest), his regiment was involved in the 1956 Hungarian Uprising, facing the 1st Russian Armoured Division. Only political intervention averted the start of WW III at the time. He returned to Canada and was honourably discharged in 1957.

Following his discharge from the army, Ralph spent forty years as a theatre technician, including a stint as an electrician for the National Ballet of Canada, and a stint as a sound technician at the O'Keefe Centre in Toronto.

He is a member of the 1st RCR Association, CAFA (Canadian Airborne Forces Association), and Royal Canadian Legion Branch 258, Highland Creek, Ontario, where he is a stalwart member of the Branch Colour Guard. He also belongs to the Korea Veterans Association (KVA Unit 59), affiliated with RCL Branch 258. He is also a well-known expert woodcarver and is a member of the Ontario Woodcarvers Association.

The "Police Action" That Was a War

There were many moments and times during my stay in Korea that I would like to forget, but somehow they seem to creep up on me occasionally. Perhaps being only nineteen years old, as were most

Infantry patrol, Korea, March 1951. Photographer L. Olson, B.U.

of my buddies, we found fear as well as excitement in our experiences. But today, some fifty years later, I remember that it was mostly fear, and the excitement was when I would be relieved from a forward position and moved into reserve, feeling I was then in a safe position.

Mostly I remember times of grief and sorrow at seeing my buddies wounded or killed in horrible ways, especially during the main Chinese attack on Hill 355 in late October 1952. Our entire area was being shelled from "the Saddle" to east of "Old Baldy." "A" Company seemed to get the worst of it. After a few days of heavy fighting, the medics were bringing the wounded and dead back from the forward listening post when I found out that my best friend, Bill Elliot, was not only a casualty but had been blown in half by a Chinese 75-mm shell.

Just prior to this, our job in my platoon was to help keep communication lines open, as we knew that a big push was under way. Otto Blain and I had the assignment of running communication lines from company to company and to the outpost, with most of our run going through the "Mad Mile." This was an area where the Chinese had their mortars set in range almost every few yards. It was like running through a maze of fire. Almost at the end of this stretch, our truck was blown off the road. We were pinned down in a culvert, where we remained until nightfall, when it was finally possible to dig us out.

We continued to check and fix phone lines, but were chased for six hours or more by Chinese mortar fire from one end of the trench system to the other, in most cases in full view of the Chinese. Needless to say, we were badly shaken up. My partner Otto was now stuttering and his hair had gone from dark brown to snow white.

There were many bad times suffered by our regiment, but there were a few good times, too. Such as the time I received a package from home with a loaf of bread in it. We all laughed when Larry Adams tore the bread apart and found a bottle of rum inside!

Another time that I now look back on as being humorous was while I was on picket duty on Hill 166. I was cleaning my .45 calibre pistol, and it went off accidentally, ricocheting into the leg of Don Campbell. On his return to our position, the officer in charge thought it best for me not to be around, as Don seemed a little upset at me. So I was given the task of lugging spools of wire around our perimeter, out of Don's sight. I later learned that in 1957 Don went on to fly with the RCAF, perhaps thinking it was safer up there than on the ground with me.

During our trip home, we had rifle drill on the deck of the ship. Suddenly the drills were stopped. As explained by the ship's captain, we were chipping the paint off the decks.

On our arrival in Ottawa, the regiment was given the keys to the city by Mayor Charlotte Whitten. But then we were given a letdown as we marched to the saluting base to find that the member of Parliament had left the saluting stand before we had even approached the area. And for the next thirty-some years we suffered the indignity of having the involvement of our forces in Korea referred to as a "police action." Perhaps if some of those politicians had served in Korea, they would have known it was actually a war.

ROGER FOOTE

ARMOURED CORPS

ROGER was born in Toronto in 1924, and attended Withrow Avenue School before joining the Queen's Own Rifles Reserve Army at age seventeen. He enlisted in the Canadian Armoured Corps Active Force in 1943.

Following basic and advanced training at Dundurn, Saskatchewan, Roger was posted overseas to a reinforcement unit in Surrey, England, and was then sent to France, where he joined the 8th Recce Regiment (14th Canadian Hussars) during the Normandy Campaign.

Roger served with the 8th Recce for the rest of the war, including campaigns in France, Belgium, Holland, and in northwest Germany. He returned to Canada and was discharged in 1946.

Roger's career was mainly with the Canadian Imperial Bank of Commerce. He retired in 1988 after twenty-five years of service. He has been a member of Royal Canadian Legion Branch 258, Highland Creek, Ontario, from 1970, serving as an active member of the Branch Colour Guard since that time. In 2000 he was elected Colour Guard captain following the retirement of Captain Al Armstrong.

COMRADES IN PEACE AND WAR (1931–?)

October 1931

New boy on the street. Roger Foote meets Al Armstrong. New boy has toy pistol, slight argument, someone gets hit with the pistol. The friendship is almost ended then. October 31st, Halloween, Roger calls on Al to go out for the shell-out . . .

This was the beginning of a lasting friendship. Our playtime was spent playing soldier. The park in that area was Withrow Park, which was our battlefield. It seems there was a constant argument about who was going to be captain. Time passed, and war began in

1939. We both got jobs working for the same company, and both of us were interested in the same young lady.

1941

Al joined The Queen's Own Rifles and, a short time after, I joined; we were both in the same "B" company. We attended camp at Niagara-on-the-Lake during the summer.

1943

We went down to the recruiting tent at city hall to make inquiries about enlistment in the active force. When we told them we'd had previous military experience, they insisted we were officer material. So they rushed us in a station wagon down to Military District 2 at the Canadian National Exhibition grounds. I was nineteen and Al was eighteen years old.

After eight days' documentation at CNC, we were posted to Dundurn, Saskatchewan. Upon arrival at camp at the end of September, snow was already on the ground. Two men unloading a truck of gear asked us what we had done to be sent to this place. They seemed to think that their particular camp was the cesspit of the world!

May 1944

I completed a course in anti-tank gunnery, and Al was trained as a dispatch rider.

I arrived in England, followed shortly after by Al in the Canadian Armoured Corps Reinforcement Unit, Surrey, where we were together again. After short courses in England, I took gunnery training in heavy armour and Al went to battle school for wireless and gunnery training.

Shortly after D-Day, Al was posted to VIII Recce Regiment and went to France. I followed a short time later, and ran into him at a reinforcement unit. Al claimed me for the VIII Recce Regiment. Al was posted to "B" Squadron, and I was posted to "A" Squadron. So once more we were serving together.

As time went by, we didn't see one another for months on end. Our paths crossed once when the regiment was together in Wamel, a town in Holland near the German border. We were on the road walking back to Squadron CP and the Jerries started to shell the town with 88s. The war moved on, and I ended up in Oldenberg in northwest Germany. Al was taken out at the German border and ended up in England.

1945

The war was over. In March 1945, Al was back in England in hospital. I arrived back in England in October 1945, and went looking for Al in Rep. Depot in Farnborough, Hampshire. Al was away on leave in Kent.

I arrived back in Canada in November 1945, and lost track of Al until May 1946. Al arrived back in Canada on his twenty-first birthday, May 15, 1946. On arriving at the Coliseum in Toronto that day, I was at the entrance, first in line to meet him. We joined family and friends for a "Welcome Home" party that night.

1946

Al and I had a falling out over a lady friend in front of her church, which ended in fisticuffs. Al had his new $22 topcoat ripped up the back. Our lady friend came out of church and was infuriated. She told both of us to get out of her life for good. Al had been drinking at the time, and this did not sit too well with her.

Al and I parted company for the next twenty-four years. In the interim, both of us married, raised families, bought homes, and settled down.

In 1964, Al joined the local Legion. In 1966, he helped organize and recruit the Colour Guard, and was elected sergeant-at-arms at the time. In 1970, a WWII reunion was held at Fort York Armouries. Al and I got together again. After Fort York, we ended up at Earl French Memorial Vets Club in the east end of Toronto, and got stinking drunk. Al had our lady friend's phone number (she had been married but was now separated). Both of us talked to her for a long time on the phone. She was very glad to hear from us, and told us to stay where we were and she would take a cab to join us. We declined, and let it go at that. Issue closed.

Also in 1970, I followed Al into the Legion. Both of us worked hard on the Colour Guard, training recruits and raising the strength of the group from ten or so to the present twenty-five. In 1977, Al took over as captain. I was promoted to second-in-command, after going through the ranks behind Al. Our Colour

Guard has an excellent record in the Legions, in respect to competitions, etc.

On December 31, 1999, Al retired as captain, and I was promoted to captain in his stead. Al is still active in parades and other functions, and is known as "Captain A. Armstrong, retired."

The wheel has come full circle. We are still playing soldiers together.

LES GOODWIN

KING'S (LIVERPOOL) REGIMENT, BRITISH ARMY

LES was born and raised in Birkenhead, England, across the Mersey River from Liverpool. He joined a cadet unit in 1941, transferred to the British Home Guard in 1943, and enlisted in the regular army at age seventeen. He was also a firewatcher from 1940, and experienced approximately 100 air raids over the Merseyside, engaging in extinguishing enemy firebombs.

Upon enlistment in the Cheshire Regiment, he trained in Belfast, Ireland, and Chester, England, and landed in France in December 1944. He went into action through Goch, and crossed the Rhine at Wesel in March 1945. He was then transferred to No. 2 T-Force, with the King's Liverpool Regiment. This battalion was engaged in reconnaissance roles, finding and occupying sensitive objectives such as rocket fuel dumps and U-boat pens in Bremen, many times ahead of forward troops, as well as rounding up, holding, and transporting captured enemy forces.

Following his discharge in September 1946 after serving in the German Occupation Force from VE day onwards, Les completed his apprenticeship, married, and emigrated to Canada in 1951. He took early retirement in 1989 after a career as a safety engineer, and is a Life Member of the IAPA (Industrial Accident Prevention Association).

Les is a past chairman of the Living History Speakers Bureau RCL Branch 258, as well as a member of the Scarborough Veterans Association. He has also served in many capacities on the executive of RCL Branch 258, including house maintenance and membership. He is currently serving as the branch service officer. He is a past president of RCL Branch 258, with a special interest in preserving wartime memorabilia and artifacts in the branch archives, and he has also enjoyed great success in past years as chairman of the Legion Poppy Campaign.

No. 2 T-Force

I joined the British Army as a volunteer in September 1943 and was called for service on October 15. I had been in the Army Cadets, and at the time of enlistment was a member of the local Home Guard unit. Being only seventeen, I was posted to be trained in a newly formed special unit called the Young Soldier's Training Corps (YSTC), one of three special units; mine was the 28th Training Battalion.

Following six months of very intensive infantry training in Northern Ireland, I was posted to Chester, the home depot of the "Cheshire Regiment," the unit of my choice. Since I had been a volunteer, we were privileged in that we were allowed to choose our branch of service or regiment.

At Chester I was trained as a machine gunner on the Vicker's heavy machine gun. Following this I went on to be trained as a universal (Bren gun) carrier driver.

I have many times been asked why I volunteered at so young an age. I don't believe that anyone who volunteered for service answers this question really truthfully. I always said, "Well, it was the thing to do," but my real motive was something much more selfish than that. As the fall of 1943 was approaching we all realized that the big day that we had all been waiting for—D-Day—was not too far away. I think we all knew that it would not be in the winter and would most likely be sometime in the spring of 1944.

Well, since my eighteenth birthday was in April, I would be getting called for military service at exactly the wrong time, and if casualties were as high as expected, I would find myself in the thick of it and possibly with only half the training necessary to survive; and a survivor I very much wanted to be.

When D-Day did come in the spring of '44, I was as physically (but maybe not as mentally) well trained as I wanted to be, so from that standpoint I was reasonably happy. But on and on we went through the summer with more and more training. At this point I wanted to get into it. I had two brothers fighting in Italy and I wanted to match their war stories after this was all over (what an idiot).

So our big day finally came. We were herded into the troop train, and down to Dover we went. Just before getting onto the ship, we were handed a blanket. I heard the guy in front of me say, "One blanket won't keep me warm—it's winter." The answer came back: "It's not to keep you warm—it's to bury you in." So with these sweet sentiments dulling our minds, we proceeded to move toward our ship.

As we marched into the dock area, we were straining to get a look at the ship that was going to take us to France, but to no avail. Well maybe it hasn't arrived yet. "Halt!" came the sharp order from somebody up front. "Right turn!" It was only now that we noticed there were four landing craft tied up to the dock wall—empty, of course.

This is our ship? They're not going to send us all the way to France in one of those silly little things? Oh, yes they are! And onto these mighty ships of his Majesty's Royal Navy we marched. Not a nice way to go to war, I thought. So away we went across the Channel after being joined by a corvette as an escort. I was beginning to wonder now if I had done the right thing by joining up, as I looked down at the "vomiting bag" that had been passed to me by someone. Other than this, I had no recollection of the trip across the Channel. The last thing I remembered was an over-the-shoulder look at the White Cliffs of Dover. *I'll never see them again*, I thought—and I never have.

I came back to reality as we arrived at Calais and quickly disembarked and were transported over to Ostende. We stayed there one night in an army barracks, and then moved on somewhere into the middle of Belgium. I was quite happy to leave Ostende. I thought the toilets there were absolutely archaic—no privacy whatsoever. You place your feet onto the designated pads, then you fall back against the wall and commence to do your duty, with all the world looking on.

We moved up closer to Antwerp, and it was here that one came very close. I had managed to survive almost a hundred German air raids on Merseyside without getting so much as a scratch, and here in the early hours of the morning, we had a very near miss by a V-1 rocket. It completely wrecked the building in which we were sleeping, but fortunately there were no serious injuries in our group.

We eventually moved deeper into Holland and on over the German border close to the Reichswald Forest. We started to move the German POWs out of the Rhineland and back into Holland. This was how I first met our adversaries. Most seemed happy to be prisoners and quite glad it was all over for them. They seemed to take pleasure in telling us that for them the war was over, but "Now you have to fight the Russians"; and we didn't know if they were right or wrong about that. It always worried me.

One morning after having had a very sleepless night due to the Royal Artillery pounding the far side of the Rhine, we heard the distant roar of engines, and for a few minutes it was difficult to tell from which direction the sound was coming. We had been caught off guard a few days earlier when a Messerschmitt 109 had flown over the trees of the Reichswald Forest, spitting out its hate at our positions, and so we were anxious to get a fix on this action.

But this was different, and it didn't take us long to realize that we were about to witness the biggest air armada that we would ever see. The 1st Airborne Division was making its assault on the Rhine, and as it approached it was like a thick, black cloud coming in low over the horizon.

We had seen the US Air Force almost daily, up in the clear blue skies at twenty-five thousand feet, with their thick con-trails following up behind, but this armada was less than a thousand feet above us, and stretched as far as the eye could see. The engine noise was so intense that it was impossible to communicate with anyone until it had passed over. This was the most powerful force that I would ever see. It passed on beyond our sight to the east side of the Rhine. Within a few minutes hundreds of the men in those aircraft would be casualties.

We continued to transport prisoners for a few days as we moved over the river. Then, suddenly, we were off POW duty and were all reassigned to new units. The army has a strange way of doing things like this. There is no such thing as giving anyone a choice—it's "You, you, and you over there, and you, and you over here," into assorted groups, and that's that. They don't think of asking you if you would like to go with your mate. It's hard to lose your friends like this, but I suppose we all faced this sort of thing at some time or other.

At times like this, days and dates don't seem to matter very much, except when you stop and write a letter. I have no recollection of the day, but somewhere around this time I had a birthday. I was now nineteen years of age.

So we moved out on the usual form of transportation, which was anything going up the line. Most of the time it was an ammunition truck. This was a great way to travel—about a dozen of us on top of the ammo boxes. These trucks had no springs, and I don't think the roads had been repaired since the war started. By the time we got to our destination we were physical and nervous wrecks and my head felt like it had been pounded with a hammer.

As we passed through Münster—which was a heap of rubble—on this hot and dusty day, my eyes became fixed on a young lady standing, it seemed, in the middle of all this desolation over to our right, and about two hundred metres away. Or was this a dream? She was, it seemed to me, dressed as if to go to a party, and she stood with her hands clasped in front of her. I never took my eyes from her as she watched our convoy pass on into the dust. I wondered if she was relieved to see us, or if her heart was full of hatred.

As it turned out, the new posting suited me perfectly. My new regiment was the 5th Battalion King's (Liverpool) Regiment, which recruited its men in my hometown area. This made me feel a little happier, and I settled in quite nicely.

The 5th King's formed the nucleus of a newly formed unit called No. 2 T-Force. This was comprised of men from several regiments transferred into the King's; also Americans, French and Dutch, as well as dozens of British civilians who were put into uniform and given commissions according to their civilian status. Majors and colonels abounded. The reason for the uniforms and high ranks was that if there were a German counterattack and they were captured, they would be better treated. However, in civilian clothes there is no doubt that they would have been shot on capture.

T-Force was created to satisfy the need of a highly mobile secret force that would have the capability of securing special intelligence targets as selected by an intelligence unit known as 30 Assault Unit, Royal Navy (later to be given the less belligerent title of 30 Advanced Unit). The high mobility was provided through the use of reconnaissance cars, of which I became a driver.

Information on targets for T-Force to investigate came from two main sources. One was the Combined Intelligence Subcommittee, which drew up what was known as the "black list." The other was the Inter-Services Topographical Unit (ISTU). The latter, which was based in Oxford, UK, had a vast store of information on targets; but being remote from the scene and out of touch with local military progress, had no idea what size units would be needed for the capture of defended points. It was therefore necessary to earmark certain units for specific military duties.

And this is where the 5th Battalion of The King's (Liverpool) Regiment entered the picture, together with three companies of the Pioneer Corps, also Royal Engineers, selected for their abilities in the removal of booby traps, bomb disposal, safe breaking, etc. These men had actually been sent on special burglary courses in England and carried the tools of the trade as part of their equipment!

This, then, was my new unit: a band of thieves and looters who would search out and secure for reparation purposes any and all of our enemy's secrets—plant, equipment, processes, documents, and people. Of course we didn't know all of this at the time, since everyone was very tight-lipped about what they did a lot of the time. We didn't even know the names of the places that we targeted. Much about our exploits was not exposed until we met at our Old Comrades Association meetings fifty years later.

The scope of operations for T-Force XXX Corps was spread across the entire front of 8 Corps and XXX Corps, from the Rhine to Bremen, the Hartz Mountains to Kiel, Lübeck and on into Denmark. The battalion was dispersed into small units, sometimes down to platoon strength, and never came together as a full unit until its mission was completed in 1947.

While most of the targets were selected by intelligence, and some by German civilians who were now anxious to show that their political feelings were not in favour of the present regime, there were also some opportunity targets that just happened to come our way.

One of these was at a town called Celle about thirty-five miles northeast of Hanover. Here we came across an underground Focke-Wulf aircraft factory that was still producing aircraft as it was taken over by T-Force personnel. This factory was said to extend about two miles underground. In another instance, an RAF unit under T-Force influence seized an aircraft factory while the directors were holding a board meeting. Under discussion was how to evacuate the plant . . .

Another very interesting target was the vast Deschimag shipyard in Bremen. The following story, entitled "Is This the Man Who Was James Bond," is taken from the October 1995 *Reader's*

Digest. This is the story of Lieutenant-Commander Patrick Dalzel-Job, commander of Team 4, of the Assault Unit 30 Royal Navy.

Information had been gleaned from prisoners that there could be as many as twenty of the newest high-speed German submarines, a prize of enormous intelligence value—but there was a problem. Artillery of the 52nd (Lowland) Division following close behind AU 30 were planning to blast the shipyard into oblivion.

Dalzel-Job entered the city on the afternoon of April 26 and was met by a policeman who asked if he would go to the city hall, where the mayor was anxious to surrender the city and all of its services to him, and gave him assurances of vigorous police action against all who failed to cooperate (notwithstanding some SS troops who were holed up in the park). Dalzel-Job radioed the army that all organized military resistance had ended, and that they did not have to shell the shipyard. But the army did not see it that way. They planned to open fire that evening, they replied, as soon as they came within range.

Furious, Dalzel-Job climbed into his scout car and headed for the shipyard, staking his life that there really would be no resistance and that his presence would keep the army from shelling it.

Then at the very gates of the shipyard he ran out of gas. When he tried to radio for help all he got was static interference. He needed desperately to tell the army that he was in the shipyard. He spotted some workers and grabbed a bicycle from one of them, and pedalled back to his unit, all the while aware that there was still enough daylight for a sniper to put a bullet in his back. As he rounded the last corner, his anxiously waiting men hauled him on board the lead vehicle, and the column sped off for the yard at breakneck speed. Inside they found sixteen brand-new submarines and two destroyers, and forestalled their imminent demolition by the technicians and directors. Dalzel-Job and his men took them all prisoner, and in a nightlong search found technical papers detailing the most recent German research, as well as machine tools of highly advanced design.

The Type XXI submarine was an enormous improvement over previous U-boats. It had twice the displacement of the U-boats in service at the time and had an underwater speed of sixteen knots for a period of one hour. An alternative means of underwater propulsion had been developed by Professor Helmuth Walter, who used hydrogen peroxide as a fuel to generate steam to power a turbine engine. Potentially such engines would enable a U-boat to sustain high submerged speeds for possibly as long as ten hours at a time; and considering that a convoy speed was normally about six to eight knots, this would have had a devastating effect on Allied shipping.

But Dalzel-Job had not heard the last of the army. Early the next morning, when experts were already examining the new high-speed Type XXI submarines, a staff officer from the 52nd Division appeared and asked him to sign a receipt implying that the 52nd Division had captured them.

This was the last straw for Dalzel-Job. He slammed the gate and had a sign posted to the effect that this was the property of 30 AU, and No. 6 platoon of "A" Company was posted on guard. I was one of those guards. As a point of interest it is suggested in this *Reader's Digest* story that the commander of 30 Advanced Unit RN, Commander Ian Fleming, was inspired by his admiration for Dalzel-Job in creating his masterpiece—which even to this day is a favourite—the master spy "James Bond, agent 007."

In March 1945, Section 6 of T-Force was given the assignment of discovering any material relating to chemical warfare in Germany. The section had been advised there was a suspected chemical warfare establishment in Germany at Münsterlager, which was about fifty kilometres north of Hanover, and only a few miles away from Hitler's extermination camp Belsen-Bergen. This was of some significance, as will be seen. Here the section found some laboratories and storehouses that looked like they had been vacated rather hurriedly—there were open notebooks lying around on desks.

The laboratories disclosed nothing of interest, but one American in the party, Captain Kraus, investigated a barn within the perimeter of the establishment. The concrete floor seemed unusually clean and he noticed a trapdoor. He found that under it was a stairway leading to an underground chamber full of furnaces, condensers and tubing. The scientists found it to be a pilot plant for the production of tabun, a colourless, tasteless nerve gas, against which the Allies had no protection at all. There was plenty of evidence of experiments around the buildings. Photographs had been taken on a progressive basis to show the full effects. Apparently the people from the Belsen-Bergen camp nearby were used in these hideous experiments. It certainly appeared that we were winning the war not a moment too soon.

The commander of Section 6, who was a major on loan from the Canadian Army when this important discovery was made, found a special satisfaction in it. Thirty years earlier, on April 22, 1915, the Germans had used gas against the Canadians at St. Julien Wood. The effect of the surprise and the casualties made it seem likely they would break through to Calais. But the Canadians held and, against all expectations, counterattacked. Their action saved Calais. It seemed appropriate that Canadians who had suffered so much from gas in WWI should track down this even more lethal form of it in WW II. I myself spent several months at Münsterlager, and was present during the infamous "T-Force Gas Attack."

(There were actually four Canadian officers with the King's Regiment in T-Force: Captains Philips, Payton, Burnaby and Keslick. Burnaby died in Guelph, Ontario, in 1995. Captain Keslick lived in Toronto and died in 1997. These were what we called Can-loan officers.)

The Gas Attack

Nobody seems to know exactly what happened, but happen it did. I had just returned from UK leave. It was January 1946, and on one of those bitterly cold nights we were awakened to find that some gas had escaped from some cylinders. Our platoon was billeted at the far end of the complex, and it was in this area that the leak had taken place. Everyone was coughing and sneezing. Fortunately this gas was not toxic. I think it was more for demoralizing troops than anything else. We called it DM or nose gas; we had been exposed to something like this in our training days. It stayed around for a few days; so, yes, we were sneezing for quite a while!

There were other episodes—maybe not as dramatic as these—in the T-Force story. Another was that of securing and transporting about seven railway tank cars of fuel (hydrogen peroxide) used to propel Hitler's V-weapons over to England. The German rocket expert Wernher Von Braun (who was later to become a key figure in the US space program) was also processed through T-Force offices. But the shining hour of T-Force was yet to come.

The City of Hamburg was entered on May 3rd, and on May 4th, "A" and "B" Companies moved on in the direction of Lübeck. A standstill order had been put into effect at this time, and no troops were to move forward beyond Bad Segeberg in a northerly direction.

However, both "A" and "B" Companies received orders to move forward to Kiel, in which it was anticipated there would be found some very interesting and valuable targets. (In point of fact this permission had been given in error.)

At 0700 the companies moved out, and were advised that they would be the first troops to enter the city. At the start line the one troop of SAS passed through at great speed, and was closely followed by the 5th King's. At Neumünster they were overtaken by 30 Advanced Unit RN driving at high speed with a white ensign on the lead Jeep.

Unaware of the error, T-Force and company moved forward through towns and villages, leaving all signs of battle behind. The company commander's Jeep driver saw several Germans dart into the woods as they passed through, but they offered no resistance as the vehicles continued on at high speed, somewhat to the surprise of the bewildered German civilians. A young sentry on guard at his post looked around helplessly, hoping for someone to tell him what to do as the recce cars of T-Force rolled by him.

The companies duly arrived in Kiel, and at a crossroads the convoy dispersed: "A" Company to the right, and "B" Company straight on. It was a queer experience to stand in the centre of Kiel on a wet Saturday morning dispersing our troops to their various targets. The German civilians stared very hard at us; but we stared even harder when we saw the German soldiers, marines, and policemen still armed. "A" Company seized its first five targets, "B" Company seized another six, and 30 Advanced Unit RN seized its main one.

Major Hibbert went to the Naval Academy and took charge there. The shipbuilding works was crowded with workers who weren't quite sure what to do with themselves. They stood around in groups and stared at us. At last they got an answer to the question that was worrying them: were we British, American or Russian? When they found out, they did not conceal their relief. In the dockyard was the cruiser *Hipper*, which was quickly targeted; the *Admiral Scheer* had capsized in the same area.

To the north of the Kiel Canal, German troops were very much in fighting order, and, unwilling to believe that things had deteriorated so fast, were not prepared to hand over anything to this small force. But they confirmed the situation by phone with Admiral

Dönitz, who was in the area and instructed them to do so. Amongst the targets taken over by T-Force were the Siemens plant, the Naval Air Station, and the submarine pens.

Officers were warned about the danger of causing an incident, yet at the same time they were told to issue definite orders to German Army personnel leaving no doubt as to who was in command. The German Navy was the most doubtful factor. The German officers were quite convinced they hadn't surrendered.

On being ordered to surrender, the commander was now asked to surrender all of their arms, for which transportation would be supplied by the British. Three trucks were dispatched to do the job—much to the disgust of the German commander, who was highly offended by the British evaluation of his command, which had in its possession over thirty tons of equipment.

It was anticipated that there would be many recriminations in high places over the mistaken permission given to 5th King's to move into Kiel. Various select bodies had been earmarked for that distinction. The Royal Navy, with some reason, claimed the right to be first to enter, even though compelled by circumstances to enter overland.

On May 8th, the Guards Brigade, believing themselves to be the first to arrive, made an almost ceremonial entry. The impressiveness was not dulled, although the edge may have been a little blunted for the brigade itself, by the presence in the town of two companies of infantry of the line, which had already been in occupation for two days.

Coinciding with the move into Kiel, another untimely advance was made by a much smaller force under the command of Captain Fackiri, MC, to the Luftwaffe Seaplane Base at Travemünde near Lübeck on the Baltic Sea. This force of nine reconnaissance cars arrived in town to find themselves surrounded by a large force of very angry German Luftwaffe personnel who had no intention of capitulating to anyone.

Captain Fackiri, who was not a big man, wore a handlebar moustache and appeared more like Flying Officer Kite than an army officer. He confronted the commandant at his HQ and demanded his immediate surrender in the name of the king. But the commandant was not impressed. As a consequence this force spent a very uneasy night under the watchful eyes of the German garrison.

The following morning, the commandant had a change of heart after consulting with what was left of the German High Command, and presented Captain Fackiri with his Luger as a token of surrender.

With hostilities now being ended, we were headquartered at the town of Winsen on the River Elbe close to Hamburg. After settling in there, we had just started to get used to the idea that we would be staying put for quite a while when we were ordered to turn in our pay-record books to the company office. We were quite indignant to find that they had had the audacity to make the following entry: "Priority, Far East I." I was being categorized to go to the Far East. But fortunately for us, the arrival of the Atomic Age put an end to that excursion.

Our companies were still dispersed across the Lüneberger Heide from Goslar in the Hartz mountains, where I was soon to be assigned, to Brunswick, Hanover, Hamburg, and up into the town of Kolding, Denmark. I never did see our battalion brought together as a single unit. Although the war had ended, there was still much work to be done by T-Force; all too often the same dangers that we faced in wartime still persisted in many of these out-of-the-way places.

I was demobilized from the armed forces in September 1946, and returned to my civilian status. I have never thought that what I did as a soldier had any significance whatsoever to the outcome of this conflict. However, what we achieved as a unit in T-Force did, I am confident, make a very significant contribution to the security of the British Commonwealth of Nations, and the freedom that we all enjoy today.

In the summer of 1947, the 5th Battalion King's (Liverpool) Regiment was relieved of its duties with No. 2 T-Force XXX Corps, and returned to regular duties as a regiment of the line.

* * *

Today I am a proud member of the 5th King's 2 T-Force, Old Comrades Association. We meet somewhere in England several times a year, where the camaraderie is second to none. This is the only coming together of the unit, as we in the Old Comrades Association represent all companies of the battalion. In May each year, a group of us takes a trip back in time to the sites of our wartime experiences in Germany and Denmark, where we have many friends amongst the Danish and German people.

One of our very good friends is the grandson of Professor Helmuth Walter, who proudly shows us over his factory that we liberated in May 1945. There is, however, one big difference in the factory. The production lines now produce, instead of those deadly war supplies, machinery for making ice cream wafers!

I suppose in a very subtle way we are still serving our country with these visits, by simply meeting our former adversaries, and maintaining an ongoing friendship with them.

TOM GREENSHIELDS   ROYAL CANADIAN NAVY

TOM was born in Montreal in 1922. His parents were from Scotland. His father was manager for Canada of the Cunard White Star Shipping Company, and his mother was a legal secretary. Tom was one of six children. Three brothers were in the services: one, a career British Army soldier, was a prisoner of war for two years, another served in the Canadian Army, and one was in the navy.

Pre-war, Tom was an apprentice steamfitter, had been a Boy Scout Patrol Leader, and played some pro hockey. He joined the Royal Canadian Navy at age nineteen and was sent to engineering school in Halifax, Nova Scotia. He was drafted to a corvette, HMCS *La Malbie*, for ten months, and then shipped to Victoria, BC, to join a new frigate, HMCS *Prince Rupert*. After twenty-three months aboard that ship, he joined the minesweeper HMCS *Wallaceburg*. Tom became a leading stoker and did twenty-six Atlantic convoy crossings in all. He was discharged in November 1945.

Following his release from the navy, Tom worked in the dry-cleaning and home-cleaning business, and then in maintenance. After relocating to Toronto he became a custodian engineer for the Board of Education, and retired in 1987. Following retirement, he engaged part time in general maintenance until several operations laid him low.

In 1950, Tom joined the Royal Canadian Legion in Montreal, was previously a member of RCL Branch 614, Scarborough, and then transferred to RCL Branch 258 in 1985. He is a member of the Seniors Association, the Scarborough Veterans Association, and is an active member of the Living History Speakers Bureau RCL Branch 258.

Tom Greenshields – Royal Canadian Navy

THE WAR—A FAMILY AFFAIR

I joined the navy at age nineteen in Montreal and spent two weeks in Halifax at engineering school. I was drafted aboard the corvette *La Malbie* for ten months and was then drafted to Victoria, BC, where I went aboard a new frigate, *Prince Rupert*, for twenty-three months. Both ships were on Atlantic convoy duty. I then joined the minesweeper *Wallaceburg*, and spent time around Halifax and Digby, Nova Scotia.

I suffered two injuries while aboard the *Prince Rupert*. I lost my hearing for three days due to a four-point gun going off while I was below it. The other injury was due to a depth charge from the starboard thrower becoming loose while they were hoisting it. It ran amok and hit me on the back of the leg while I was at my action station on the port side at the thrower. I landed in sick bay, and stayed there until we reached port. Then I was shipped to the hospital in Newfoundland to have my broken bones put together. I rejoined my ship on the next trip.

When I was drafted off the *Prince Rupert*, I had a leave that I spent in Montreal, and enjoyed it very much. While on leave, I had quite an experience. My wife Bunny (who was my fiancée at the time) and I went to a show and dinner after. When I went to pay the bill, I found I had no wallet. Luckily, Bunny had enough money to pay for our dinner—otherwise we would have had to wash dishes!

The best part of this lost wallet incident was that a young girl working as a housemaid in Outremont found it in the snow on St. Catherine Street. She had the woman of the house phone my mother to ask if she had a son in the navy. My mother came to my room and woke me up and asked if I had lost my wallet. Well, you should have seen how fast I went to that phone. I identified what was in the wallet, so the woman gave me her address. My wallet contained roughly $300, my train ticket to BC, and all my other papers. What a stroke of luck. When I offered the young girl a reward, she wouldn't accept anything. She said she had four brothers in the army and if anything like that happened to them, she just hoped things would work out as well for them. Since she refused a cash reward, I went to a drug store a few blocks down the road and bought the biggest box of chocolates they had and took them back to her. She didn't even want to accept that. That was my happy experience. My leave was very good.

I also had three brothers in the services. My eldest brother was a career soldier in the British Army and served through many campaigns. He was also a prisoner of war for about two years. While a prisoner, he punched a guard and was stabbed in an altercation. My second eldest brother served in the Canadian Army. My second-to-youngest brother served in the navy, also on convoy duty. My youngest brother was too young to get into any branch of the services during the war.

ALBERT (BERT) HOWARD

Royal Artillery, British Army

BERT, from Lancashire, England, left school at age fourteen to become an apprentice baker, then was conscripted into the British Army in May 1943 at age eighteen. In the army he was trained as an infantryman, then as a driver of heavy vehicles, and then assigned to the 15th Medium Regiment, Royal Artillery.

The Regiment hit the beaches of Normandy at Graye-sur-Mer in June 1944 (D+2 weeks), with Bert driving gun-towing tractor vehicles responsible for positioning the 5.5" guns. The regiment was attached to the 1st Canadian Army on their attacks towards Falaise, and was regularly under fire (sometimes friendly) from artillery and planes. After Falaise, it supported the Canadians in their sweep up the coast of France, Belgium, and into the Scheldt estuary. They wintered in Nijmegen, Holland, and provided support for the Rhine Operation, which ended on VE day. Major battles along the way included the beaches of Normandy, Caen, Falaise Gap, and Nijmegen Bridge.

After VE day, Bert was assigned to the 5th Battalion Somerset Light Infantry for training in jungle warfare, pending being shipped to the Far East to invade Japan. After VJ day, he was assigned to the Suffolk Regiment for a tour of duty for two years in the garrison troops in Jamaica, after which he returned to England and was released from military service.

Post-war, Bert worked with a maintenance unit of the Royal Air Force, serving four years as an apprentice mechanic on heavy vehicles, and then six years as a mechanic. He immigrated to Canada in 1957, and was employed as a bus vehicle repair mechanic with the Toronto Transit Commission until 1990, at which time he retired after thirty-three years of service. He then worked part time with a local YMCA health club, where he still enjoys his involvement with them as a volunteer.

A widower, Bert has one daughter, two grandchildren and a great-grandchild. He belongs to Royal Canadian Legion Branch 258 and is a founding member and immediate past chairman of the Living History Speakers Bureau RCL Branch 258. In 1999, Bert was named Branch 258 Legionnaire of the Year in recognition of his efforts involving Living History.

OFF TO WAR I GO . . .

I was born February 14, 1925, in Rochdale, Lancashire, England, a small town outside Manchester. I finished public school in 1939 and joined the workforce. In 1939 every member of the family went out to work, since money was not easy to come by; 1939 was also the year war broke out.

War at that time didn't mean much to me until the Germans started dropping bombs on Manchester, as that was the area where the famous Lancaster bomber was manufactured. The defences in that area were good, which meant that bombs missed their targets and the outskirts of Manchester got hit, Rochdale being one of the towns. At this time I was seventeen, and the British Government sent me for my physical prior to enlistment into the British Army. At that ripe old age, I was old enough to join the LDV (local defence volunteers). Too young to bear arms, we were given pick handles instead. The purpose of the LDV at that time was just to patrol outside the towns and report to the local authorities anything unusual, such as downed aircraft or parachutists.

I turned eighteen years old and the time had come. A letter arrived at my home bearing "On His Majesty's Service," saying, "God Save the King and welcome to His Majesty's Forces." It contained a railway ticket, a food voucher, and directions to the army barracks down in Aldershot.

On May 6, 1943, off I went at 6:30 a.m. to the Rochdale railway station with suitcase in hand. The train stopped at every station, and what did we see at each one but other young men, suitcases in hand, no doubt on the same mission.

Finally we reached our destination: Aldershot. At the station were rows of troop-carrying vehicles waiting to take us to our assigned barracks. On the vehicles we rode, and when we reached the barracks, we were directed to the gym. There were tables all over the place and, as a start, I had to find one with my last name and initial on it. My particulars were taken, and I was told that I was now a member of His Majesty's Forces (God Save The King).

They gave us dog tags, told us to look at the number—that's what we were now—and remember it so we'd know it backwards. Welcome to the British Army. Then we left the gym and received our mess tins—knife, fork and spoon, not forgetting our tin cup—and off we went to the cookhouse to line up, mess tins in hand, while the cooks slapped mashed potatoes, beans and bangers in our tins along with tea (one bag per gallon of water). I said to myself, *this is something to look forward to.*

Day two, clothing issue. In the British Army you are big or small, no in-between sizes. One good thing: the boots fit. Next came inoculations and vaccinations. We knew this wasn't going to be fun when they gave us forty-eight hours off to recover. The British Army does not give you time off for no reason.

Then followed the real stuff: physical training, foot drill, arms drill, route marches, war games—you name it, we did it. We did the route marches in full marching order, even with water bottles full. No water bottles full (on a charge), ten miles run and walk. Some of the men fell out with sore feet or legs. Trucks came along and picked them up without question. (Oh, this didn't seem right to me!) Next morning, five a.m. reveille for those who fell out without completing the march, plus doing the assault course. What a lesson to be learned. Nothing easy in the British Army.

Now I had completed six weeks' preliminary training and was ready for posting. I was selected to be posted to a parachute regiment, but before we got our assignment an emergency order came through for drivers, and off I was posted to a heavy vehicle training school up in Yorkshire. Training was on heavy equipment towing and recovery of off-road vehicles, including tanks. Six more weeks went by, and I was posted to the 15 Med Reg Royal Artillery in Guildford, Surrey.

Week in and week out, we played war games; we took the 5.5 med guns out to the coast and fired them out to sea at targets towed by small craft. We got used to going on war games.

But one day in June, things seemed different, somehow. Everybody packed up and nothing was left behind. This time we travelled south to the dock area. It wasn't long before we got some idea of what was going on. Troops, tanks, and guns were all going in the same direction—towards the docks. We arrived at Tilbury docks, where the guns and vehicles were loaded onto the ships.

One interesting story, though, I must tell. On the way down to the docks, the convoy stopped for a break. One of the gun crew said he lived in the area, and, wouldn't you know, down the road came his father and two lovely sisters! They talked for a while and then off we went. Believe it or not, he was one of the first men in our regiment to get killed. The last I saw of him, he was wrapped up in an army blanket waiting for burial. My mind went right back to when he last saw his family. These are the sad times that stick in your mind. Nineteen years of age and life taken away, and for what reason?

We were now on board ship—troops and equipment—and off we sailed into the English Channel. It wasn't long before we got our first taste of battle: aircraft, shells, you name it. We were lucky, although others around us were not so lucky. We were in sight of the beaches of Normandy. We stopped; backup was forming. This made us nervous, a sitting target. But luck was on our side. Then we started to move closer to the beaches, but not too close. We dropped anchor. Up the side of the ship came the landing craft, over the side by crane went the guns and equipment, down the side of the ship on rope ladders went the troops, and off we went to the beaches of Normandy. Don't look around; you would not like what you saw. Landing craft being hit gives you a funny gut feeling. Just cross your fingers and pray.

Suddenly we hit the beach, down went the ramp, and off we went, luckily into only two feet of water. Not so lucky for the landing craft next to us. They hit a sandbank and *thought* they had hit the beach. A Jeep drove off the craft and vanished in about fifteen feet of water. There are more ways of dying than you know. Just hitting the beach you could be drowned, shot, shelled, bombed—and if that's not enough, you can stand on a land mine.

We landed at a place called Graye-sur-Mer, but having no place to position our guns, we had to hide them and other equipment in the town out of sight. Then the word came to move out. We proceeded on to the outskirts of Caen, where we dug in and fired 5.5 med guns with open sights. Those guns soon became hot with the amount of shells we were delivering to the enemy's Tiger tanks. It took quite some time to remove the German line of defence from this position. After Caen came Falaise Gap. Lack of communications saw our own aircraft drop bombs on our own troops, despite our displaying the yellow triangle flags. After Falaise Gap, we proceeded to Rouen, up the coast to Boulogne, Calais, Dunkirk, to Bruges and up to Nijmegen, where we finished in May 1945.

This war now over, the regiment was sent back to England, reformed and posted to Light Infantry, and trained with Somerset Light Infantry for jungle warfare. We traded in our vehicles for mules. All this for the invasion of Japan. But then bombs were dropped on Japan and that war was also now over. Transferred to another regiment—Suffok Regiment. This regiment was assigned to Kingston, Jamaica, as a garrison troop, since Jamaica was a colony of Great Britain. We thought this was going to be a holiday in the sun. Little did we know that we were there to defend the country from enemy attack, and also to help the local police keep peace during riots.

It wasn't long before our first encounter. A ship returning from England with Jamaican RAF personnel stationed in England was taken over. A female on board was raped, and crewmembers were injured. The men now in control of this ship refused to bring it into dock, but at that time the British Navy was in the area on some kind of mission and was called upon to escort this ship into Kingston Harbour. Then the army took over, and the RAF personnel were escorted into compounds and the guilty parties sorted out for trial.

Our second encounter was when Kingston had a riot, with fighting in the streets, looting, you name it. This was just up our alley. They were up against seasoned troops. We had no trouble with that problem.

This is a funny one. One day, while walking through the barracks during lunch time, I happened to be with my Jamaican ATS girlfriend, and we were holding hands. The company clerk came up to me and said I was wanted in the company office. On arriving there, I was informed by the CSM that I was on a charge for something like "improper conduct unbecoming an NCO." At nine a.m. the next day, I was up on company orders, and the company commander said he would have to hand this charge over to the CO. At nine a.m. the following day, I was up in front of the CO, stripped of my corporal stripes, and confined to barracks for fourteen days. This caused a stir within the ranks. I didn't see my girlfriend for a few days, but when she found out, she went to see her commanding officer of ATS. Within days I was reinstated to corporal with back pay.

In 1947 our tour of duty in Jamaica was over, so back to England we sailed, and I was ready to be released from His Majesty's Forces. While waiting for release, all NCOs were given the job of escort duty. I got a good one, from the south of England to the north of England, just ten miles from my home. I had three days at home, and decided to visit my girlfriend whom I left before going abroad, only to find out she had married a Canadian sailor and moved out to Chapleau, Ontario. Not a good start after going through WW II.

Anyway, back to the barracks for release and goodbye to the British Army. I was issued civilian clothing, and was off on the lone train ride home to Rochdale. On returning to Rochdale, there was a welcoming party with flags flying everywhere and everyone making whoopee—but not quite everyone, as some had lost their sons or husbands at war. It was not easy, but we talked to all the families that had lost relatives, and they joined in and made the best of it.

RONALD F. JOHNSON BRITISH PARATROOPER

RON was born and raised in London, England, and was bombed out as a child during WW II. As a boy, he was active in Cubs and Boy Scouts, as well as the Boys Brigade, and played a lot of soccer. He enlisted in the British Paratroop Regiment at age eighteen, in September 1956, and served with the SAS in Gibraltar, Cyprus, and Jordan until being discharged in September 1959. He wears the 1958 Jordan Medal presented by a grateful King Hussein for services rendered. He has been in Canada since January 1969.

Ron joined the British Legion in 1960 and the Royal Canadian Legion in 1969, and is now a member of RCL 258, Highland Creek, Ontario. He is also a member of the Governor General's Horse Guards in Toronto, the BAFA, and the Scarborough Veterans Association.

Ron is an avid sportsman, enjoying squash, tennis, skiing, scuba diving, skydiving, parasailing and water skiing, as well as ice- and roller-skating. One of Ron's prized possessions is an embossed and signed Certificate of Pilgrimage to the Holy Sepulchre in Jerusalem in 1958.

ON THE JOB IN THE MIDDLE EAST

I went into Para Regiment because I was afraid of being a cook (that's not really true). I was attracted to the Berets, but my sister said they wouldn't take me.

Out of the 120 young men that started in my platoon, nineteen got wings. After joining Battalion (3rd), two of us were put in "A" Company 3 Platoon 3 Para, where I met Ted ("Ack") Acton.

The time came for my first parachute drop, from a Hastings aircraft. I was about number eight on that stick. I don't remember seeing the door, but I do recall that it was the softest landing I have ever had—all heather. Another jump—or perhaps I should say, no-jump—that comes to mind is the time that I was about to go out of the door but couldn't. I was afraid of the court-martial and terrified of the outcome of 184 days at Colchester Jail for refusing to jump, so I tried my damnedest to get out of that plane. But eventually I gave up, and was left with my legs dangling, just sitting at the door. I later found out that two dispatchers were actually holding me back, as the winds had come up high and the drop had been cancelled, even though half of the stick had already gone!

It was nothing but training until I was shipped out for a short stay on Gibraltar before going off to Cyprus. I was really scared when Punchy, our sergeant, told us to load just five rounds, as we were now on active service, but nothing much happened. A few days later, we were sent out on "keeping curfews and chasing terrorists," which was interesting.

I got a bit worried when Ack and I were together covering each other in Nicosia and he disappeared. I had a Bren in my hand, but it didn't really help, because it was rocks that were coming out of windows, not bombs, so I couldn't fire. I made a hasty retreat, only to find my buddy in a nearby establishment, where he had a local against the wall with his hands held high. Instead of taking out my anger over Ack's disappearance on him, I took it out on the local, and escorted him down to the police station, leaving Ack standing there.

One time, I was on escort with my Bren atop a three-tonner and was fired upon (actually somebody threw a bomb), but my platoon commander wouldn't let me fire back, because we had little red cards stating that we could only do so if we were hurt or if there was damage.

Another time I remember being nervous was when I was in Jordan, where we were again training for something that was expected to happen but didn't. My job was to get on top of a roof with my Bren in order to cover my platoon on fallback. On one particular occasion I was on the roof, and none of my platoon were in sight, which worried me. I wondered what had happened to them, and became rather nervous. Eventually I decided to make my way back to camp, only to find everyone laughing at me. While I was busy scrambling up the back of the house to get on the roof, the exercise had been cancelled and they forgot to let me know. Big joke for them, terror for me!

In Nicosia, when Charlie C. caught a piece of shrapnel in the rear end, he must have dropped his pants a dozen times just to show everyone where he was hit. He had a nice tush, but a bit bloody. He was sounding like a hero, but he said all he actually felt was something like a little razor slash. Of course, for the next two years we lived with how Charlie was wounded in action. As for me, I just remember being in a doorway when it happened.

On guard duty in Amman one night, I was confronted by a Jordanian soldier who was also on guard duty patrolling the area. He cocked his rifle, or at least I think he did—it was pitch black at the time. I just hit the deck and fired one shot—but where, I don't know. I then heard some screaming in Arabic and got up and walked warily to where the noise was coming from. I saw this poor guy, hands in the air, rifle on the floor, apologizing to me for upsetting an English soldier. It took a while for me to give him his rifle back. After that, I was worried about the spent round that I had used but nobody questioned it. I had a few spare rounds anyway. Even if they had asked, I didn't know anything anyway. I must admit, when he first confronted me, I was scared witless. I think that was why I fired the shot.

There are several other stories I would like to share regarding my tours of duty, but unfortunately most exploits of the SAS are still classified and those of us who took part in them are sworn to secrecy. Perhaps someday the powers that be in the British government will release more information concerning events that took place during the war, but it may not be in my lifetime.

GWILYM JONES, MM, MID

ROYAL CANADIAN ARMOURED CORPS

A NATIVE of Wales, Gwilym moved with his parents to the United States in the early 1920s. As a teenager, he joined the US Army Reserve Officers Training Corps, spent his summers with the US 7th Cavalry, and qualified as a machine gunner. After WW II broke out in 1939, he became a student at Columbia University in New York City.

Following a foiled attempt to join the Royal Air Force in Montreal, Gwilym joined the Canadian Grenadier Guards at the end of 1940. Following training and stints at Camp Borden, Camp Valcartier, Halifax, Sussex and Saint John, NB, the regiment was converted from an infantry battalion to a tank regiment at Camp Debert, NS, and arrived in England in September 1942.

After completing various training courses, including commando training and mine clearing, Gwilym was sent on an exchange draft to the Three Rivers Regiment (TRR) Recce Troop, 1st Canadian Armoured Brigade, in Italy via North Africa. His baptism of fire was clearing mines and booby traps during the battle of Ortona in December 1943. His regiment then fought its way through a number of battles including Cassino, the Gustav Line, the Liri Valley, the Hitler Line, Lake Trasimeno, and the Advance to Florence; and then held static positions in the mountains north of Florence during the winter of 1944–45. These 253 consecutive days under enemy fire was the longest unbroken period for the entire Canadian Army.

Gwilym was both Mentioned in Dispatches and awarded the Military Medal during this campaign. The TRR moved to Northwest Europe in March 1945 and saw action in the Reichwald Forest, the Ijssell River, Arnhem, and ended the war beyond Apeldoorn near Amersfoort, Holland.

Gwilym returned to university following his discharge. He holds a bachelor's degree in Commerce from Sir George Williams University (Concordia) and bachelor's and master's degrees in Social Work from McGill University. Following early retirement from Dupont Canada after thirty years' service, he engaged in private social work in Montreal, involved primarily with the administration of employee assistance programs for staff and teachers of various school boards. He was also a guest lecturer from time to time at McGill and local community colleges in the Montreal area for courses involving industrial social work. Gwilym volunteered his services to the Boy Scout movement, the Kiwanis Club and the Board of Trade, and is a past master of his Masonic Lodge.

He relocated to Toronto in 1984, where he became engaged in various freelance activities, including serving a term as services officer at his local Legion branch. Since that time he has completed his wartime memoirs, *To the Green Fields Beyond: A Soldier's Story*, published in 1993; a book of favourite recipes; and a book of poetry, *Random Thoughts*. He continues to write and to paint with oils.

Gwilym also enjoys being a member of the Royal Canadian Legion Branch 258 and the Scarborough Veterans Association; and being secretary of the Three Rivers Regiment Veterans Association, Toronto Chapter, as well as an executive member of the Living History Speakers Bureau RCL Branch 258.

In December 1998 Gwilym was privileged to form part of a pilgrimage to Italy to celebrate the fifty-fifth anniversary of the Battle of Ortona, and to attend a reconciliation dinner with former enemies, members of the German 1st Paratroop Division. He also attended the celebrations of the fifty-fifth anniversary of the Liberation of Holland in Apeldoorn, in May 2000.

Gwilym's family has a long history of service to the British crown. His great-grandfather, who was with the 17th Lancers, was in the Charge of the Light Brigade during the Crimean War, and his great-uncle commanded the Royal Welsh Fusiliers during WW I. His father enlisted in the King's Liverpool Regiment and survived fifty-six days in the trenches and gas attacks during the Battle of Ypres, but was badly wounded on the Somme.

Gwilym Jones, MM, MID – Royal Canadian Armoured Corps

"THE MAD WELSHMAN"

Choosing my most memorable wartime experience is, to me, like attempting to select the most palatable strawberry in a basket. Some are sweet and juicy, some overripe, some still green, some not fit to eat. During my five-year wartime enlistment, I accumulated many memories—some were precious, some were unforgettable, others I would much rather forget.

Some of the ones I think about today involve the exhilaration felt on seeing places or things for the first time. Still vivid in my memory are my first few days in Montreal, visiting old Quebec City, being stationed at the Citadel in Halifax, experiencing the troopship voyage to England, seeing the green hills of Ireland as we sailed around her north coast, landing in Liverpool, being on leave in London during an air raid and working backstage at the Garrick Theatre, having tea with fellow Welshman actor/playwright Emlyn Williams at Lyons Corner House, standing fire watch with actress Ann Todd, buying drinks for Dylan Thomas, swapping lies with ex-boxer Tommy Farr in his pub in Brighton, visiting my grandfather in North Wales, defusing my first Teller mine on a mine clearing course in Yorkshire, experiencing the horrors of a Luftwaffe attack on our troopship near Algiers and witnessing the torpedoing of a nearby hospital ship by a Messerschmitt, touring the Casbah in Algiers and viewing the ruins of Carthage, seeing the red roofs of Naples from the bay— and then, on shore, its filth—and clearing mines and booby traps during the battle of Ortona in my baptism by fire.

Crossing the Rapido River near Cassino after the biggest Allied bombardment of the campaign to date, and being mentioned in dispatches at that time, was also a particular highlight. Memories of our battles up the Italian boot now sometimes swirl about in my mind's eye like a kaleidoscope. In each city we captured, I endeavoured to get a glimpse of Italy's glorious past—museums, art galleries, architectural wonders, ancient cathedrals, Roman ruins and other historical marvels. A nine-day leave in Rome was fascinating, topped off with seats in Mussolini's box at the Royal Opera House with a lovely *signora* by my side, watching *Il Trovatore*. Fighting alongside the Italian and Russian partisans in Florence before its capture ranks high in my thoughts, along with wonderful memories of forty-eight-hour leaves in that beautiful city afterwards.

Other memorable experiences in Italy include nightly foot patrols, sometimes with infantry troops, in the mountains south of Bologna, being decorated with the Military Medal at Castel Del Rio, and winning seventy-seven thousand francs in a crap game at a debarkation camp at Leghorn. A three-day pass in Paris also stands out, during which we blew all the winnings.

On a more poignant note, receiving news of my mother's death by way of the Red Cross in Switzerland a month after the fact was hard to endure. Being part of the food convoys into Amsterdam three days before VE day and the fantastic reception by the Dutch people as they were liberated was unforgettable, as was the peaceful sojourn in Friesland while waiting for a ship home. The victory parade in Trois Rivières, Quebec, on our return to Canada was also a highlight.

Memories I would rather forget invariably relate to incidents involving the deaths or wounding of some of my buddies, and I prefer not to relate them here.

Most of what I experienced during the war is included in my book of wartime memoirs, *To the Green Fields Beyond: A Soldier's Story*. I wrote this book on the premise that as we old soldiers die off, so do the first-hand accounts of our experiences.

However, despite having recorded an account of my wartime experiences, it was not until Christmas 1998 that I finally came to terms with my feelings towards our wartime enemies. I was privileged to be part of a pilgrimage to Italy to celebrate the Fifty-fifth Anniversary of the Battle of Ortona. Also invited were members of the German paratroop regiment we fought against during that battle. On Christmas Eve we sat down together at a dinner table in a church where, in 1943, Canadian troops had also celebrated Christmas.

Together we took part in an ancient Roman ceremony for making peace with an enemy—we each ate a chunk of bread, drank a goblet of wine, saluted each other, then shook hands while the band played our national anthems. As a result, in my case—and I'm sure with others who participated—all feelings of hatred towards things German disappeared from my psyche. It was a long-delayed catharsis, for which I am most grateful. Currently, I exchange regular correspondence with one of my newfound German friends and we have become quite close. As to the war: they did what they had to do, as did we.

Gwilym Jones, MM, MID – Royal Canadian Armoured Corps

As my most memorable wartime experience, I have chosen to relate an incident that occurred following our crossing of the Rapido River in Italy during the final battle for Cassino in May 1944. I am not proud of my actions that day, but I do not apologize for what I did, as I am still a firm believer that we are all equal in the eyes of the Supreme Being; and caste, colour, and creed have no bearing on how we treat our fellow man.

The following is an excerpt from my wartime memoirs (pp. 85–87). This chapter gives an account of the Three Rivers Regiment tanks crossing "Oxford" bridge near the village of Cassino on May 14, 1944, and launching an attack across the higher ground to take its objective.

> After the higher ground had been secured, the Recce Troop moved to replenish supplies. In actions like this, we used our Honey tanks to carry ammo and petrol to the Shermans, so we were busy for a few hours. As we neared the slope after traversing the flat ground, we got a blast on the side of the tank and we bailed out fast. I dove head first, landing in a somersault on rocks. (I limped for a long time after that.) There was no damage to the tank, so we remounted. The infantry in the meantime had pushed forward, and we could hear the battle raging further north. I stopped at one point and picked up an officer wounded in both legs and hauled him into the tank. As I tried to inject a hypo of morphine, I accidentally jammed it into my own thumb. I held him in my arms back across the river to the BDS, but I was like a zombie for a while from the effects of that shot and lack of sleep.
>
> On about the third day, after refuelling, we stopped to catch our breath and count casualties. I had almost run out of steam at this point, dashing back and forth across the open ground and guarding the bunkers. Then I learned that Wally Burnett had been killed crossing the flat ground; but we had to push forward then, so we could not look for him. We could see puffs of smoke over to our right and just knew the Kiwis and Poles were having a rough time of it trying to take the

monastery. It went on like this for a couple of days, then quiet. The Gustav Line had been breached and Cassino had fallen.

My patrol (two Honeys and eight men, four in each tank) moved back to the river to try and find Wally. We found that the Gurkhas had already buried him, wrapped in a blanket and straight up, as is their custom. I obtained permission from their Lance-Naik to disinter him, and my boys started to dig a grave in a plot near the bunkers where the Canadian dead were being buried. The ground was solid rock, so we used hand grenades to blast a hole. While the patrol was so engaged, I went

RCL Branch 258 mural depicting the Battle of Ortona, Italy, December 1943, with branch artist Joe Evans and donor Gwilym Jones, Ortona veteran.

back across the river to fetch the padre. Being a French-Canadian regiment, our chaplain was Roman Catholic. When we returned, the boys had finally dug the hole large enough. The padre checked Wally's dog tags, and exclaimed, "*Un Juif,*" and told me he would not bury him. My boys, tired and short-tempered by this time, started to mutter. I saw red; I pulled my sidearm, pointed it at him and said, "Padre, you bury him or we'll bury you." And he did.

The next day I received orders to report to RHQ; the colonel wanted to see me. When I got there the RSM was like a hen on a hot griddle, wanting to know what had happened. I told him and he escorted me to the colonel. Nobody had asked me to remove my beret, so I knew I wasn't on charge—yet. The padre was with the colonel, as was the 2 i/c. The colonel asked me what had happened and I told him. A man of few words, he ordered me back to my tank, and turned to the padre and said, "I want to talk to you." I never saw that padre again. He is now deceased.

It so happened that this incident spread through the troops and the story grew in the telling. I soon learned that I had a new nickname—*Le Maudit Gallois*, roughly translated as "The Mad Welshman."[1]

Some years after the war, I composed the following poem in commemoration of Wally's death:

1 Prior to the publication of my book, considerable pressure was brought to bear on me to delete this episode. The colonel disclaimed any knowledge of it having occurred, as did the brigade chaplain. I therefore had to obtain first-hand witness corroboration that it actually happened, despite claims in some quarters that it was a figment of my imagination. The ecclesiastical arm is long and far-reaching!

To Wally, Killed In Action
Cassino, Italy, May 1944

The sun was high where olives grow,
The plain was long and wide.
Grapes were bursting on the vine,
With chaff wheat side by side.

Mountains ringed the valley's neck,
Their crests were shorn and bare,
Overlooking luscious growth,
A place to stand and stare.

This sun-drenched plain in days of yore,
Was Caesar's private fief.
His Legions here fought Tuscan foes,
Before he came to grief.

Later then the Visigoths came,
The Franks, the Gauls, the Celts.
The battle cries of many men,
Have thundered through these welks.

What thoughts are there beneath this turf,
If fallen foes could speak,
|Of life, of love, of kin and kith;
The brave, the gods, the meek.
A bugle sounds, the drums do roll;
'Tis time to gather round.
Another group of heroes brave,
To sleep beneath the ground.

They join the ranks of ancient dead,
Who've slumbered eons through.
Like mighty armies of the night,
Their names are known to few.

But overhead beyond the stars,
A roll is kept, no doubt,
Of heroes clad in princely robes,
Who fought both keen and stout.

The ranks that line across the square,
Look sadly at the cross.
The trumpets blare, and Last Post sounds,
A hymnal for our loss.

Is this the price we have to pay,
To clear the Boot of hate,
What came of love, of peace 'tween men;
Who turns the key of fate?

These thoughts came rumbling through the tears,
As Last Post faded past.
So join the ancient shroud, Old Friend,
You're equal too, not last.
To me, forever, you will be
A memory God has cast.

GEORGE KERR

ROYAL NAVY

GEORGE was born and raised in Scotland. He was a pre-war member of the Boys Brigade for eight years and served in the British Home Guard for three years before enlisting at age twenty-one in 1941 as an engineer in the Royal Navy. He served on HMS *Princess Astrid*, HMS *Caernarvon Castle*, HMS *Emperor*, HMS *Arbiter*, HMS *Reaper*, and HMS *Glengyle*. He was involved in the D-Day invasion, the South Atlantic patrol, North Atlantic patrol, Antarctic patrol, the bombing of the *Tirpitz*, the invasion of the South of France, and in clearing the enemy from the Aegean Sea. He also served in Japan, Australia and New Zealand.

Following his release from the navy in July 1947, George worked in the engineering field, mostly in tool-and-die making, and in aeronautics at A.V. Roe. He emigrated to Canada in 1966 and has had a lifetime career in this country as a life insurance broker.

An entertainer all his life, George trained as a concert singer in England. He was a member of the Scarborough Choral Society, the Toronto Musical Theatre Society, and the Unionville Arts Society, and was MC of the Baron Show Band for twelve years, entertaining seniors and many others. After his accompanist passed on, George decided to accompany himself, and learned to play the guitar at age sixty-five, then the fiddle at age sixty-eight.

George has been married for fifty-four years. He is a lay preacher at St. Giles Anglican Church, a Royal Canadian Legion chaplain, and padre of RCL Branch 11, as well as an active member of the Living History Speakers Bureau RCL Branch 258.

THE SINKING OF THE *TIRPITZ*

One of my most memorable—and frightening—experiences during the "Big One" (as Archie Bunker called it) was due to the *Tirpitz*, the largest, fastest and most powerful battleship ever built for the German navy. At 52,600 tons, she was bigger than the *Bismarck* and could steam at thirty-one knots, faster than any British battleship. She was 828 feet in length—almost three football fields long—and her beam was 119 feet. Launched on April 1, 1939, she was intended to be the pride of the new German navy.

Captain Karl Topp took command of *Tirpitz* on January 25, 1941, at Wilhelmhaven. He had spent his early career involved with U-boats and destroyers, and had the reputation of driving the giant ship like a destroyer. Hitler was to visit the *Tirpitz* on the following day (the 26th) and it was Captain Topp's intention to request permission to sail on a three-month cruise on the Atlantic trade routes with the *Bismarck* and *Prinz Eugen*, both of which were also in harbour. His request was refused. No ship could hope to be battle ready until sea trials had been completed, and her crew conversant with all the intricate instrumentation and armaments.

The *Tirpitz* sailed for the Baltic Sea, away from British bombers, to complete her battle- and sea-training. These extensive trials carried on through the summer and fall. She had one opportunity for action in September 1941 when a large task force consisting of *Tirpitz*, the pocket battleship *Admiral Scheer*, and some light cruisers, minesweepers and destroyers stood by near the Aaland Islands for a sortie with the Russian fleet. The Russians, however, stayed put in Krondstadt, so *Tirpitz* returned to the Baltic to finish her trials.

Hitler was so certain that Britain intended to invade Norway sooner or later, that he insisted the seaward defences had to be strengthened as soon as possible. To this end—and also to save the *Tirpitz* from suffering the same fate as the *Bismarck*, which had been sunk in May 1941—*Tirpitz* sailed for Norway. As she sailed north, Hitler said, "Every ship that is not in Norway is in the wrong place."

Tirpitz was soon safely at anchor at Trondheim, where a snug berth had been prepared for her. She was only forty miles from the sea, so she presented a serious threat to convoys sailing to Russia.

The arrival in Norway of the *Tirpitz* was immediately conveyed to the Admiralty in London, as they had a Norwegian underground worker in Trondheim who sent a signal as soon as the great ship arrived.

Prime Minister Winston Churchill was so concerned about the threat *Tirpitz* presented that he wrote: "The destruction or even crippling of this ship is the greatest event at sea at the present time.

No other target is comparable to it. I regard the matter as of the greatest urgency and importance." Churchill had good reason to be concerned, since the presence of the *Tirpitz* forced the Admiralty to keep three battleships at Scapa Flow to protect the northern convoys—battleships that could have been used elsewhere.

Sinking the *Tirpitz* now became an obsession with Churchill, so he began a series of attempts to fulfill his ambition—attempts that were to cost many lives and millions of dollars. Starting in January 1942, there were sixteen sorties made to cripple or sink the *Tirpitz*, culminating in her being sunk on November 12, 1944, by Lancaster bombers flying from Lossiemouth in Scotland. The sixth attempt was the one in which I was involved.

I had joined HMS *Emperor*, an auxiliary aircraft carrier, on March 11, 1944, and spent the next two weeks on manoeuvres in the Firth of Clyde off the west coast of Scotland. We had two squadrons of Grumman Hellcats, single-seater fighters capable of carrying a 1,000-lb bomb. The Hellcat was the most successful carrier-based aircraft during the war, much superior to the Seafire, which was a Spitfire adapted for carrier duty. Early in the war, the Fleet Air Arm was equipped with Fairey Swordfish planes, then Albacores, but these were slow compared to the Hellcat, which had been specifically designed for carrier duty.

Our aircraft were flying daily, but we were more interested in another plane that we saw flying from the two big aircraft carriers, *Victorious* and *Furious*. This plane was a new dive-bomber that had been specially designed for vertical dive-bombing. It was a peculiar-looking plane with holes in the wings. During our workup, we saw some of these planes—Barracudas—dive straight into the sea. We wondered what action we were training for, but were no wiser when we joined a convoy sailing north to Scapa Flow.

We arrived at Scapa Flow on March 28th and left on the morning of the 30th, joining a convoy that had left Scotland a few days carlicr. This convoy, bound for Russia, was J.W. 58 and consisted of forty-nine ships protected by a strong escort. A German reconnaissance plane spotted them on the 30th, the day we left Scapa, but our fighter aircraft reacted immediately and shot down six German planes.

Included in the escort were Admiral Bruce Fraser's flagship, the battleship *Duke of York*, and the battleship *Anson*. (Admiral Fraser was one of the few naval ratings who ever made it to admiral. He started as an ordinary seaman.)

Shortly after leaving Scapa Flow, we were informed at last that our mission was not to protect the convoy, but to attack the *Tirpitz*. There was great excitement throughout the ship, particularly among the pilots who were at last going into action.

The original plan had been to sail due north for two days, then east for one day and attack the *Tirpitz* on April 4th. However, at 2:30 p.m. on April 2nd, Admiral Fraser decided that the operation would be advanced by twenty-four hours, so we changed course to northeast for eight hours, then east to a rendezvous about 200 miles north of our target, which was in the very narrow Kaa Fjord. The *Tirpitz* was anchored right next to the cliff face, making it a very difficult target to bomb.

The afternoon and evening of April 2nd were very busy and exciting times for all on board; we looked forward with anticipation to the following day, although, as we were on an aircraft carrier, most of us would not be involved unless we were attacked.

In the wardroom that night, I was having my usual drink, and one of the pilots, a good friend of mine, John Brine from Cornwall, was bemoaning his fate. He was not flying with the squadron to protect the bombers, but had been assigned to protect the fleet. We all left the wardroom about ten p.m., early for us.

My watch in the engine room was from four to eight—the morning watch—so I was up by 3:30 a.m. and could hear the activity above on the hangar deck. After a quick coffee, I went up to the flight deck at 3:50 a.m. The noise was deafening. All the planes were running their engines, while the plane handlers were trying to get the frozen snow off the wings. We were just south of the Arctic Circle and it was mighty cold. Anyone in the water would die in two minutes.

Zero hour was 4:15 a.m. The Barracudas took off, followed by twenty-one Corsair fighters, one for each Barracuda. Then the Hellcats joined in the formation. By 4:37 a.m. all planes were in position and took off for their target, 120 miles away.

The attacks—there were two, one hour apart—were intended to be massive, sudden and unexpected. They were. Each attack lasted only a few minutes.

Of the forty-two Barracudas taking part, ten carried one 1,600-lb armour-piercing bomb, twenty-two carried 500-lb semi-armour-piercing bombs, and ten carried high-explosive anti-submarine bombs.

It was a beautiful morning on the day of the attack, and when I went on deck at about 5:45 a.m. our planes were already returning, just as the second strike was taking off.

There was one Barracuda lost in each strike and one Hellcat had to ditch in "the drink," as his landing gear did not work. The pilot, the squadron leader from our ship, *Emperor*, was picked up in minutes and rejoined us later in Scapa.

My friend was not so lucky. After all of the attacking planes had returned safely, he continued to fly round the fleet waiting for an order to return. However, the weather suddenly changed, and we started rolling and pitching, causing planes to break from their moorings. There was so much confusion on deck that John was signalled to remain up until some planes were lowered to the hangar deck. By the time the deck was clear, the seas had become mountainous, and even down in the engine room, where there was less motion, we were holding onto stanchions and railings to avoid falling. John was signalled to land, but just as he came over the stern, the ship pitched, the bow went down, the stern came up, and his arrester hook caught the end of the deck instead of the arrester wire. The hook was wrenched from its socket and the plane flipped over upside down. John had a fractured skull and died the next day. We buried him at sea, and that in itself was a nightmare, since it was almost impossible to stand, with the ship rolling and pitching.

For some unknown reason, *Emperor* was the only ship in trouble. The rest of the fleet returned to Scapa Flow, arriving on April 6th to a rousing welcome from the ships in harbour.

We continued to roll a steady 30°, which is very dangerous, and twice we did 45°, which is usually fatal. Eating and sleeping were practically impossible. Crockery was smashed and planes were wrecked, so we turned into the wind to alleviate our problems. Our nightmare continued for six days before the seas and winds abated—the waves had to have been fifty feet—and we could sail back to Scapa Flow for a well-deserved rest before preparing for D-Day.

I learned a few months later that we had been given up for lost for six days, and for some years after the war I had nightmares about being on a ship that turned upside down, but the only one to do that was the *Tirpitz*, a few months later.

After our dangerous sojourn in the far north, D-Day was an anti-climax.

We had seven days' leave, and then proceeded to the River Foyle in Northern Ireland, just off the port of Londonderry. Our planes were kept busy doing all kinds of manoeuvres, for what purpose we did not know. Things were quiet, but we felt something big was on the agenda.

At last, on June 3rd, we sailed for Anglesy in North Wales, to learn that the invasion was to take place on June 6th. However, a burst steam pipe in our boiler made it necessary for us to sail for Belfast for hurried repairs, which were completed in twenty-four hours.

We left on the morning of June 5th for our station off Bordeaux, in the Bay of Biscay. The morning of June 6th was so foggy that we could not fly, and it continued all day. The following day we sailed south to the Mediterranean and the Isle of Malta, with a stop at Gibraltar.

We spent an idyllic month from the middle of June to mid-July, basking in the sun, swimming, sightseeing and generally having a good time. This life could not last forever, and at last we sailed out into the Med to do some flying. Through the last week in July and the first week in August, our planes were taking off and landing all day, but not attacking anyone.

On the morning of August 12th, they flew off and were gone for some time. When they landed, the pilots were very excited—they had been attacking gun emplacements around Marseilles and Toulon. After refuelling, they were off again. These attacks continued during daylight for the next two days.

The morning of August 14th was bright and clear, and when I came off watch in the engine room at eight a.m., I went on deck to see an amazing sight. As far as the eye could see, to left and right, were ships—battleships, cruisers, destroyers, escort vessels, landing craft and escort carriers—from five navies, American, British, Australian, French and Greek. It was a sight almost impossible to take in. I stood there in awe.

When I came up after breakfast, the view was the same: a continuous line of ships from one horizon to the other—more than 1,000 ships in all.

Hitler had been expecting the invasion to be at Genoa, and to convince him that he was correct, extensive attacks were made in the area. We joined the armada, but naturally on the outside, since our aircraft were still pounding the German defences continually. As soon as a plane landed, it was refuelled and rearmed, and then took off again. There was dawn-to-dusk activity.

The invasion of the South of France commenced on the morning of August 15th with amphibious and airborne landings. We could not see the beach landings, since we were about a half-mile offshore, but it was quite a memorable experience to see thousands of parachutes in the air at one time as relay after relay of aircraft came over. There was no retaliation from German aircraft, although sixty managed to get off the ground. They were quickly shot down—they were outnumbered ten to one.

On that single day, August 15th, allied aircraft flew 4,250 sorties and the fleet fired 50,000 shells. By evening 60,000 troops had been landed with 6,000 vehicles and 50,000 tons of *matériel.*

Two days later, we were granted forty-eight hours' rest off the coast of Sardinia; then it was back again to support the invasion.

One of our Hellcats was shot down by a river patrol boat, as our pilot had gone very low on a strafing run. He managed to get out of the aircraft and was picked up by the Maquis (the French underground) and hidden for two weeks until the south of France was liberated. He rejoined our ship in Alexandria, Egypt, a few weeks later, when we were attacking German boats trying to escape from Crete by way of the Aegean Sea. That was a memorable experience, since many of the islands were German-occupied. One in particular had large gun emplacements embedded in the cliff faces, and no matter how low we bombed them, they kept firing. We even landed commandos, but they were repulsed. Eventually the powers that be decided to use the *King George V* battleship (which was on its way to the Far East) to dislodge the guns, but to no avail.

We cleared the Aegean after four months of continual attacks, and arrived home in February 1945, after a very memorable year.

Two months later, I was in Australia, and then headed north to attack Japan—but that is another story.

George Kerr – Royal Navy

WWI – Navy Mural – Cdr. Richard Burke, V.C.

DAVID LEA — ROYAL CANADIAN ARMY SERVICE CORPS

DAVE was born in Hillier, Prince Edward County, Ontario; raised in Unionville; graduated from North York Collegiate in 1938; and was employed by MacLean's Publishing when WW II commenced. As a teenager he was a senior cadet. He enlisted in the Royal Canadian Army Service Corps in September 1939. After basic training, he was promoted to senior transport sergeant, and sailed to England in December 1939. In England, he experienced the Blitz, with most of his service time spent in transporting supplies to various camps. He was also involved in transporting evacuees from Dunkirk to camps throughout England in the summer of 1940.

David participated in the invasion of Sicily, from Pachino to Regalbuto. During the Italian Campaign, his unit supplied the 1st Canadian Division through to Ortona, where David received his first wound stripe. After convalescing in England, he returned to action in France, Belgium and Holland. In February 1945, David was severely wounded by German shellfire, was comatose until VE day in hospital in England, and suffered a total loss of memory that persists, in part, to this day. He has managed to piece together most of his previous life with the help of friends, relatives and documents. He was discharged in September 1945 after six years and eight months of overseas service.

Following his discharge, Dave sold life insurance and real estate before settling into a career position with John Mansville, retiring as a factory quality controller in 1981. He joined the Royal Canadian Legion in Port Carling in 1959, and transferred to RCL Branch 258 in 1972. He has served this branch in many executive positions over the years, most notably as services officer for the past twelve years. In latter years he has been a prominent speaker throughout the community in Legion Poppy Campaigns. David is also an active member of the Living History Speakers Bureau RCL Branch 258.

World War II Experiences, 1939–1945

On September 10, 1939, my brother and I and three friends joined the RCAF at Manning Pool, the Coliseum in Toronto. Later that day, I met a friend downtown who was headed for the Armouries, already in his RCASC uniform. He said to me: "Come on with me and join the Service Corps. We will be overseas this year waiting to go into action in France, and this war will be all over before you young guys are called up to get your wings. Meet me tomorrow morning at 7:30 and we'll come down here and join the army."

I enlisted in the Army Service Corps on September 11, 1939, and went over to England in December of that year as an NCO. We spent the winter in Aldershot Barracks marching around the whole county of Hampshire. In June 1940, we were issued British right-hand-drive trucks to drive on the left side of the road. We stayed on the southeast coast of England awaiting orders to head for France in June 1940. A few advance First Division guards did go, but were shipped back home forty-eight hours later. Shortly after came the Dunkirk retreat.

Instead of taking petrol and ammo to the boys in France, we picked up the troops that had managed to escape at Dunkirk and took them to our old winter barracks at Aldershot. The bombing raids started the summer of 1940. After we, the Canadians, received our trucks from home, we were kept busy at various jobs, including transporting goods that came in from America, Glasgow, and other places, down to the south of England for distribution to proper regiments.

At one time, bringing a convoy of thirty-odd trucks down to the south of England from Glasgow, we were dive-bombed by German Stukas that shot up the drivers' side of the trucks. Fortunately, these trucks were for use in Europe where they drive on the *right* side of the road, so the only damage was a few holes in the sides of the trucks where there were no drivers!

Two things happened to me in the next two years that are very vivid in my memory. First, I was on leave in London, where I had some friends. We were in a hotel room on the third floor and we received a direct bomb strike on the hotel. It might be hard to believe, but I ended up still in bed, unhurt, on the main floor! As far as we could figure, the explosion had blown the lower section out onto the street, and my floor dropped right down and was covered by the other wall at an angle over the bed. We crawled out with only a few slight cuts and bruises.

The second close shave came at a time I had reserved a table at the Café de Paris in London to celebrate a friend's twenty-first birthday. It turned out that I was on duty at our camp that weekend, and couldn't change it or trade with anyone. I phoned my friend at Military HQ in London, and told him to keep the reservation and get another friend to take my place. He did that and they had a direct hit from an enemy bomber; the four of them were instantly killed. In five years and eight months overseas, this was the only pass I ever lost.

We went down to the Mediterranean and into Sicily in July 1943. I was wounded in Italy, but it was only a broken arm and some small shrapnel in that arm. I was sent back to England in May 1944, and over to France in July. I was back in transport, mostly POL (petrol, oil and lubricants), from port up to the front line.

I was blown up by a German shell in north Holland on February 25, 1945. The next thing I remembered was VE day in an English hospital in May 1945. I was sent home to a Toronto hospital in August, and discharged in September 1945, after six years in the army.

CLINT G. McCORMACK RCAF

CLINT was born and raised in Toronto, and at age thirteen learned to play the trumpet, subsequently marching in the Boys Brigade band. He later became an aero-engine mechanics helper in the Malton Air School Unit.

Clint joined the Royal Canadian Air Force at age nineteen in August 1943. He took training as an aero-engine mechanic and became a leading aircraftman, qualified on all RCAF aircraft. He was also directly involved in the training of aircrew.

He was honourably discharged in March 1946, at which time he joined RCL Branch 13, where his father was a member. After leaving the service, he was employed by Rogers Radio for five years in sales and service, then spent another five years with Underwood Typewriter. He then went into the life insurance business, in which he is still active as an insurance broker and advisor, having held a government license for over forty-five years.

In 1985, Clint joined Royal Canadian Legion Branch 258 and immediately volunteered as a member of the Branch Colour Guard, where he now holds the rank of staff sergeant. He enjoys acting as MC for various entertainment functions, and has devised a number of comedy and musical routines. Some years ago, he started the Branch 258 Players, and with Peter Prior and Harry Bull and other branch members has staged several outstanding productions with huge success, including a wartime parody, "We'll Meet Again." Clint also takes great pleasure in his involvement in various other activities at his Legion branch, especially in being a member of the Living History Speakers Bureau RCL Branch 258.

CANADA AT WAR, 1939–1945

I was fifteen when, with permission, I left school to go to work. I guess permission came easily because, before the war, money was not too plentiful in my family of Mom, Dad and five children, with only Dad working as an instrument mechanic for CNR. As I remember, the Canadian economy wasn't that good in the pre-war years, or maybe it was just at our house. (When the garbage truck came down our street, we were the only family that took some!)

Before I was sixteen, I had bought my first car. My dad co-signed for a 1931 Model A Ford convertible. I mention this car to show how sometimes moves we make in life can determine future moves. In my case I'm sure it was for the best. In those days, Danforth Avenue was five miles of car lots, all with sales people wearing checkered suits and smoking big cigars. Of course, I had bought myself a lemon, $295 worth of trouble. Used car dealers for the most part have not changed (buyer beware).

I decided I was going to keep that car, so I took the motor out of it and carted it down to the basement and worked on it all winter—not without research and good advice. It turned out beautifully, A-1.

I could talk for a while longer about that car. However, my mentioning it has a point. It proved to me that at a young age I was a very good auto mechanic with a good understanding of the workings of the gasoline engine. This experience gave me what I needed to get a job at age sixteen at Malton Airport, or No. 2 EFTS (Elementary Flying Training School, RCAF). I was hired as a mechanic helper, working on Tiger Moth aircraft and Avro Ansons to be used in the elementary training of pilots for the RCAF. Malton was part of the British Commonwealth Air Training Plan (BCATP). After a year of working on the Tiger Moth aircraft, I had become very familiar with them. During that year, I went up many times and on many occasions I was allowed to take over the stick. I was getting to be a pretty good pilot at age sixteen going on seventeen. Little did I know what this was to lead into later on.

My next two years were spent building transmitters, walkie-talkies and radio equipment at Rogers Radio on Fleet Street in Toronto. When I left, I was building the transmitter rack for the air force. Most industries were converting to wartime products. Rogers changed from victrolas, radios, car radios, etc., to radio equipment for our navy, army and air force. Massey Ferguson converted from farm equipment—at least about 90%—to the mass production of vehicles and equipment for training in Canada for the armed forces here and overseas. General Motors and all the major car companies retooled to building vehicles for the armed forces—trucks, tanks, guns, etc. I was witness to the greatest industrial changeover in the history of this world. Most factories were working three shifts, going twenty-four hours a day. No one was out of work.

When Canada entered the war, all of our eligible men that were of age, medically fit, and not in jobs where they could not be spared, were going into the services. This opened up thousands of new jobs, and so the women of our country joined the front line of our home defences and became the greatest work force of the war, learning and doing all those jobs that previously would have been done by our men. These women were doing jobs such as building ships, aircraft, army vehicles and ammunition; and learning to weld, rivet, and operate heavy machinery. To prove themselves even more invaluable, they entered the armed forces, creating the women's division of the air force, army and navy, joining our men in being posted wherever they were needed.

I would like to say at this point that ever since the war ended, we have celebrated every year our victories in World Wars I and II, and paid our respects to our comrades who didn't come home, and rightly so. I would like to say that we should also remember the ladies who stayed in Canada working in factories and shipyards, sometimes seven days a week in good weather and bad. They were making the guns, bullets, bombs, tanks, aircraft, trucks and all the equipment needed so badly. Without them we would surely have lost that war. They surely were part of the "combined effort," as we say. A lot of them died giving their all on the home front. I say now: We will remember them.

My part in the war began on the day I joined the Royal Canadian Air Force.

WW II had been in our news for a few years, and, as I grew older and said goodbye to a few of my close friends, it was time for me to follow their example and get involved and get in uniform.

Going back to my experience with my first car and my job as a mechanic's helper at Malton Airport, I guess the only thought in my mind was the air force. My brother Alf was already in the air force in New Brunswick. All airmen think about being a pilot, but my experience as an aero mechanic pulled me in that direction. So down I went to the Manning Depot in the Exhibition Grounds. I had previously received my letter of acceptance and date to report to the Ex. I was excited, to say the least. I had said tearful goodbyes to my family. As I walked through the gates of the Ex and into the Horse Palace, I suddenly realized I was not the only applicant for this job. There were bunk beds as far as you could see!

Getting inducted into the air force, as far as I can remember, consisted of a medical, the issue of an air force uniform that didn't fit, a haircut from a butcher, and a bunk bed in the middle of a huge cement floor with about another thousand or more men (all applicants for my job).

After about two weeks confined to barracks with no leave, I had made a few new friends—but not for long. We were notified that our postings were on the bulletin board. My first posting was to Uplands Ottawa, an elementary training school. We had to wait a month for our course to start, so we were put on a landscaping detail to plant trees and flowers. I enjoyed it, and our station was the most beautiful in Canada. One month later, I was on course helping out with on-the-job training on Harvards, Tiger Moths, and other craft. The course was completed in six months and I received my status as aero engine mechanic, along with a raise in pay.

Ottawa was okay. I could get a forty-eight-hour pass every two weeks and take the train home. Ottawa at Uplands in the winter was colder than Portage and Main in Winnipeg. It didn't matter how cold it was, pilot training and flying still went on. The cockpit of a Harvard can be as cold inside as it is out. As an engine mechanic, same as airframe, all ground crew were always ready during the cold winter days. Ground crew engine mechanics would check gas and oil, start the engine, check oil pressure, and warm up. When all was checked out the pilot would be ready for takeoff. Ground crew would pull chocks, and perform other last-minute operations. This was all done regardless of weather. Engine and airframe mechanics made sure pilot training continued. Pilots and crewmembers were second to none in the world.

For the basic training of pilots, the RCAF used the de Havilland Canada DH-82C Tiger Moth, a biplane two-seater. This was the primary basic trainer during the war years. From this you graduated to the North American Harvard RCAF-HC-8956, the sweetest all-round basic trainer ever built—ask any RCAF pilot, or anyone who ever worked on it or had any contact with it.

As the BCATP got underway, production of Harvards for training could not meet the demand. In typical fashion, the Canadian government had committed its forces to tasks for which sufficient resources were not available. A lot of the Harvards used by the RCAF were on loan from the USAF to bridge the gap between supply and demand. As an aero engine mechanic, I became very familiar with the Harvard. It was easy to work on and great to fly in.

This is a good time to tell you about a never-to-be-forgotten experience of mine involving the Harvard aircraft. It's true that the RCAF would fly in just about all kinds of weather, which reminds me of Christmas season 1943. I was stationed at Uplands Ottawa, an elementary flying training school. At the time, I was a qualified aero engine mechanic familiar with the Harvard trainer. On this day, an airframe mechanic and I were selected to volunteer to do some repairs on a downed Harvard trainer somewhere north of Smiths Falls, Ontario. My partner in this venture was James (Jim) Callahan. The airman, who was on a solo training flight, developed engine trouble, so we were told, and in a bit of a snow squall he crash-landed in a farmer's field about ten miles from nowhere. In performing this emergency landing in the snow-covered field, the student pilot did a great job, considering the shape this farm field was in. However, he did manage to bend one blade on the prop and damage one of the oleo legs (wheel mechanism).

So on this cold winter day, Jim and I were sent by air force truck to the scene of the crash. Arriving at the farm, we had to go 'way around the other side from where the craft was, and in through the gate. We met the owner and his family, and, after a little conversation, were told the best route to reach the craft.

Coming towards the plane, it looked like a downed bird. The student pilot had given a good description of the damage to the plane, and Jim and I, along with the F/S driver, began to unload the equipment from the truck: a bench to stand and work on, jacks, new oleo leg, propeller parts, our tools, etc. We took note of all our parts, and the F/S driver took off back to Uplands, saying he would be back when needed to pick us up. The farmer said that in an emergency we could use the phone in his house, which was about a two- to three-mile walk through snow.

The idea was for us to repair the plane and the driver would bring back one of our pilot instructors to fly it out of the field and back to the station. Jim and I discussed over and over the chances of this being possible, because of the poor condition of the ground, the presence of the snow, and the wind, along with poles and wires to contend with.

However, this was a few hours away, we thought. We worked as fast and with as much precision as possible, because we wanted the plane to take off in daylight. It had to. With help from Jim, but with all kinds of setbacks, we finished the propeller (this Harvard had the aluminum prop, feathering type). We both worked on the oleo leg. The biggest problem was jacking up the plane. It was not easy working with bare hands in the wind and snow, and it was cold, cold, cold! (It was so cold that Jim and I saw the farm dog chasing a cat and they were moving in slow motion—true.)

We finished our repairs, cleaned up the mess, and sat in the plane for a break. It was colder in the plane than outside, so we got out. It was about four p.m., as I remember, and very dull. We opened up a lunchbox packed for us by the mess hall crew. It consisted of about a dozen jam sandwiches and an apple each, but nothing to drink. Who said the air force had it easy.

We tossed a coin to see who would make the trip to the phone. I won the toss and started out for the farmhouse. The people were great. They were all ready for Christmas, and made us up a real lunch, pie and all. Our flight sergeant told us to hang in there. He was trying to round up a pilot instructor, but most of them were off the station for Christmas. He told me the plane had to be kept under guard at all costs.

As you may have guessed by now, no one came to pick us up that day and we spent a great night trying to keep warm. People heard about the plane down in the field and drove out to take a look. The fence was lined with people and cars waiting to see if, indeed, it would be flying out of this field.

The following morning was Sunday, and the townspeople offered to drive us one at a time to the local Mass. It was a wonderful morning. The sun was up, and it was cold and dry. It was about noon when a sheepish-looking F/S drove the air force truck across the field with our pilot instructor. Perfect timing. We had each been to church and back. The road around this farm was lined with cars and townspeople, all having heard the news from, I think, two uniformed airmen who had been to attend Mass at the local church and couldn't keep it a secret.

After loading all the equipment onto the truck, the F/S moved off towards the road. I had already started the plane and had it all warmed up with everything checked out A-OK. The pilot had walked quite a bit of the field, and I was impressed when he asked Jim and me what we thought of his decision to taxi the plane down to the other end of the field and take off over the road (as there were wires at this end). He felt that the bit of wind he would fly into would help lift him up and over the road.

Looking at this young man, only three years my senior, I could see the positive attitude in him and the confidence in his decision. We all agreed. We helped him into the cockpit, strapped him in, closed the top, and gave him thumbs-up.

He slowly turned the plane around and started taxiing down to the other end of the field. We didn't have to clear the people away from this end—the mini-snowstorm that the Harvard created did it for us. Our pilot reached the spot where he felt he had enough ground in front of him to take off. He turned the Harvard around and took a few more minutes to warm up and recheck everything. Then we could hear the increased rpm and see the tail section bouncing and eager for takeoff. Releasing the brakes, the pilot taxied down the field towards us. What a picture this plane made: the motor roared, and for a moment we could barely see the aircraft because of the cloud of snow behind and all around it. It seemed it had not travelled very far, and it was trying to leave the ground and yet looked as though it wasn't going to make it. As the plane passed by us, it was only about two feet off the ground and we all gave it another thumbs-up. I'm certain our pilot returned it to us. In the very next second, our plane turned upwards and was headed into a beautiful, clear blue sky. At about 300 feet he made a circle and as he went back over us he tipped his wings to say goodbye and all's well. We stood and watched with a little choked-up feeling, and, I believe, a few were close to tears as pilot and plane went out of sight, clearing the hydro wires by about thirty feet.

It was this event that drove home to me just how important *my* position with the air force and the BCATP was. It was a great feeling to see that plane take off and go back into action because of the repairs Jim and I had performed in that field. We had a direct hand in the training of pilots and aircrew that played a big part in the outcome of WW II.

I spent close to one year at Uplands and learned a lot about the Harvards and the twin-engine trainer known as the Avro Anson.

It may not be a well-known fact, but it remains true: Most men who became pilots also became addicted to the experience of being in command of a plane. So much so, it became the number one event in life. Should a pilot lose the right or ability to fly, drastic things could sometimes happen.

When these men graduated from Harvards and Ansons to Mitchels and Liberators, they were among the best pilots in the world. As such, a pilot could have been tempted to try manoeuvres that were not in the training program. If word got back to Command about this, he could and would be grounded—sometimes for a month or more, depending on how serious the charge was. He could even lose his wings.

I mention the above to preface an incident that happened when I was stationed at Boundary Bay, BC, flying Mitchels and Liberator bombers, two- and four-engine bombers and fighters.

I was living off base in New Westminster at the time, and I would hitchhike approximately twenty-five miles every day to Boundary Bay. One morning as I was walking across the New Westminster Bridge, as always looking up and down the water to see the goings-on, I was really jarred and stunned to see a Mitchel bomber coming up the river about thirty feet above the water and coming fast towards the bridge. As I stood there, looking out and down, he went right under the bridge and, as he did, I could see as plain as day that the pilot was not dressed for flying—no parachute, no helmet or radio phones, just his blue air force shirt and trousers. As he went under the bridge, I tell you he scared the hell out of me. As he passed under me and out from under the bridge, he started up, increased speed, and took off in the direction of Boundary Bay.

When I arrived at the station, it looked like everyone was out around the tarmac; there were an ambulance and a fire truck, and there was all kinds of activity up in the control tower. It looked like some crews were getting ready to go up, but were waiting for something. That something suddenly showed. It was the Mitchel that I saw in New Westminster. He came straight across the airfield about ten feet off the ground, and at the end of the field he took that plane up as straight as could be. I was told later by another pilot that he didn't think it could be done. This man put on a show for about another half hour. Apparently he had taken the plane up by himself without permission because he had been grounded for a record of unauthorized moves in the past.

The tower could not talk to him because he would not plug in. He must have known he was running out of gas, and when he did he was up about 2,000 feet and put the plane into a nose-dive. As we all stood and watched, he came down and exploded in a field in the small town of Ladner, BC, about a mile off the station. The road from the station to Ladner was jammed with cars, people and police, all trying to get a look and take photos of the very unfortunate death of a top-notch RCAF pilot. By those who knew him, his death was considered to be a suicide. I have heard of others, but this was the only one I ever witnessed. I say he was another casualty of WW II.

In closing I would like to say that I am very proud to have been able to take part in and contribute to the outcome of World War II. We pray, never again.

GRANT McRAE RCAF/POW

GRANT was born in Quebec City in 1922, and lived in Montreal and Vancouver prior to relocating to Toronto in 1959. As a youngster, he was active in the Boy Scouts. In March 1942, at age nineteen, he enlisted in the Royal Canadian Air Force.

Trained as a bomb-aimer with Bomber Command, Grant was on operations with 619 Squadron RAF at Dunholm Lodge, Lincolnshire, England. He was shot down over Stuttgart, Germany, on July 25, 1944, on his thirteenth operation, and became a prisoner in *Stalag Luft* III, Sagan, then in *Stalag* IIIA, Luckenwalde, Germany.

Grant was discharged in September 1945, and ended his career with Safeguard Business Systems as national operations manager. He was for a number of years a director of Sales and Marketing Executives in Toronto.

Grant is past chairman, the Aircrew Association, Metro Toronto Branch, and past executive, National Prisoners of War Association. He is a member of the RCAF POW, Bomber Command, RCAF, and 619 Sqdn. Associations; and is a member of the Royal Canadian Legion.

Much of Grant's wartime experiences during WW II were featured in various news articles, and a TV series last fall entitled *Grant's War*. As a valued member of the Living History Speakers Bureau RCL 258 he is still active in addressing students and others regarding his air force and POW career, primarily in schools located in the western part of Greater Toronto.

A Close Call

In August 1943, I was stationed at an RAF Advanced Flying Unit near Wigtown, Scotland, a town located south of Ayr. One night shortly after takeoff on one of our flying exercises, the starboard engine of our Anson aircraft caught fire. At the time, we were flying over the Irish Sea at a ceiling of approximately 4,000 feet. Rapidly losing height, our skipper gave us instructions over the intercom: "Dinghy—Dinghy prepare for ditching!" Immediately, all members of the crew took their ditching positions.

Then, suddenly, to our amazement and good luck, we broke cloud at approximately 200 feet and, to our surprise, were flying over land. Our landing wheels were up and our engine was still on fire. I was sitting beside the skipper, who immediately signalled to me to lower the undercarriage. I quickly wound the wheels down by hand, which was required on this model of Anson. Miraculously, as we were about to land, bright lights came on and fortunately we were over a landing strip of an airfield. On landing, the lights went out again. Right away a fire truck came out and extinguished the fire in our engine.

We did not know where we were, as our navigation and wireless instruments were not functioning. The rescue unit told us that we were in Llandudno, Wales, and that we had landed at an RAF fighter observation base. We were also told that we were in the middle of a German air raid! We remained at the station for a few days waiting for our aircraft to be repaired. We were in no hurry, as the meals there were very good. This was the first close call of my air force flying experiences. A lot more were to come.

"For You The War Is Over"

On the night of July 25th, 1944, fourteen Lancaster aircraft from No. 619 Squadron, RAF Bomber Command, were assigned to attack Stuttgart. Our aircraft, *"K" King*, was the only one that failed to return. Our crew consisted of our pilot, who was from New Zealand, our navigator, wireless operator and rear gunner from England, our flight engineer from Scotland, and our mid-upper gunner, who was an American from California who had joined the RCAF. I was the only Canadian and was the bomb-aimer.

We were coned by searchlights on our run over the target—some railway yards—and it was clear as daylight in the bomb-aimer's compartment. On our return course, our wireless operator noticed a blip on the green H2S radar screen. The blip became larger and larger, and he believed it had to be another aircraft. Alarmed, our skipper altered course fifteen degrees into German territory. If it was an Allied plane, it would continue on its course back to England; if it was German, it would follow us.

Suddenly underneath us was a German ME-410 Messerschmitt fighter with a rotating turret that fired upwards, striking our starboard engines. With our plane on fire, our skipper began evasive action, and started manoeuvring the aircraft. He veered left, then sharp right, and then a dizzying hairpin back to the left. Our gunners strained as they fired on the Messerschmitt, but they could not actually see it. Our port side engine had been hit, too. Our skip ordered us to bail out. I watched our plane explode and was relieved when the fine bits of shrapnel missed my parachute. It was an abrupt landing when I hit the ground.

It was now July 26th at approximately two a.m. I released my parachute and quickly buried it. I was very fortunate to land in an open field. I then made a fast getaway, as it had started to get light. My plan was to hide in a wheat pasture the next day. Then I opened my escape kit, which was a small package we had to sign for and take with us on each flight. It contained German money, a map, water tablets and a highly condensed energy chocolate bar. I was starving and ate the whole bar, which was supposed to last me for a few days. The next day I started out in a southwest direction, as I had figured out by my map that I was in the vicinity of Strasbourg. I had the intention of crossing over to French territory, then heading south towards Switzerland, with the possibility of being interned there for the rest of the war.

I made good progress, but was hampered by having only slippers on, having lost my flying boots when I bailed out. I was able to climb a few fences and cross fields at a slow pace. I had to hole up overnight in a wooded area under a few trees, where I got quite wet, as it rained very heavily that night.

The next day I watched a few German farmers at work, and must say that I had a few close calls. The next evening, I walked into a barn looking for something to eat or a place to rest. I woke up all the animals and managed to clear out in a hurry. As I was resting the next day, I was kicked by a boot, and, as I looked up, I saw that it wasn't a soldier but a civilian who was working in the field. He spoke French and my fractured Montreal French suddenly became very helpful. Noticing that I had no boots, he told me that he would return in an hour with some food and a pair of boots. When he did return, not only did he bring me a loaf of dark brown bread and some boots, but also a bottle of red wine. I was lucky—the boots were just the right size. I thanked him very much and he hurried on his way. I knew that if he had been caught by the Germans, he would have been shot for aiding an enemy airman. He gave me the energy to last a few more days. I made good progress over the next few days, evading capture, ducking fences, even mistakenly hitching a ride deeper into Germany on a sooty boxcar.

The following day, as I was lying down in the woods after walking all night, I got up to relieve myself when suddenly a dog appeared in the clearing. The vicious German police dog started barking and baring its sharp teeth. He sure wasn't friendly. A few moments later, a young German foot guard showed up with his rifle over his shoulder. I knew then that my freedom had come to an end, and that I was in the power of my enemy. I spent the rest of my starvation vacation in the land of culture.

"For They Shall Grow Not Old"

Some time later, while being interrogated by a German officer one day, I was saddened to learn that three of my crew were killed when our aircraft blew up. It was difficult for me not to show any emotion. They made the Supreme Sacrifice.

MAY O'BRIEN — BRITISH NAVY (WRNS)

MAY was born and raised in the East End of London, England. She and her family survived the worst days of the Blitz, sleeping most nights on the floor of a dugout shelter. May became a stenographer with an oil company that eventually evacuated its staff to an estate in Crawley, Sussex. In 1941, at age eighteen, May enlisted in the Women's Royal Navy Service (WRNS), was trained as a teletype operator, and stationed on the north coast of England. The German planes came over almost every night, dropping their leftover bombs along the coast.

In 1943, May married Pat O'Brien, a member of the Royal Montreal Regiment. She was discharged from the WRNS in 1945, and, five months pregnant, came to Canada as a war bride. She and her husband relocated to Toronto in 1957. After a twenty-year career at Centennial College, May retired in 1989. The O'Briens have three daughters and a son, nine grandchildren, and one great-grandchild.

May joined RCL Branch 258 in 1984, and is also a member of the Ladies Auxiliary and the Scarborough Veterans Association. May's life during the London Blitz, as an evacuee, and as a member of the WRNS, combine to make her wartime experiences a compelling story in her presentations as an active member of the Living History Speakers Bureau RCL 258.

My Wartime Experiences in England

At the outbreak of World War II, I was fifteen years old and living in the Isle of Dogs area of London, England. This area, also known as Millwall, was the docklands and a prime target for the German bombers. A neighbour who was used to locking her door when she went to the bomb shelter looked at her mostly bombed-out place and said, "Why bother, you can crawl through wherever you can get through!"

I cannot describe to you how terrible it was. But that was life. We became accustomed to it, and lived through it as best we could. Can you imagine being bombed night after night, for over two years? I will never forgive the Nazis, never. However, we lived through it, and I would never wish it on anybody. I often think how fortunate I was to come to this country. I have never regretted it.

The Germans started their bombing during the daylight hours, but they met with opposition from the Spitfires. The Germans then decided to do their bombing during the nighttime, when they were less visible.

To get to Greenwich we had to use a pedestrian tunnel under the Thames River. At the outbreak of the bombing, the tunnel was a target. It was hit directly, and, to this day, you can see the blister where it was hit.

Before I enlisted in the WRNS, I worked in London as a stenographer. It was difficult going to and from work, as the streets had been bombed and were filled with craters. We had to climb down and up the other side of them to get to and from work. It sometimes took two hours to get to work, and they had to let us go home at three p.m. before the bombing started.

We had to change into our dugout clothes before going to the crypt of the church, which was our bomb shelter. The crypt was about one hundred feet long and thirty feet wide, with single mattresses laid out in rows on each side.

We found out that the Germans were using the tall steeple of the church as a landmark. That could be why the church didn't get bombed. This shelter was quite a distance away, and we had to duck in and out of other shelters to avoid being hit by bombs. One night the ARP saw us and hollered, "Take cover, you silly pair of cows!" After a while, taking cover became second nature. To while away the hours in the shelter, I learned to play cribbage—and I'm still learning.

Once, after the pub closed, my dad came into the shelter singing. As a teenager, I thought this embarrassing, and asked him to shut up. One night he lost his baked potato, and, as he couldn't find it, he hollered, "There are thieves in this here church!" Another night, a woman said to her husband, who was sleeping in a reverse order to her (his feet up at her face), "At least you could take your bleedin' boots off!"

I became tired of the long journey to work, and looking out the back room of my dad's house I could see a company called Snowden's. I applied there for a secretarial position and got it.

The bombing was so bad every night that they evacuated the office staff to a beautiful forty-acre estate in Crawley, Sussex. Across the highway was an army base of British soldiers. When they were sent off to North Africa, the Canadians moved in. We invited them over for a dance and social evening and we also went to the base to attend their dances.

At the estate, we had to give in our ration books so that we could get fed. We had three maids, so all we had to do was make our beds and do our personal laundry. The gong would sound for each meal, and if you didn't answer, you missed out.

I had a foster mother, and spent some of my time with her and some of my time with my dad. The woman I called my mother was deaf. One day she went to visit one of her sons, who was a stevedore. He lived up some stairs and when she got there nobody was home. When she came back down the steps, an ARP told her that there was an unexploded bomb up there and to clear away. That was a close call for her.

One night when my dad came home he found a bomb lying beside his bed. My sister Vi, who served as an air raid warden, had to carry it out to the ARP.

It was when the Canadians moved in that I met my future husband, Pat, who was a sergeant in the RMR (Royal Montreal Regiment, Machine-Gun). When the Canadians moved out, one of them shouted at me, "Hey, Red, you think we are bad—wait till you see the Americans!"

My foster mother had daughters living in the countryside—Cowley, Middlesex or Denham, Buckinghamshire. She would go to visit them, and I would go back and stay with my dad while she was gone. When the bombing started, she got worried about us and came back.

My dad, who was too old to re-enlist, spent most of his idle time in Kingsbridge Pub until it closed. Then he would come home singing. He had a hook go through his hand while working as a stevedore, and, because of this, lost his ticket for steady work. He only worked when they needed extra men.

May O'Brien – British Navy (WRNS)

When I came of age to join the forces, I enlisted in the WRNS, as my only brother, who is the best brother a girl can have, was in the navy serving on submarines. My dad was also navy. My brother's wife, Maureen, was also in the WRNS and was stationed in the south of England. I was stationed in the north of England, so we used to send teletype messages to each other.

I was nineteen years old when I got married in December 1943. I had to borrow a wedding dress, and have it cleaned before returning it. I came to Canada in 1946 aboard the *Queen Mary*. At that time, my husband was a lieutenant. His function was to muster all the war brides bound for Canada. As I was five months pregnant, he ensured I was on my way to Canada. Otherwise I would have had to stay in England until after the birth. We both wanted our child born in Canada.

MacGREGOR ROULSTON

Canadian Army/ The Black Watch

MAC was born and raised in Lancaster, Ontario. At age nineteen he joined the Glengarry Highlanders. He moved to Montreal in 1937 and joined the Black Watch (Royal Highlanders of Canada).

In 1939, the Black Watch was mobilized to guard the Soulanges Canal, and Mac became the recruit instructor at Camp Huntington, Quebec. Following the heavy losses suffered by the 1st Battalion at Dieppe in August 1942, Mac was involved in the formation of the 2nd Battalion as replacements. He then trained for several years in the south coast area of England, where they endured Nazi air raids and V1 and V2 rockets, which caused heavy casualties.

The Black Watch landed in Normandy on July 6, 1944, endured the bombing of Caen (3,000 bombers), and engaged the enemy at Hill 67 and St. André, where Mac was wounded twice and taken prisoner after heavy fighting and many casualties. Mac was released from prison camp by General Patton's troops following the capture of Brest. He was shipped back to Canada and discharged.

Mac has spent a lifetime since the war in sales, and at age eighty-three is still actively engaged as a manufacturer's agent. A sought-after speaker, Mac is a valued member of the Living History Speakers Bureau RCL Branch 258.

The Black Watch

As a teenager, in 1935, I joined the Glengarry Highlanders. This was in Cornwall. I had been in the Highland Cadets in high school and loved the kilt and the sound of the pipes, so it was natural that I had been attracted to a Highland regiment. In 1937, we spent two weeks at Barriefield, and I enjoyed it thoroughly.

That year, I found a job in Montreal, and shortly afterwards joined the Black Watch. I started my job at the fabulous salary of $5 per week. At that time there was not too much talk of war. We did hear rumours that things were not too good in Europe, but that was far away and really did not involve us (how naïve we were). Our big concern was making a living and surviving.

The unit held a parade each week. There were dances and weekend outings at local camps. We went several times to a shooting range at Pointe-Aux-Trembles for target practice and slept in tents. For the weekend we received the sum of $0.50. For the centennial in Sherbrooke, the battalion, along with the Grenadier Guards, was asked to participate.

We wore scarlet tunics and feather bonnets, along with all the appropriate regalia. It was a great thrill for a country boy. By this time, it was beginning to reach us that we were being trained for a purpose. In the early part of 1939, we had a visit from King George VI and Queen Elizabeth. I was chosen to be on the guard of honour. We did not know at this time how close we were to war.

On a sunny day in August of that year, I had planned to go swimming with my girlfriend. I received a telegram (delivered by a boy on a bicycle) to report to the armoury with all my equipment. This ended our plans to go swimming at Ste. Helen's Island; in fact we never kept that date.

The battalion was bussed out to Soulanges canal to do guard duty. This canal was the only water connection between the Great Lakes and the sea. It was a strategic point should the American German *Bunds* (German patriots) slip across the border from the US and disrupt communications. We were issued with live ammunition, but I don't think we had had adequate training to handle a serious attempt.

We watched boats from the Great Lakes pass up and down the canal. We were, on occasion, the recipients of some of the excess from their galleys, which was very welcome when army food became monotonous (which was most of the time). One day we were called to a meeting and told that we were at war with Germany. It would be very short—over by Christmas. They didn't say *which* Christmas.

I received my first stripe here, followed by two more a short time afterwards. A month or more later, we were replaced by a veterans' guard unit, "Old Sweats from WW I." Since I had some military training, I was sent to Huntingdon Basic Training Camp. Here we received about 250 men right out of civilian life. We gave them basic training and shipped them off to various camps in Canada for further training in their own particular branch of the service.

In Huntingdon we had a regimental sergeant major (RSM) who was thoroughly disliked by the rest of the training staff. He had won his position by turning king's evidence on a number of NCOs who had gone AWL with him.

To aggravate us, he called a parade at six a.m. each morning. This was in the dead of winter. Cold and half asleep, the men turned out at his bidding, but they had their plan. Obscenities were called out at him. But in the darkness he could not identify the culprits. The parade ceased!

The camp had an excellent bugler who had played in a jazz band in civilian life. He was good! At the end of many of his calls, he would break into boogie-woogie, much to the annoyance of the RSM, who would take off after the bugler. He could never find the one in question, who was quick and would slip away, and all would be calm—until the next day.

Then there was a company sergeant major who would broadcast orders over the PA system. One particular day this man was bothered by flatulence. There were some unusual sounds broadcast across the camp that day; fortunately the RSM never found out who the broadcaster was.

In the mess at night, the cook would lay out a roast of beef with all the trimmings. The RSM was always hovering around, and if he saw a new sergeant who had not heard his story, he would descend on him and start recounting his adventures while serving in India. "Once bitten, twice shy," is the old saying. So the next time, you watched to see how near he was to the roast and to whom he was talking, before making a quick sandwich and retiring somewhere out of reach.

In the spring it was decided to form the second battalion of the Black Watch in Montreal. We were all given the option of going in that direction, or remaining at the training centre. My choice was easy, and without hesitation I decided to join my buddies and hear the welcome sound of the pipes. We had a visit from the 186th Artillery Battery from Brooklyn, New York (by this time the US was also at war). The 2nd Black Watch was in its infancy, and had but six pipers and two drummers. We looked pretty small as the US band entered our parade ground six abreast, with trombones, cornets and various other instruments, and with much more fanfare!

It was a wild weekend with exchanging uniforms, lots of music, and quite a few drinks. It was something to behold to see these fellows trying to get on a kilt. It all made good international relations, to say nothing of a few big hangovers.

We moved from one camp to another until we arrived in Halifax. I had taken a course on poison gases and had a few small pieces of CAP (tear gas) with me. One night I came in late and placed one of the harmless-looking stones on the hot stove. The reaction was immediate. The boys were out of their beds in an instant with tears streaming down their faces, which continued until the gas cleared. Next day the RSM was out to find the culprit, and closed the bar until he was found. I was teetotal at that time and it didn't mean anything to me; however, what did bother me was the fact that the boys who enjoyed their drinks had to be deprived because of some unthinking member. I went to the RSM and admitted my guilt. He gave me a mild dressing-down and all was forgotten. (CAP gas is really a harmless type of irritant. It clears the sinuses, and is soon over and forgotten. However, I didn't repeat that prank.)

We had regular dances with the local girls. Some of us had our wives staying in rooms nearby. One of our members was the regimental quartermaster (RQ). He was very businesslike at his work during the day, but when night fell (and he'd had a few drinks), he was a different person. During a break in the program, he and a few others decided to do cartwheels down the centre of the dance floor. Now, please remember, we all wore the kilt and were told to dress properly. I don't know if that was the proper term but it meant that we wore nothing under the kilt. Need I say more?

It was strange to learn that the navy did not have an adequate mess of their own, and of course asked us if they could use ours. We were agreeable, as it would give us extra revenue. All went well for a time, until one of the navy guys punched our barman in the face for closing the bar at closing time. The Black Watch was a close-knit regiment. When you hit one, you hit them all. Pandemonium reigned immediately. Innocent "tars" sitting around, not knowing anything of what happened, were punched, and all were thrown out of the mess. It was closed to the navy until well after a written apology was received.

In Halifax, we occupied half of a sports field with army huts all around the border. The other half was occupied by the Canadian Women's Auxiliary Corps (CWAC). How could we have been so lucky? There was a heating unit in one corner, with the pipes crossing under the parade ground. The space was large enough to walk through, with access to this tunnel from both ends. One opening was on the Black Watch side and the other opening was at the CWAC barracks! There was more activity after dark in this tunnel than there was on the parade ground during the day. Ah!

However, all good things must come to an end. The openings were discovered and blocked up. The Black Watch took it in stride, but the CWAC were vicious. They vented their feelings in language that would curl one's hair.

Then there was a dance for the air force. I was taking my wife back to her room when two members of the air force saw us and said, "Two girls, one for each of us!" (I was wearing the kilt.) The battle lines were drawn, and another of our number, a Greek chap as I remember, was nearby, and yelled out, "Hold them there, Sarge, I'm coming!" It all ended amicably, with the flyboys apologizing and saying they had had a few drinks and did not mean any insult. The kilted lads are real family.

At the end of another dance, the boys were ready to leave when the colonel's driver pulled up at the sergeant's mess, and left the staff car to deliver a message. One of our number said, "Here is a car for us, hop in and I'll take you all and deliver the ladies back to their homes." In my innocence I went along with it, but just before we left, someone called me back. I don't remember what the message was, but it saved my skin. The four who did go were privates the next day.

In the early spring, a draft was sent to England from our battalion. I did a great deal of the work, but at the last minute I was taken off, much to my disgust. A second draft was organized, and again I did much of the work arranging for embarkation leave, etc. This time I made it, and went on the draft. We were marched down through the streets of Halifax by our pipe band, much against the rules of military headquarters: This was to have been as secret as possible. As our boat passed through the boom, all was quiet—not like the former draft, who were given a farewell from our boys on York Redoubt. That time, they had their knuckles rapped for such a demonstration and waste of valuable ammunition.

It was very early in the morning when we slipped out quietly past the light ships as the submarine nets closed behind us. It was not until years later that I learned that the wolf-pack submarine attacks were at their worst just at that time. We encountered none, and the crossing was without incident. Nor did we have an escort. For myself, being a very poor sailor, I travelled by "rail" most of the way. Thinking of all the possibilities on the way over, it was reassuring to see an RAF plane circling us as we drew near Liverpool.

England was fresh and colourful, with the periodic rains we passed through on our train trip to Aldershot. We marched to Farnborough, and were billeted in permanent buildings; for the next few days we did nothing but lie around on the grass and attend the mess three times a day. One night, one of our sergeants was asked by a female member of the British Army (ATS, or auxiliary territorial service) if he knew of a place where she could stay the night. She had arrived a day early to meet her boyfriend, and he could not meet her until the following day. Being a typical soldier, he gentlemanly offered half of his bed, which she accepted with all the side benefits that went with such an invitation. When reveille sounded and the duty sergeant came to wake the billet, a khaki skirt on a hanger was the last thing he expected to see. She was piloted away without the authorities finding out.

From our area we could see what I later found out was a jet fighter flying from the experimental station a few miles away. I had never heard of a plane without a propeller. Later, I learned the capabilities of such a plane, as applied in the form of a flying bomb—the V1.

I was sent down to Borden in charge of a section to guard the buildings housing the tank supplies that were going to the 8th Army in North Africa. There were two officers, myself, a corporal, and a lance corporal. The two officers were well below the standard set for the Black Watch. I saw this right away. I don't know how they won their one pip, but somehow they did. They were not from the Black Watch.

After a few days, one of the privates went AWL, leaving us one man short for the guard. The officers approached me and said they were going to put the lance corporal on in the missing spot. I flatly refused. They asked me if I knew their position. I assured them that I was fully aware of what they could and could not do. They said,

"We have never had trouble with sergeants before." When I asked if they ever had a Black Watch sergeant, they answered in the negative. I said, "Well, you've got one now, and I will not allow my lance corporal to go on guard." Unbeknownst to me, they asked the NCO in question if, as a favour, he would go on, and he agreed.

I had become friendly with a British officer who shared my "esteem" for the two "one-pip wonders." He reported the incident to Canadian Military Headquarters, and they never rose beyond their original rank. By coincidence, one of them married a girl from my hometown, and, when we met, he voiced his opinion about my action. I assured him that he might have done much better if he had listened to me. Fortunately I never saw him again.

While in Borden, there was a fifteen hundredweight (1,680 lb) truck available, so even without driving orders I used to visit my guards, usually late at night. On one of my visits, I found a guard asleep with his rifle propped against a wall. I had a decision to make: to charge this man and create another vacancy in our guard, or forget about it and leave things as they were. I woke up this sleeping beauty and chewed him up good and proper, with a warning that if he were caught a second time, I'd throw the book at him. No one knew of our conversation, and all went well for the remainder of the tour of duty.

Farnborough was a holding centre, and soon we were to move down to our respective units. Again, as in Canada, we were given the choice of which unit we wished to join. There was no hesitation on my part. I would rejoin the Black Watch. Soon I was at Pullborough, where the colonel gave each of us the "opportunity" to take down our stripes. I refused, and soon we joined the balance of the battalion at Hove.

Now the real test began. Many of these boys had been here for some time and were anxious for promotion. Every trick in the book was tried on us. Some didn't make it. In my case, one day I was battalion orderly sergeant and had to parade the defaulters. One man didn't turn up until the parade was nearly over. After enquiring about his absence and finding that there was no good reason for his being late, I put him on charge. To the best of my knowledge, no one had seen him join the defaulters, yet I was summoned to the RSM's office and asked who the latecomer had been. "What have you done about it?" he asked. I said that he was on charge, and the RSM said,

"Good. If you had let this go, I would have had your stripes." Some of our NCOs didn't fare as well.

At the end of 1943, the regiment went by rail to the north of Scotland to commence training. At Oban we went by landing craft tank (LCT) down the Sound of Mull. Our rations were deliberately kept meagre so we would become familiar with eventualities that were sure to arise when the invasion began. We did boat landings from the sea with associated noises, etc., of a defending force. There were thunder flashes buried in the sand that were exploded as we ran. Parachute flares floated down, showing us up in the darkness. One landed near me, and I reached out to pick it up. A burst of well-aimed machine-gun fire changed my mind quickly, and I left it to the next inquisitive soldier.

The ingenuity of the army always intrigues me. Since we were all hungry due to our meagre rations, our quartermaster, a born Scot, found a way to help cure the situation. Four of us went out on a cold moonlit night with pails and shovels. We dug cockles and fried them in margarine. What a treat! They were gritty, but oh, so good!

Our training finished, we returned to billets in Hove on the south coast and were moved to other billets in Folkstone. We had been trained in what I think was called *battle drill*. When you came under fire you went to ground. The platoon commander, the sergeant and one corporal withdrew a short distance, planned a form of attack, a Very light was fired, and the platoon made its attack. It was found that the enemy used this same routine and knew our every move. Without hesitation this plan was scrapped, and we concentrated on creeping barrage.

While at Folkstone, two of us were sent to Hythe to the Officer Cadet Training Unit (OCTU) pre-selection board. Here we were given a number of tests, written and tactical. We wore numbered shoulder tabs, and were watched as we marched to attention, even to the ablution hut. We ate with high-ranking officers who watched our table manners and listened to our conversation. On our return, we were told by the colonel that he would watch our progress in battle, and if we measured up we would be sent back for our commission. He did not last long enough to carry out his promise.

The days were moving on now, and rumours of an invasion were rampant. The question was not *if*, but *when* and *where*. I had not had a steady officer in my platoon for some time. One would arrive, and, in a few days or weeks, would be gone. Our company commander, John Taylor, spoke to me regarding his concern about the situation. I replied that I didn't have time to train an officer now that things were moving towards invasion. He questioned my remark, so I replied that the new man would have to do what I said, not vice versa. John just shook his head and walked away. I never got an officer.

One day, small boats were seen passing near the shore, and we had our suspicions. Next day it was confirmed. The invasion had started. We wondered why *we* were not in these boats. We were told that there was a place for us to fit in, but we would have to wait. A month later, we sailed on the *Isle of Orleans* as night fell. I slept little. Next morning, we saw the silent white beaches of Normandy. There was no opposition, as the fighting had moved inland. After a few miles' march, we took over the slit trenches that had been dug by the enemy at Beny-sur-Mer, and, since our place was not ready for us—believe it or not—we played baseball!

We viewed the bombing of Caen from a distance, and in a few days we moved up in the dead of night to the outskirts of Ancient Abbey of Ardennes, where Kurt (Panzer) Meyer had shot Canadian prisoners for the bombing of Berlin. We did see places where these murders had been carried out. We received a bit of shelling, and one of our lads was killed.

I cut the German eagles from the tunic of a couple of dead SS members and sent them home to my wife. That was July 1944. She is still waiting for them. The army mails are so slow!

We marched through the ruins of Caen to the Iona piper Geordie McKay from my home county of Glengarry, to the tune of "Australian Ladies." Some women appeared and handed my men pieces of purple sugar. I ordered them to be thrown away. They were likely poisoned. We could not take any chances.

In Caen we settled down for further instructions near a small racetrack, and one of my boys who could speak French talked to a native, unknowingly giving away our position. We were immediately machine-gunned, but there were no casualties. So much for fraternization with the French.

That night we crossed the Orne River with little opposition. I was given one house to clear. I crept silently up the stairs and opened a bedroom door. All seemed clear—nothing to be seen—nothing under the bed—and I was about to leave when a scream froze me to where I stood. Then a cat tore past me and flew down the stairs! It sure gave the nerves a shaking up.

We marched down the road the next day. At the intersection of the Ifs road we ran into machine-gun fire, which was quickly stopped by a bulldozer. At Ifs we had some sniper trouble, but the forward company looked after that in short order. We were just a mile back of Hill 67, and a day or so later, the enemy staged a counterattack on the hill and broke up one of our Canadian battalions. We were ordered forward and took the hill with little or no resistance.

That night, we had orders to make contact with the Calgary Highlanders. I volunteered and took in the first patrol. We were nearing the village of Ste. Martin when a voice out of the darkness called "Halt!" Our password was a joint one: It was "strike," and the answer was "a match." I gave the first word, but the answer did not come back. Instead, a Very flare was fired and a machine gun opened up on us. We went to ground, and when the darkness returned we moved fast and were all separated. I wandered around in the dark trying to get my bearings and get back to our lines. I reached out and touched something cold and metal and heard a Canadian voice say, "Hey, there's someone out there." Like lightning I had a pistol poked in my back, and a voice said, "Shut up and keep marching." Knowing it was one of our lads, I tried to identify myself, but I was kept under guard until they radioed back and confirmed just who I was. That was a relief. By a stroke of good luck I had run into the Calgary Highlanders.

A little later, a voice from the darkness called "*Kamarad!*" A young soldier just back from the Russian front came in asking to be captured. His uniform was clean, not like our muddied ones. The Calgarys took him back. I was taken by carrier back to my lines, and, after a good tot of rum, I had a welcome sleep. Later, a counterattack came in. There was a burst of machine-gun fire, and the enemy could be seen running in our direction, then another burst. Our CO called down the artillery and that ended *that* operation.

Then the Big Day arrived. At three a.m. we started from Hill 67 down to Ste. André. Here we encountered some machine-gun fire. We tossed a few grenades over the stone walls. Our company got off lucky. Not so some of the others. The colonel was killed climbing over the wall. The 2i/c and a number of the other officers were knocked out, and by the time we were ready to move again the NCOs were playing a strong role in the operations. One company was headed by a sergeant.

By now, the enemy was well aware of our intentions, and was ready for us. The battalion snaked along the road in as open a formation as possible, and entered the mine road. I had been sent forward to see if we could get transport into this area. As I returned, we were moving up, so I joined my company and got ready at the start line. Intelligence had been remiss in their work, for what we did not know was that the building we had just passed under was packed with Germans arriving there along the underground mine shafts!

Another danger point was the innocent-looking haystacks on Verrière Ridge about a mile away—our objective. We headed for the ridge with bayonets fixed. Cruel 88 airbursts began to rain down on us with their deadly load of shrapnel. My boys were being hit. Some I urged on, and we continued in open formation to the hill. As we might have known, the fire was coming from the haystacks and from the mine buildings behind us. SPs and Tigers were dug in, with their guns pointing through the haystacks. By this time, what with losing my boys, I am told I was screaming savagely and disposing of the enemy as I encountered them.

I reached the hill, and the acting colonel was there and realized how hopeless the situation was. He turned to me and said, "Let's get the hell out of here," so we took off. I had gone but a short distance when my leg went numb. I had been hit in the thigh. The Germans came and herded us into a shelter and bused us back to their lines. My leg was hurting and the blood was caked on my muddy trousers. What a terrible feeling I had. Could I have done more? How were my boys faring? Did they know where I was? I dared not even think of home and my loved ones. Fifteen returned from this battle and I was not one of them.

The bus ride was long. At nightfall we were bedded down in a stable, and the next night we reached Rennes and had beds to sleep on. This had been a girls' school. There were, alas, no girls, but there were French nurses. These gals wore cloaks, and when the German officer in charge left for the day, they dished out jam and butter that they had concealed under their cloaks.

Before the German officer left, he would point out the less wounded to be taken out and marched into Germany. Any who could not make it were shot—no questions asked. Before we reached this school there were some SS kids around. They looked on us Canadians in a queer manner, for we were classed as the SS of the Allies. We were more than a match for them, I can assure you.

I had some escape tools, and when I met a dental officer from Canada, I tried to pass them on to him. The German guard saw this and questioned my movement. The officer covered it up with some remark. It saved my skin.

By now my leg was aching badly with all the mud and exposure, and my appetite had gone. I was taken to a makeshift operating room to have the wound "reamed" out. A chloroform-soaked rag was put over my nose, and the procedure was begun before the anaesthetic took effect. I remember screaming, and then the next thing I knew, I was back in the dirty old bunk.

Things improved medically from then on. During the time I had no appetite, an American soldier asked me if I would sell some of my small loaf of black sour bread because his brother was hungry. I almost cried. Never would I sell food to a brother prisoner like myself. I gave it to him freely. Some years later, I learned that a politician from Montreal had sold food in a POW camp. On return to civilian life, he tried to collect, and was punched and kicked down a flight of stairs.

An RAF officer had a radio hidden somewhere and when the German officer left for the morning, he would get it out and report how near the Americans were, and how soon we would be released. The Americans didn't know we were there, and shelled the town. The retreating Germans saw the makeshift US flag that the nurses had made, and they shelled the hospital.

Knowing how close General Patton was, and in fear of being encircled, the Germans made a hasty retreat, leaving behind their vast store of French wines. Then they set the hospital on fire. After all I had been through, I had great forebodings that I might not make it through this new threat. But the fire was put out, and we were carried down and housed in Nissen huts in the compound. To further protect us, we were told to get under our bunks and leave our mattresses on top in case we got a direct hit. Getting down on that hard floor was no picnic, nor was it any easier to get any sleep with an aching leg.

The great day finally came and the American army arrived. There was a slight downside to this, however. The GIs soon found the booze and helped themselves most generously. We needed help, but little came.

The next day the medics and a hospital moved in. We were housed in good bunks, all in tents. They treated us royally, asking us what we wanted for dinner. I've had a soft heart for them ever since. One of our lads had one leg removed. He cried like a baby, as he was sure it was okay and should not have been taken. It was heartrending to see his reaction.

Great news arrived: We were going back to a hospital in England. Before we left, a padre came by and handed out V-mail forms so we could write to our loved ones. We were told that they would receive our letters in three days. That was July 1944. I am writing this in the middle of May 2000. The message hasn't arrived yet. Any day now!

We left by DC8s and arrived in Swindon and from there travelled to Aldershot. There, I met some of my officers, and learned there was a shop about a mile away that would serve you a fried egg if you asked for a "special." A few of us hobbled down on our crutches. How sweet it was to taste an egg. The government had requisitioned all eggs, but must have missed our shopkeeper.

By this time, my leg had improved somewhat, and I was put on permanent camp orderly sergeant for Aldershot. Things in Europe were drawing to a close, and I was shipped back to Canada. Three days later, the European war ended, and it was back to university for my BA.

My armed conflict was over, but my battle for a pension went on for several years. I eventually received a small pension, and was told I had received all I deserved. Funny how attitudes had changed from the day I joined up.

MacGregor Roulston – Canadian Army/The Black Watch

WALTER S.C. RUDOLPH

Royal Canadian Regiment - Korea

A FIFTH-GENERATION Canadian, Wally was born in Toronto in 1929, the son of a WW I veteran. His mother was a registered nurse. He joined the Canadian Army Special Force 2nd Battalion Royal Canadian Regiment (RCR) on August 15, 1950, and was posted to Dog Company, taking basic training in Camp Petawawa. He received advanced training at Fort Lewis, Washington. Wally sailed for Korea with the battalion in April 1951, and was involved in actions with Dog Company throughout the year as a private and acting section leader. He returned to Canada with the second half of the battalion in May 1952, was hospitalized twice during the following three months with malaria, and honourably discharged in August 1952.

Wally was employed for five years as an auto body and fender man. He then obtained an auto body license, and in 1957 obtained employment with the Canadian General Insurance Company. He worked at various times in his career as appraiser/adjuster, property supervisor, service office supervisor, and bodily injury specialist. He took early retirement at age fifty-eight after thirty-one years of service, but was rehired on a contract basis by Canadian General for a further eleven years, retiring permanently at age sixty-nine.

Wally is a past president of the Korea Veterans Association, Unit 59, having been active in that organization for over twenty years, and is currently honours and awards chairman of that unit. He is also an active member of the Living History Speakers Bureau RCL 258.

"Operation Pepper Pot," or the Raid on Hill 166, October 23, 1951

Our Dog Company of the Second Battalion RCR had been dug in on Hill 187 since the brigade push or advance on October 3,

Infantry patrol. Korea, March 1951. Photographer Bill Olson.

1951. We were on the Jamestown line. This was at the 38th parallel, and the same position the United Nations held until the end of the Korean War.

Our company was selected for the raid on Hill 166. There were about 100 men involved. Also, Dog Company of the Royal 22nd Regiment was making a similar attack on our left, and "A" Company of the First Battalion Princess Pats was attacking on our right. Our company left the lines at about four a.m. Our platoon was selected to lead the raid, and I was the first man in the lead section. This raid would be the deepest any Canadians, except for prisoners of war, would penetrate into enemy territory during the entire war.

We did not know if the Chinese positions were mined. We started off and went down Hill 187 through our barbed wire, then through our minefield and started across the valley, which would be about 1,000 yards to Hill 166. We were supported by our machine-gun section, our mortar section and the field artillery.

As we reached the Chinese positions (we had crossed the valley in single file), the enemy opened up with heavy machine-gun fire. I could hear the bullets cracking as they went by my head. Our first casualty was our new platoon sergeant, Harry Rowland. Harry was hit in the left shoulder. At that time he had almost reached the bottom of Hill 166. Harry was lying on the ground and swearing loudly. He said he had been hit in the *right* shoulder on the first day of action in the Second World War. Now the same thing has happened to him in Korea, only it was the *left* shoulder this time! Our medic attended Harry. That was the last time I saw him. He was sent back to Canada with his wound.

We continued up Hill 166, which was heavily occupied by the enemy. I saw tracer bullets coming from about halfway up the hill. I reported this to Captain O'Dell, who was our company commander for that day. He called artillery down and it wiped out that machine-gun nest. My platoon, No. 12, continued on up the hill, and then we were instructed to stop and give covering fire for our other two platoons, Nos. 10 and 11.

After they went through us, we dug in as best we could. I dug in with Pte. Tom Dyson. The Chinese opened up with artillery and shelled us for the next six to eight hours. Our company reached the top of the hill, wiped out several machine-gun nests, and took care of the snipers.

We captured one prisoner. He was very reluctant to go back with us. He got away from us and was run down by Pte. Ezra Steen. The prisoner had to be subdued in order to bring him back to our lines. He was still conscious when we got him back, but he was in pretty rough shape.

Corporal Eugene Wazny was with 10 Platoon that day. He was near Corporal Evans when Evans was shot through the chest trying to spot a sniper. Evans died before the medics could get him back to our lines. There were five other casualties in our company that day. The VanDoos and Patricias had a similar number, although the Patricias suffered about ten further casualties on their own land mines, when a section got lost on the way back under the heavy smoke cover. We inflicted about twice the amount of casualties on the enemy as we had.

We stayed on the hill until about four that afternoon, and then withdrew. Our artillery laid down a heavy smoke barrage in the valley to help us get back to our own positions. We returned in the same order that we went over, with my section leading the company in single file back across the valley. We did not have any casualties on the way back. Our Lieutenant Red Hamilton, who had been left out of battle, greeted us on our side of the valley and congratulated us on a good job.

General Rockingham and his staff had watched the raid from our side of the valley. Rocky said we put on a grand performance. However, no medals were given out for our "grand performance." We were given a big shot of rum when we got back, and then we went back to our dugouts on Hill 187.

On the night of November 2nd, the Chinese put in a grand-scale attack of about a battalion on our "A" company, who were on our direct left on the Songgok spur. Number 2 Platoon of "A" Company had sixteen casualties. The Chinese got the worst of it again. They left about twenty-five dead, plus whatever wounded and dead they carried back with them.

Operation Pepper Pot was the first and largest raid the Canadians put in across the valley, which we named "The Bowling Alley." It was also one of the most successful. There were numerous subsequent raids up to the end of the war. These were mostly night raids and of much smaller size, about ten to twenty men.

TOM STEVENS Royal Canadian Army Service Corps

TOM was born in rural Scarborough in 1922 into a family of seven children. He graduated from Oakridge School after grade eight and worked at a number of jobs before joining the army in 1941. He received basic training in Chatham, Ontario, and advanced training in Red Deer, Alberta, before shipping overseas to Farnborough, England. He was then assigned to the Royal Canadian Army Service Corps (RCASC) as an attached to infantry driver. He later was posted to 41st Company RCASC for the invasion of Sicily in August 1943, following his company into Italy in September to supply the Canadian 1st Division all the way to Ortona, where they spent the winter. In May 1944, his company was involved in the Liri Valley campaign.

Tom returned to Canada via New York in December 1945. He worked at a variety of jobs before starting a career with the Scarborough Fire Department. This included several years as a captain and a stretch as acting district chief before retiring after thirty-five years of service.

Tom married Betty France on June 26, 1948. They had four children—Carol, Bill, John and Cathy—and at present they have ten grandchildren and five great-grandchildren, with two more expected before summer's end (2001).

A member of Royal Canadian Legion Branch 258 since 1963, Tom has served on the executive and was made a life member in 1995. He is a member of the RCL 258 Seniors Association and the Scarborough Veterans Association, is a retired drummer from the Highland Creek band, and is an active member of the Living History Speakers Bureau RCL 258.

TOM'S STORY (COMPILED BY HIS WIFE)

At age seventeen, Tom joined the RCASC. Basic training was in Chatham, Ontario, which then led him to Red Deer, Alberta, for advanced training in first aid and male nursing.

Tom was then sent overseas and was stationed in England for approximately one year, at which time he left England for Sicily and fought there until the hostilities ceased. Tom was attached to the 41st Company RCASC (First Canadian Infantry Division) for the invasion of Sicily in July 1943.

During fall and winter, the fighting in Italy had slowed or gone static. Tom had to bring supplies to Ortona in jeeps and trailers, with which he began to bring out sick and injured personnel and transport them back to the Fifth General Hospital. While in Italy, when Tom called sick parade in the mornings, it got to be that there were more civilians than servicemen seeking medical attention. But these people were treated as well, even though they had no medical benefits.

Tom was reassigned to the Medical Inspection Room (MIR), where he used his medical training on the sick and wounded personnel. He accompanied his regiment through the assault on the Gustav Line and the Rivers campaign in northeast Italy, and then was shipped out to Marseilles, France. After approximately two months of healing and strengthening up the troops, Tom, along with the rest of his regiment, moved north through France and Belgium, then joined the push across the Rhine, by which time Canada had liberated Holland.

Tom met a lot of very nice people in Holland, and stayed friends with them for many years after the war. They came over to Canada and stayed with his family. Tom and his wife, Betty, also went to visit them in Hengelo. While there, they were taken to see the war graves for Canadian servicemen, which are very well kept.

Tom recalls that after the liberation of Holland, all married men in the 41st Company had first choice of going home, which was well received by all. Tom was single at the time, and single men were left to handle transportation of supplies and personnel from Germany to France. As part of the army of occupation, Tom stayed there until it was time to move back to England to await transport home.

In December 1945, Tom was shipped home in time for Christmas. He arrived in New York via a US ship. Tom then boarded a train for the trip back to the Exhibition Grounds in Toronto, where a joyful family reunion took place. Tom had been gone for so long, when his younger brother Joseph came to greet him (in his air force uniform), Tom did not immediately recognize him. In January 1946, Tom was honourably discharged from the forces.

ROBERT CHARLES STONE Royal Canadian Navy

BORN in 1926 and raised in Toronto, Bob was in the Naval Cadets from 1936 on, including the Ark Royal as a petty officer in 1942–43. He enlisted in the RCN at age sixteen in 1943 as a naval cadet and was promoted to midshipman in May 1945, RCN Executive Branch. He was promoted to lieutenant in July 1947, and discharged from the service in February 1948.

During Bob's tour of duty in the navy, he served on the HMCS *Uganda*, with training duties on the frigates HMCS *Matane* and *Grou* and the destroyer *Gatineau*, and on HMCS *Stadacona* and HMCS *Athabaska*. He was also appointed on loan to the battleship HMS *Nelson*, and served on the sloop HMS *Cygnet*, identifying and destroying wrecks in the English Channel. As well, he took part in training sailors on the corvette HMS *Tintagel Castle*. He had a brief exposure to the shooting war in Palestine in 1947 aboard HMS *Black Prince*. An unpleasant experience occurred there, when he was ambushed on the road to Jerusalem. After discharge, he served as 3rd officer aboard the Victory ship SS *Walton* on the Atlantic during the summer of 1948, prior to entering university.

Bob's unforgettable experience was aboard the HMCS *Uganda*'s goodwill tour around Cape Horn, January to April 1946, with the ship's whaler under his command. All told, he served with the British Pacific Fleet, and in South America, the English Channel and the Mediterranean. On his return to Canada, he was appointed training director on the admiral's staff, East Coast Command, until he retired in 1948.

Bob's family was also fully involved in wartime activities. His sister Margaret Annice, who was a swimmer on the 1936 Canadian Olympic team, met with Marshall Hermann Goering, Field Marshall Werner Von Blumberg, and minister of propaganda Joseph Goebbels, and secretly took photos. Later, in 1941, she was recruited for William Stephenson's espionage group (Intrepid). In 1942, she was appointed to the British Admiralty Delegation in Washington, DC, and served as secretary to Admiral Sir Percy Noble, C of C of Western Approaches.

In 1942, Bob's sister Bernice joined the New York espionage group and in the following year joined sister Margaret in Washington at the Admiralty Delegation. Bob's mother worked as an inspector in a munitions plant, making Bren guns. Bob's father, Matthew, went overseas to Scotland in December 1940, landed in Normandy on July 6, 1944, and fought throughout the entire Northwest Europe campaign as senior NCO of an Advanced Workshop Detachment (AWD) in 6th Brigade. He was awarded the British Empire Medal, and died of wounds in October 1946.

Following his discharge from the service, Bob entered the University of Toronto and received a degree in Political Science and Economics in 1951. In 1966, he earned a CFA at the University of Virginia. He worked for the Canadian Bank of Commerce from 1951 to 1953, and then set up one of the first investment research departments in Canada for F.H. Deacon & Co. He later became a shareholder and a vice-president of Deacon, and a director of several public companies. He was chairman of the Scarborough Board of Education in 1965 and 1966. In 1970 he became a vice-president of Yorkton Securities, and in 1988 he retired to undertake private investment banking, project financing and other occupations.

Bob is the author of two unpublished works, *The Ancient Origins of French Canadian Separatism*, otherwise known as *Hadrian's Legacy*, and *S/Sgt Matthew Charles Stone, B.E.M., Letters 1940–1946*. Bob is also a member of Royal Canadian Legion Branch 258 and is an active member of the Living History Speakers Bureau RCL Branch 258, currently serving a term as secretary.

THE HORN

Wednesday, March 20, 1946, 56° 09' S–67° 31' W

"Between 0900 and 1000 the Ship passed between Ildefonso and the Diego Ramirez Islands, the latter group considered to be the southernmost land of South America. They are forbidding pieces of real estate rising out of the sea to mountainous heights and cold enough for snow caps. At 1245, the Ship slowed and both whalers were sent away, the port whaler with a photographer on board to record the *Uganda* rounding the Horn, which was about two miles off to port. The sea was running high in long hill-sized swells about thirty feet from trough to crest.

"Three ridiculous filthy black 'sails' were hoisted on board the Ship from the forestay, the aircraft crane amidships and the mainmast to simulate sailing round the Horn. The sails had been improvised by the bo'sun from canvas that had seen better days. The rigging was under the personal direction of the commander, Edward Finch-Noyes. In this remote and improbable propaganda exercise, the Ship made the passage of the Horn seven times, to get it right. After all, it would be another fifty years before another Canadian warship was in these waters, although we didn't know that at the time, of course.

"The Horn itself is a cliff projection rising sheer from the sea, covered in green moss liberally decorated with several tons of guano, the product of a prolific bird life. Under grey skies, the Horn is uninspiring for all its legend but certainly ominous and threatening."

From the Journal of Midshipman Robert C. Stone, RCN

Uganda was a modified Fiji class British cruiser of 8,800 tons displacement built by Vickers Armstrong at Newcastle-on-Tyne, and launched on August 7, 1941. She was armed with nine six-inch guns in three triple turrets, eight four-inch high angle low angle guns, two quadruple 40mm Bofors guns, and three quadruple pom-pom mountings. Just for good measure, she mounted two triple twenty-one-inch torpedo mountings, one on each side. Her 72,500 hp steam turbine plant could develop thirty-three knots.

Commissioned into the Royal Navy, she served in the North Atlantic and the Mediterranean. In 1943, she was crippled by a radio-controlled bomb that entered the ship through the after director, penetrating through the after engine room to explode under the keel. This blow knocked out three of her four shafts and broke her back. Nevertheless, *Uganda* proceeded under her own steam at sixteen knots to Gibraltar, and then as a private ship without convoy to Charleston, South Carolina, for repairs and refit. Very tough ships, these cruisers!

In October 1944, *Uganda* was re-commissioned into the Royal Canadian Navy, with Captain E.R. Maingay in command, and was directed to the UK for some minor alterations and additions and, after workups, to join the 4th Cruiser Squadron, an integral part of the British Pacific Fleet. With the BPF, *Uganda* participated in several shore bombardments and many air defence actions to protect the fleet's carriers.

I was appointed to her in June 1945 as a midshipman, having entered the service as a naval cadet aboard HMCS *Royal Roads* in September 1943, graduating in May 1945.

By the way, the original idea was to rename *Uganda* to *Quebec*, but renaming was deferred during hostilities at the request of the Colonial Office. In the Canadian Navy, she was usually referred to as the "*Mighty U.*" Her sister ships were *Ceylon* and *Newfoundland*. *Uganda* was not renamed *Quebec* until 1952.

In 1946, while Canada was still in a legal and technical state of war emergency (until March 31, 1946), *Uganda* was sent on a goodwill and training cruise to South America.

While this voyage had some of the characteristics of the Never-ending Party, *Uganda* was still very much a commissioned warship that went to gun drill every forenoon with communication and transmitting station crews closed up for exercises under the beady eyes of commissioned gunners and gunnery lieutenant specialists. Every dog watch, the ship's whalers were sent away on man overboard drills, laying Dan buoys or practising torpedo retrievals.

My sea duty station was coxswain of the starboard whaler, and that's how I found myself in command of a twenty-seven-foot whaler with its five-man crew and numerous passengers. We were off Cape Horn in a slight breeze, riding seas that from a sea-level viewpoint were cliff-like, and I was wondering how we would get back on board the *Uganda* in such a seaway without harm. More to the point, how successful would I be in this manoeuvre with the eyes of God, the captain, and all his entourage upon me?

As we came alongside, the slowly rolling steel hull of the *Uganda* showed her bilge keel and armour. I instructed each man in what he was to do, and when he was to do it. A touch too much rudder, and we'd be caught by the bilge keel and instantly recycled into matchsticks.

As it turned out, the repeated drills and a lifelong exposure, all nineteen years, to small boat behaviour did the trick. As soon as we were hooked onto the gear, executed by my love-of-life-inspired crew, I shouted, "Hooked on in the boat!" and the lieutenant on deck (Freddie Frewer) ordered, "Hoist away!" In a twinkling we were lifted up off the top of a convenient—but also calculated—swell, clear of the sea and inboard.

Hey! There's no blood and guts in this story, no heroics, just another incident at sea. But I would rather have brought that whaler, her crew and passengers safely back on board *Uganda* that day than win a medal or another degree!

Suetonius says that the Emperor Tiberius was a famous and victorious commander because "his drills were bloody battles and his battles bloody drills."

It has always been that way with the Royal Navy and its successor navies.

ROBERT J. TAGGART — FIGHTER PILOT – ROYAL CANADIAN AIR FORCE

BOB was born and raised in Toronto and served with the RCASC NPAM in 1939 and 1940. He enlisted at age eighteen in the RCAF, and was trained as a pilot, earning his wings in 1942. Posted to the RAF, he served with 167 Sqdn, 1435 Sqdn Malta, and 404 RSU 2nd TAF. He had several kills during his sorties against the enemy, and was later a test pilot. In 1943, during his second tour of operations with RCAF Sqdn 402 in France, Holland and Germany, he was shot down over Sicily and rescued by a high-speed launch that took him back to Malta. He retired from the air force as a flight lieutenant.

Bob was discharged in 1945, and graduated in 1950 from the University of Toronto as a Doctor of Veterinary Medicine, practising first in Saskatchewan, and then relocating to Toronto in 1954.

Bob is a member of the Canadian Fighter Pilots Association, RCL Branch 165, the Royal Canadian Military Institute (RCMI), and is a valued member of the Living History Speakers Bureau RCL 258.

THE JOY OF FLIGHT

I was born in Toronto in July 1921, attended school in Toronto, and graduated from fifth form in 1938. My father was CSM in the RCASC NPAM, so I joined and went to camp at Niagara-on-the-Lake.

When war broke out, I tried to join the RCAF as aircrew, but was turned down. I was told that I was colour-blind. They offered to enlist me as ground crew, but I figured that if I had to be on the ground, I might as well be in the army. So I transferred to the RCASC permanent force. I was stationed at MD2 in Toronto and lived at home.

When hitchhiking home one evening, I was picked up by an officer in the Medical Corps. I told him about being turned down for aircrew because of my colour vision. He tried me on the colours of neon signs, and told me to go back to the recruiting office and ask for the Eldrich Green Lantern Test. When they asked me how I knew about that test, I told them who had told me about it. I passed this test and was classified as "red-green defective safe." I then went back to my colonel and was granted a release, conditional on making aircrew.

I went to Manning Pool at the Exhibition Grounds in Toronto. I was sent to Picton for a period of guard duty, and then back to the aircrew selection centre for testing on Link Trainers, where I was selected for training as a pilot.

My next station was No. 3 Elementary Training School in May 1941, where I was trained on Fleet Finch biplanes by civilian instructors. After twenty-nine flying hours' solo time and twenty-six hours' dual time, I was considered competent to proceed to a Service Flying Training School.

Before reporting to the SFTS at Camp Borden, my fiancée and I decided to get married. This we did on July 12, 1941. However, the RCAF decided that we could not receive marriage allowance until I finished my training.

We then moved to the village of Angus, a few miles from Camp Borden. I commenced training on Yale and Harvard single-engine aircraft in August 1941. By October, I had done thirty-nine hours' dual time and forty hours' solo time for a total of 144 hours' air force flying time. I was made a sergeant and received my pilot's wings.

I then went to Halifax and boarded the armed merchantman, *Chiteral,* and we sailed solo rather than in convoy to land at Greenoch, Scotland, nine days later. From there we were sent to Bournemouth to await posting to an operational training unit for conversion onto either fighter or bomber aircraft. I was posted to No. 58 OTU at Grangemouth, Scotland. Here I was trained on Miles Masters and Spitfire I and II aircrafts. While there I developed appendicitis and was operated on. Consequently, I didn't complete my training until the middle of April 1942.

I was then posted to No. 167 Squadron at Scorton, Yorkshire, flying Spitfire VBs. There, in May 1942, I was involved with a

Junkers 88, and this was my first kill. The squadron was temporarily moved to Castletown on the Pentland Firth, where we carried out convoy patrols over ships entering Scapa Flow in the Orkney Islands. It was strange being so far north. It was daylight twenty-four hours a day, and we were on readiness at all times.

In September, I was sent to Inverness for an interview with the air officer commanding, 83 Group, Air Vice Marshall Ray Collishaw, a WW I hero. The purpose of this interview was to determine whether or not I was to receive a commission. My interview apparently was successful, as I was appointed as pilot officer, backdated to August 10, 1942. The squadron was moved to Ludham in Norfolk, but after one flight there I was posted to "Prefix Draft," Gibraltar.

There seemed to be a cock-up, as Malta had ordered a number of *airscrews*, at that time the RAF terminology for propellors. Some person in Air Ministry had sent that number of *aircrews* to Gib en route to Malta! As they didn't know what to do with us, we were given the chance to fly some replacement Spitfires to squadrons in North Africa. After two of these ferrying trips, I managed to catch the last Liberator to Malta. The pilots who were left at Gib were sent to Casablanca in North Africa to be part of a ferry pool.

On Malta, I was assigned to 1435 Squadron at Luqa airfield flying Spitfire VBs. While there, we did island patrols, scrambles when enemy aircraft were approaching, and offensive sweeps to Sicily. We also bombed power stations, carrying a 250-lb. bomb under each wing, and two aircraft rhubarbs to destroy locomotives and railway signal boxes.

On March 3, 1943, our CO attempted to get permission for a flight of four aircraft to go on an offensive sweep over Sicily, but was denied this operation. He then asked for permission to take a flight of four up practice flying; and asked for three volunteers to go with him to Sicily. He chose me to be deputy leader—his number three—and two others to act as his number two and number four.

We kept at deck level until we were in sight of Sicily, to evade both our own and enemy radar. When we reached 3,000 feet, our control told us there were six-plus enemy aircraft approaching from the north. As we headed towards them, we were told there were another six-plus to the south of us. The leader told us to turn slowly to this second bunch, but my wing man broke violently, so to try and protect him I had to break, too. Then I heard a loud bang! as my aircraft was hit, and I saw two Messerschmitt 109s climbing away. I pushed my throttle through the gate after them, but my engine had seized and the recoil from my guns when I fired them sent me into a stall and a spin. When I recovered from the spin there was no one to be seen, so I glided out over the coast and transmitted for a fix on my position for rescue purposes and bailed out into the Mediterranean.

Four more Spits came out to cover me, and the Germans sent a Junkers 88 as well. The Spits shot him down, but one of ours was hit by coastal flack. He got halfway back to Malta and the air/sea launch that picked me up picked up the other pilot on the way back. The CO got back to Malta, but his aircraft was a writeoff. We never heard about our other two, so it was a poor show altogether. We lost five Spits and two pilots for one Ju 88.

The CO was given a disciplinary posting to a refuelling post in the western desert in Africa—all of which goes to show that Flying Control knew what they were talking about when they said the operation was too dangerous. I was given a week's leave to Tripoli before flying on ops. After that I resumed the routine scrambles, bombing attacks, rhubarbs and patrols.

On one of these bombing runs we went to Syracuse harbour and sank several seaplanes with bombs equipped with three-foot rods attached to the nose to cause them to explode in the air, hurling shrapnel into the hulls to sink them.

After six months on Malta, because of the lack of food due to the submarine blockade of supply ships, the medical officers declared that we were no longer in good enough health to fly. I was sent back to England and assigned to a Repair and Salvage Unit in 2nd Tactical Air Force. This unit repaired any aircraft that could be repaired in a week. My duties were to test-fly them before they were returned to active squadrons. I was fortunate enough to get to fly Mustangs, Typhoons, Hurricanes, and all marks of Spitfire. Our unit also did inspections on the light aircraft used by the artillery as spotters, and after they were finished I tested them and flew them back to their unit.

It was enormous fun landing in the postage-stamp fields surrounded by trees in remote parts of France. I had been taught how to lose height in a hurry by slideslipping. One of the colonels took exception to this and asked me where I had learned to fly. He then took me up to show me the proper way to get into a small tree-surrounded field. He did this by bringing the craft to the point of stall with three-quarter throttle, then cutting the throttle and sticking the nose down to make a landing. I was never so scared flying, and was on the point of saying that I was surprised he had lived long enough to make colonel, but, being a lowly flying officer, I held my tongue.

My CO asked me if I would like to go back on ops with a Typhoon Squadron that was being formed to be taken over by the RCAF. As I had a tour of ops under my belt, I stood a good chance of being promoted to flight commander. I was all for it, and was posted to No. 245 Squadron. After less than five hours, the CO looked in my logbook and saw that I hadn't completed a tour of rest. He returned me to the R&SU.

Near the end of 1944, I was promoted to flight lieutenant and sent back to Canada for a month's leave. It was great to be back with my wife. When my leave was up, we went to Montreal, whence I went on to Halifax and then back to England.

I was sent to No. 61 OTU at Rednal for a refresher course on operational flying, then to 83 Group Support Unit for conversion to Spitfire XIVs. In April 1945, I was posted to my first RCAF unit, No. 405 Squadron, which I joined in Holland, but we soon moved on to Rheine in Germany. It was from here that I was able to destroy three enemy aircraft. We did several fighter sweeps and moved to Wünsdorf near Hamburg. On May 3rd, the ceasefire in Germany was ordered, and on May 8th Prime Minister Churchill proclaimed VE day. During June and July, we practised flying and generally showed the flag by flying wing formations over German cities, and even to Copenhagen in Denmark. On July 11th, I flew to Dunsford in England and prepared to return to Canada.

After returning, I attended the Ontario Veterinary College at Guelph and received a Doctor of Veterinary Medicine degree from the University of Toronto in June 1950.

I was in practice in Saskatchewan when I had a chance to be in the reserves and go to Gimli, Manitoba, and fly Harvard aircraft. I was offered the chance to go to Chatham, New Brunswick, to convert onto Sabre jets and go to Korea but, by this time, I had not only a wife but two children, so I turned the offer down.

In 1954, having moved back to Ontario, I went to Trenton as a reserve officer and had the chance to fly the Silver Star T33 jet trainer. That finished my flying of powered aircraft, but during the summer of 1998, I went up to Georgian Bay on weekends, this time accompanied by my wife, and learned to fly gliders.

WWII, Air Force Mural – Spitfires / Battle of Britain

DON TORNEY

ROYAL CANADIAN AIR FORCE

BORN in 1921, Don was raised in Ottawa and Kingston, Ontario, and served in the Royal Canadian Army Medical Corps (corporal, No. 1 Field Ambulance) for three years before enlisting in the Royal Canadian Air Force in April 1941. Trained in electronics, he was shipped overseas to 219 Squadron RCAF to further train on radar transmitters and receivers. He then maintained a radar system for 71 Wing. He re-mustered to aircrew, received his navigator wings, became a flight sergeant, and was serving as a Mosquito navigator when the war ended. He was discharged in October 1945.

Returning to civilian life, Don attended Peterborough Normal School and graduated as a teacher in 1948. He taught school in Hamilton, Ontario. He then earned a B.A. at McMaster University, and later a B.Ed. and Master of Education at the University of Toronto. Moving to Scarborough in 1967, Don became academic director at Maplewood Vocational, and in 1968 transferred his Legion membership to RCL Branch 258. He is currently enjoying his retirement, and is an active member of the Living History Speakers Bureau RCL 258, in Highland Creek, Ontario.

NOT ALL HEROES

It was time to change the watch on the RDF station in the north of Scotland and just south of Aberdeen. It was our custom to pair up and march the half-mile to the Rx and Tx areas. A WAAF contingent of eight girls led the column. We mechanics followed. As we marched along, we nattered back and forth about the girls being slow.

We were approaching a 90° turn in the road, keeping to the left shoulder to face oncoming traffic, even though we seldom met any. A young lady on her bicycle pedalled past us just before the turn. Suddenly, out of nowhere, a lorry skidded around the corner and hit the cyclist. She went straight up in the air and landed on her head on the pavement. The lorry stopped just inches away from our marching column.

One of the men ran back to our camp to get a medic. Another ran across the field to a doctor's house. The victim was bleeding from the ears, but was still alive.

The driver of the lorry, an FO, was explaining to his passenger that he couldn't help it. It seems that the proper driver had been ordered by this flying officer to let him drive, even though he didn't have a licence. The other passenger, an NCO, was licensed to drive, but also had to obey orders.

The girl died in hospital that night. The FO tried to commit suicide in our hospital tent that evening, but lived to face careless driving causing death charges. Only two of our group were allowed to give evidence. The FO was acquitted when the wing commander said he was a valuable cog in 71 Wing staff.

But for a young farm girl, a whole watch of radar people might have been killed.

* * *

Here I was at No. 54 OTU Charter Hall, three-and-a-half years after I had enlisted in the air force. It was nice to see the Mosquitoes dispersed around the airport. There were about half a dozen of us navigators looking to team up with a pilot. I was lucky. WO2 D.L. Grummett (Danny) was the only Canadian available. I paired up with him immediately.

The Mosquito was quite a plane—two powerful engines attached to a plywood body. The cockpit was fairly narrow. Danny took the port seat and I had to squeeze into the starboard, which was slightly behind the pilot's seat. The entrance or escape hatch was right at my knee. To exit, I had to stand up and back out under the ladder. When we were using our radar set, I had to unstrap myself and kneel on the seat facing backwards. Most of the time, however, we were just familiarizing ourselves with the plane and each other.

The Mosquito was equipped with two twenty-gallon tanks, one at the outer edge of each wing. There were 200-gallon tanks on each side next to the fuselage. The engines burned 100 gallons an hour when we cruised at 240 mph. The pilots were supposed to take off on the outer tanks, then switch to the inner ones, and switch back to outer tanks for landing. However, the plane was more manoeuvrable if the outer tanks were nearly drained first.

It was slightly overcast. Danny, another crewmember, and I were sent up to do a bit of map reading. When Dan and I reached our height, we were above clouds. We had to search around for an opening in the clouds to orient ourselves with the ground before starting our trip. I finally discovered that we were over Ballater in Scotland, not far from Balmoral Castle. I gave Dan the course to set.

We had barely started when the port engine started to splutter. Dan was on the radio immediately to let base know we had a problem, but he assured me that Mozzies could fly on one engine.

There were a couple of idiots from our satellite 'drome discussing the conquests of the night before. The pilot of our other crew yelled, "Get off the air, you ***, we have a plane in trouble!" Meanwhile, the starboard engine started to splutter, and the port engine stopped completely. Dan went through the cockpit procedure. Fortunately he came to "petrol" before he came to "parachute"! He reached behind his seat and opened a few taps, and the engine caught and started to run smoothly. While searching for a place to start, we had forgotten to switch from outer to inner tanks.

We radioed base that we had overcome our problem and finished the exercise. When we landed, Dan was called into the adjutant's office. There, he found the other pilot being chastised for swearing on the air. No charges were laid when the episode was explained.

The two jocks from the satellite had their promotions deferred for three months. I consider myself lucky that I didn't qualify for a "caterpillar pin" for using silk to save myself. If we had had to jump, there would have been real trouble when the investigators found that we were using the wrong tanks.

* * *

I had reported to Manning Depot and Lakeside in Toronto to wait for an ITS class to start. To earn my keep, I was appointed orderly sergeant (OS). There were two of us for daytime duty. Our duties started by raising the flags in the morning. At nine a.m. one went through part of the barracks with the orderly officer. He checked the security posts in the afternoon and was free for the day. The other OS checked the other barracks, the guardhouse and the mess. That ended our duties until the next morning.

There were a few instances that are worth mentioning. One morning after a very late party, we didn't have time to shave and shine before the flag raising. As luck would have it, the wind was quite strong that morning. The rope on the flag slipped out of my hand and knocked the wing commander's hat askew. As quickly as possible, we marched off as the CO was inspecting the ranks. I never shaved and polished my shoes and buttons faster than I did that morning. We had just finished our ablutions when the CO came racing in, demanding to see us. He told me I should get a better grip on the flag rope in future.

We had a large Newfoundland dog as a mascot. One AC2 used to get put in detention just so he could groom the dog. When his time was up, he would commit another misdemeanour to get back to the dog. One day when the AC2 was free, I was taking the dog for a walk. It was difficult to control him when he decided to do something. This day, a CWAC was strolling along eating an ice cream cone. The dog pulled me towards her and bit the ice cream cone from her hand. I had not been told that he liked ice cream! I made an appointment with the CWAC to reimburse her for the cone—and we enjoyed a movie together.

The orderly officer and I walked into the mess. I shouted out the usual "Orderly officer, any complaints?" Much to my surprise, an airman at one table stood up and said, "Yes, sir!" The orderly officer walked to the table to see what was wrong. "There's a fly in the milk, sir." The orderly officer ordered me to pick up the ewer and follow him to the kitchen. There he ordered me to empty the ewer into the sink. One of the kitchen staff was upset. He said that they could have strained the milk and used it for cooking. "That's why I had the sergeant pour it into the sink," said the officer.

The air force finally found room for me on a course. I was given fourteen days' leave and ordered to then report to No. 6 ITS at Church and Gould Streets. I was finally started on my quest for wings.

FRANK WEST PARATROOPER

BORN Francis George West in east end Toronto in 1925, Frank served as a teenager in the militia with the Queen's Own Rifles (1941–42). He enlisted at age eighteen in the Royal Canadian Armoured Corps (1943–44), and then transferred to the 1st Canadian Parachute Battalion (1944–46), serving both in Canada and the United Kingdom. He was discharged in June 1946. Later, from 1960 to 1963, he served as a leading air craftsman in the Royal Canadian Air Force.

Post-war, Frank became a successful self-employed carpenter. In 1952 he joined the Royal Canadian Legion, Woodbine Heights Branch 22, and in 1955 transferred to RCL Branch 258, Highland Creek. He is also an active member of the 1st Canadian Parachute Battalion Association, having recently played a prominent role in the dedication of that battalion's mountain monument, "Ex-Coelis" Mountain, in Alberta. Frank has served RCL Branch 258 in many executive capacities over the years, currently as president of the branch. He is also the liaison officer to the Living History Speakers Bureau RCL Branch 258.

THE CASE OF THE HIDDEN BLOOMERS

I have had many memorable moments during the years I served in the armed forces. However, one particular episode stands out in my mind. When I was an eighteen-year-old soldier, I was returning from a brief visit in Yonkers, New York. I was with my mother, who was also in the Canadian Army. After our visit, I had to return to Toronto via the train, and my mother remained in Yonkers.

Unbeknownst to me, my mother had placed a few of her personal articles in my duffle bag. When we reached customs at the border, I was asked to make a declaration of any purchases in the

United States. I said that I had nothing to declare. He looked at me skeptically and asked to see what was in my bag.

To my great astonishment, and especially to that of the customs officer, out fell a beautiful pair of bloomers and a corset (my mother's, of course)! The others on the train didn't know what to think, especially when he held up the bloomers in a way that, to me, was a warning to any other soldier that might have a similar pair of silky possessions. The redness of my face was the most profound form of embarrassment that I have ever experienced.

DONALD E. WILSON

Royal Canadian Corps of Signals

DON was born in Manitoba in 1918, raised in Northern Ontario, and studied at Danforth Tech in Toronto. As a member of the Boy Scout movement, he became proficient in Morse code. Upon enlistment in December 1941 at age twenty-three, he was assigned to the Royal Canadian Corps of Signals (RCCS), took his basic training in Camp Borden and qualified as a wireless operator at Vimy Barracks in Kingston, Ontario.

Shipped to England in December 1942, Don served as a signalman in Algeria in September 1943, then shipped to Italy attached to the 1st Canadian Armoured Brigade (1CAB), Headquarters Communication Unit. He was with the brigade as it fought its way through Ortona, Cassino and the Liri Valley, and on to Florence, as part of the British 8th Army. The brigade was moved to Holland in March 1945, and re-united with the 1st Canadian Army at Arnhem, reaching as far as Hilversum and Utrecht by VE day.

Following his discharge in October 1945, Don began a career in cost accounting, retiring from Canada Wire in 1983. He joined the Royal Canadian Legion, Signals Branch, in 1949, transferred to RCL Branch 258 in 1962, became a life member in 1968, and was awarded the Legion Meritorious Service Medal (MSM) in 1994. He has served as branch chaplain since 1964. Don is also a member of the Signals Association (known officially as the "Jimmy Association"[2]), the Scarborough Veterans Association (chaplain),

---

[2] "Jimmy and Associates" is composed of former members of the Corps of Signals, formed shortly after the war. How the name "Jimmy" became associated with Signals is unclear, but it may have had some connection to Mercury, the messenger of the gods, whose image appears on the corps cap badge. The association holds periodic reunions at the farm of Frank and Patricia Freeman, north of Toronto. Frank is an ex-WO II Signals and Pat is an ex-CWAC. Both are members of RCL Branch 258.

the Ontario Regiment Association, and the Living History Speakers Bureau RCL Branch 258.

Why On Earth Did I Do This?

I was born on November 2, 1918, just nine days before the close of World War I. I pride myself on being a WW I war baby, and also that the Kaiser, upon being informed of my arrival, didn't take long to throw in the towel.

We moved, first to Winnipeg, and then to Ontario—northern Algoma-Hornepayne—where Dad worked as a baker. We then moved to a hamlet called Oba, near the 49th parallel. Yes, it was very cold. There, we got possession of a store where the CNR crosses the Algoma Central Railway, and this was where I spent the early years of my childhood. After a few years there, we decided to move "back east" to the Toronto area, and we finally found our way to a permanent area of identity in Toronto's vast east end.

Turning twenty-one in 1939, and not being from a military family, it did not occur to me to join up until two years later. So, mounting the steps of what is now known as Old City Hall, I was confronted by a recruiting sergeant with "What is it you want here?" To which I responded, very carefully, "I want to join the army." The good sergeant said, "You are too small for the infantry. Do you know the Morse code?" Believe it or not, I said, "Yes, I think I do." As a Boy Scout, I had earned one badge—Signaller, in Morse and semaphore.

That got me an enlistment into what was then known as the Royal Canadian Corps of Signals, now renamed Communications and Electronics, and very soon after that I was awarded a place on the crowded back of a stake model truck.

It was on that truck that I first started to ask myself: *Why on earth did I ever take a notion to do this?*

I was asked this question not too long ago, by a British comrade: "Did you fellows here in Canada really say you had joined for the defence of king and country?" To which I replied, "Yes, we certainly did." I interject this to assure you that if anything I say seems grudging in that respect, it is not intended to be. Like an old Britisher I knew years ago, wounded serving in WW I at Passchendaele and left totally blind: when I asked whether, if possible, he would go again, he replied, "Well, now, we couldn't have those other fellows coming over and telling us what to do, could we?"

Meanwhile, back on the truck, and on to a restaurant for dinner, then to the Exhibition Grounds, to the Horse Palace, and to a stall that was to be my bedchamber for the following month.

That was December 4, 1941, three days before Pearl Harbor, with me suffering along with thirty or forty others from heavy inoculations. One month later, we were sent to Camp Borden for basic training for three months, then to Kingston, home of the Royal Canadian Signals, for "trade training," to train as an operator. We had the rank of "wireless & line, 2nd class," which was as far as we could go in wartime.

Later that year, in early December 1942, we were off to Halifax to board the steamship *Queen Elizabeth*, arriving at Greenoch, Scotland. From there, we went by train to a camp at Crookham Crossroads in southern England, where we stagnated throughout the winter.

After spending the summer months working in communications somewhere west of London, in September 1943 command decided I was to be one of a number of signallers to work high-security wireless at an outpost south of the Mediterranean, in Algeria.

That assignment being completed, I was dispatched across the Mediterranean to Italy to the holding unit at Avellino, about fifty miles due east of Naples. They all told me how lucky I was when the posting came. I was to go as reinforcement to the 1st Canadian Armoured Brigade, which was then positioned somewhere south of Ortona. What a challenge. It scared the daylights out of me, until it was pointed out to me that Armoured Corps was the best place to be.

So I joined 1 CAB as an operator at the small Adriatic town of San Vito di Marino, then moved over to Lanciano due south of Ortona. The Battle of Ortona took place at Christmas 1943.

The following spring, we moved across the peninsula to the area of Monte Cassino. Cassino fell in May 1944. Some months later, we were stationed in a town many miles north named Fiesole, near the city of Florence. It was our last encounter with the enemy in Italy. We had pushed him up into the Appenine Mountains, and the opposing commanding general, Erich von Kesselring, let it be known that he was quite willing to let it go at that. Did he have a premonition as to what May 8th the following year (1945) would bring?

Along with the rest of the 1st Canadian Corps, we sailed from the port of Leghorn to Marseilles, then to Belgium in mid-March 1945. We moved to a lovely little town named Lauwe, then to the last battles of WW II in Holland: Arnhem, Appeldoorn and Ede. On May 8, 1945, our war was brought to a conclusion.

After another four-month wait, yours truly found himself aboard the steamship *Isle de France* bound for Canada, and then discharged in October 1945.

* * *

If I were asked what was my most dangerous experience, I would say there were a few, but the first that comes to mind might be that first night in action near Ortona in Italy. The enemy was not too amused by our successes against him, and our command positions were given spasmodic shelling—possibly he was trying to let me know he was aware of my arrival. He hit us pretty hard that night, zeroing in on our officers' mess. Instantly, I thought: *This is even worse than that truck ride to Richmond Street!* And, yes, I again asked myself the question: *Why did I ever . . . ?*

But then the image of the star of the film *Sergeant York* came to mind. It occurred to me I should take it upon myself to play that role; and, well, look: fifty-six years later, I am still here, safe and sound.

My most entertaining experience? There were actually two of them. One was when the play *My Son My Son* came to Phillipeville in Algeria. I believe it starred Ethel Barrymore and Brian Aherne. The other was when Yehudi Menuhin, the violinist, toured Italy, and one of our sergeants graciously insisted I accept his ticket. I am not expert at either music or theatre, but it is amazing how valuable entertainment can be in wartime.

And, oh yes, I must describe my most disappointing occurrence: the wounding of our sergeant, Rod Prest. He suffered a nick in the temple, costing him an eye and diminished mental capacity—and costing us the presence of a very fine young man from Vancouver, the father of Prescilla Prest, at that time a very promising Hollywood child starlet.

In summing up, I would say merely this:

It has been said that the soldier's willingness to die for his country, although prominent, should really be secondary in order. The first, of course, is to work it so that the fellow on the other side dies for his.

The First Canadian Armoured Brigade spent approximately twenty-two months in action, and I was with them for thirteen of those. I often think that if our freedom were threatened again, and 1 CAB wanted us again, there would be a lot of us out there on crutches tomorrow morning.

At the same time, I must say that danger in wartime varies in intensity with different occupations, but in any theatre of action, a goodly degree of danger is always there. So it follows that the people who want war the least are those who have been through one. And I am certainly one of those.

NICK W. ZIEMNICKI

Polish Army

NICK was born and brought up in Poland. In February 1940, at age eighteen, he enlisted in the 2nd Polish Infantry Division, with whom he took part in the campaign in France during May–June 1940. He was interned in Switzerland, but made his way via France and the Mediterranean to Gibraltar, and thence to the United Kingdom, where he enlisted in the First Polish Armoured Division. His squadron fought its way through France, Belgium, Holland and Germany from July 27, 1944 to the end of the war. During these campaigns, the Polish Army, under the command of Lt.-General Stanislaw Maczek, was an integral part of the Canadian Army 2nd Corps.

After the war, Nick graduated in Electrical Engineering in England, and completed a two-year postgraduate course. In 1952 he emigrated to Canada, where he worked for General Electric as a professional engineer until retirement. He also taught evening courses for engineers at Ryerson Polytechnic Institute. He has written two reference books for engineers, and has been granted several patents. His unpublished wartime memoirs, *The Land and Sea Borders I Crossed*, is a book of reminiscences about the turbulent six years of Nick's life during World War II, and is a true story of a young man's efforts to escape from occupied Poland and reach the West to fight against the Germans.

Nick is a member of the 1st Polish Armoured Division Association, the International Society of Poets, and an active member of the Living History Speakers Bureau RCL Branch 258.

Reminiscence of a Chilly Day

As we drove from the frosted banks of the immense river separating us from the enemy, the chilly November day grudgingly began to break. The depressing greyness of the landscape, enveloped in a heavy dense fog, resembled more the dark remnants of an uninviting cold night than the feeble pronouncement of the new day. The grim scene of war, so familiar to us, unfolded once again in its total wretchedness. Flooded countryside, heavily damaged or completely destroyed houses, grotesque-looking branches of bare trees that had suffered directly from the gun shells, and a lonely track partly submerged in water—a poor reminder of the once excellent highway now barely distinguishable amidst the overflowing water. This was Holland during the Second World War, in the late fall of 1944.

Still shivering from the penetrating dampness of the night, we silently reflected on the task given to us. The mines were solidly planted on the enemy's bank and luckily, under the darkness of night, we were back on our way to a designated assembly area. The satisfaction of a job well done helped temporarily overcome the gnawing and shaking from the cold caused by a strong wintry wind blowing at us in an open army half-truck.

The state of reflective mood in which we all were deeply immersed did not last long. The explosion of an artillery shell nearby made us aware that the enemy had detected us, and that we now were the target for its fire. The second shell fell not far ahead. It hit the road and tore off a considerable portion of its side. The adjacent water instantly filled up the newly formed crater, leaving just a narrow stretch of the road surface barely wide enough for the vehicle to pass through.

Clutching the steering wheel, with the accelerator pedal pressed down, I focused my already strained eyes on the only passable stretch in front of me. A fortunate blend of instinctive driver's judgment and the maximum speed of the heavy armoured car worked. I was able to make it through, leaving the badly damaged part of the road behind.

But now, with the rising morning mist, the improved visibility made the shelling more frequent and closer to us. Huge jets of water, propelled high up in the air by the force of exploding projectiles, temporarily obscured my vision. Our solitary presence on the deserted road in the vast expanse of a flat land totally submerged in water made us now more and more conspicuous. There were a few more close encounters with exploding shells as we raced full speed forward, and then, to our relief, the fire stopped. The engineering section leader sitting beside me calmly lit up a cigarette and said, "Well done, Nick."

I felt happy, but even more so when I sensed the gratitude of all my ten friends sitting behind in the open part of the car.

Several minutes later, we stopped in a wooded area of an abandoned farm. Hot, black coffee with rum—a standard soldier's treat on damp, wintry mornings—awaited us in a big military pot suspended over an open fire. (It has been said that the addition of rum to coffee for consumption by the army constituted a transgression of an old navy tradition.)

Absolution granted, feeling cold and tired, we all came close to the fire where radiating heat and a strong coffee-rum aroma permeated us with a rare sensation of physical comfort. Relaxed, listening to the crackling sound of burning logs, and watching the dancing flames springing high up, I conjured visions of "Once upon a time in faraway lands . . ."—visions of peace, harmony and happiness—a magical transformation from the realities of perpetual conflict in the realm of human destiny seeking its resolve in never-ending wars.

For a moment, my eyes drifted towards a cluster of tall, dignified-looking trees that surrounded us. An air of sadness seemed to encompass these mute and passive witnesses of many wars past, these true living monuments of history. Noticing their age-riddled trunks, my musing was interrupted by a sight of a few German prisoners, hands firmly placed on their heads, led by our men—all marching towards us.

The group was small. It consisted of three POWs and two Polish Force allies. The prisoners were brought near to the fire, allowing us full view of them. At first they looked frightened, but later, after they were permitted to take their hands off their heads to receive some hot coffee, they appeared less scared. The oversized, dark-green German uniforms partially concealed their true identity: They were not Germans—they were Asians. Short, haggard, with flat features and round heads, oblique-eyed, they were pitiful-looking characters, a far cry from the propagated image of the invincible German *Herrensfolk* army.

Towards the end of the war, the retreating Germans on all three fronts suffered heavy losses of men. Desperate to replace them, they even drafted some of the Russian POWs, of which two representatives were now with us.

While I watched our captured visitors, sudden flashes of the medieval history of Europe created an unexpected metamorphosis. Through the images formed in my mind, I no longer saw the emaciated POWs. I now saw, standing in front of us, proud, awesome warriors of Genghis Khan, whose unconquerable armies were formed from Asiatic tribes of Tartars and Mongols. In the thirteenth century, under the successors of Genghis Khan, the Tartars made their last rush upon Europe, reaching the western borders of the present Poland.

None of the three prisoners spoke German, but they all understood Russian. In response to a question asked if they were hungry, one of them—I believe the shortest one—to the astonishment of everyone watching, drew from inside his large coat something that resembled an enormous wooden spoon. Its immense size and crudeness were startling. It was the largest spoon I have ever seen, and probably the largest handmade spoon in the world. It was soon put to its functional use, and the sound and the sight of voraciously consumed soup provided its best evidence of the test well passed.

Has the *Guinness Book of Records* missed something? I wonder.

MAPS

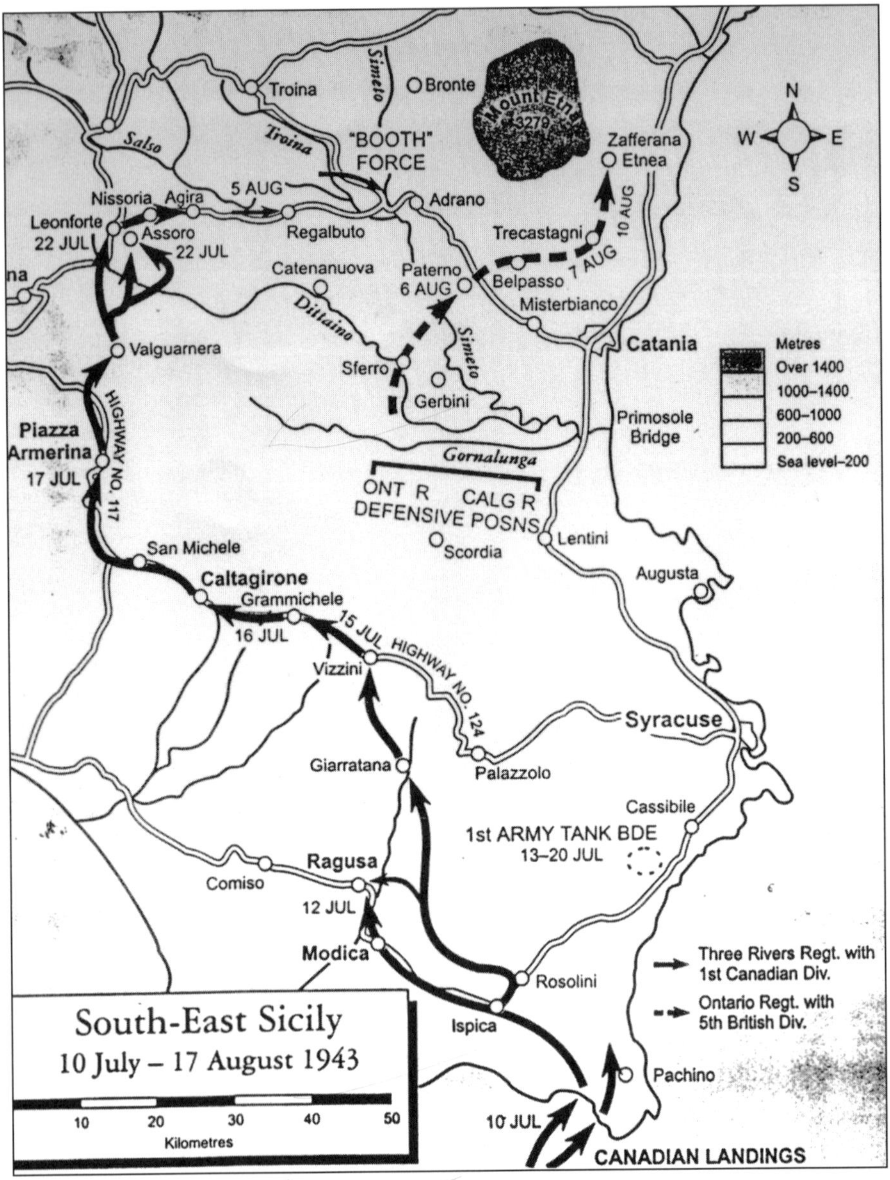
South-East Sicily
10 July – 17 August 1943
10
20
30
40
50
Kilometres
Troina
Bronte
Simeto
Mount Etna
3279
Salso
Troina
"BOOTH"
FORCE
Zafferana
Etnea
N
W
E
S
Nissoria
Agira
5 AUG
Adrano
Leonforte
22 JUL
Assoro
22 JUL
Regalbuto
Trecastagni
10 AUG
Catenanuova
Paterno
6 AUG
Belpasso
7 AUG
Misterbianco
Dittaino
Simeto
Valguarnera
Sferro
Gerbini
Catania
Metres
Over 1400
1000–1400
600–1000
200–600
Sea level–200
Primosole
Bridge
Piazza
Armerina
17 JUL
HIGHWAY NO. 117
Gornalunga
ONT R
CALG R
DEFENSIVE POSNS
Scordia
Lentini
San Michele
Caltagirone
Grammichele
16 JUL
15 JUL
HIGHWAY NO. 124
Augusta
Vizzini
Syracuse
Giarratana
Palazzolo
Cassibile
1st ARMY TANK BDE
13–20 JUL
Ragusa
Comiso
12 JUL
Modica
Rosolini
Ispica
Three Rivers Regt. with
1st Canadian Div.
Ontario Regt. with
5th British Div.
Pachino
10 JUL
CANADIAN LANDINGS

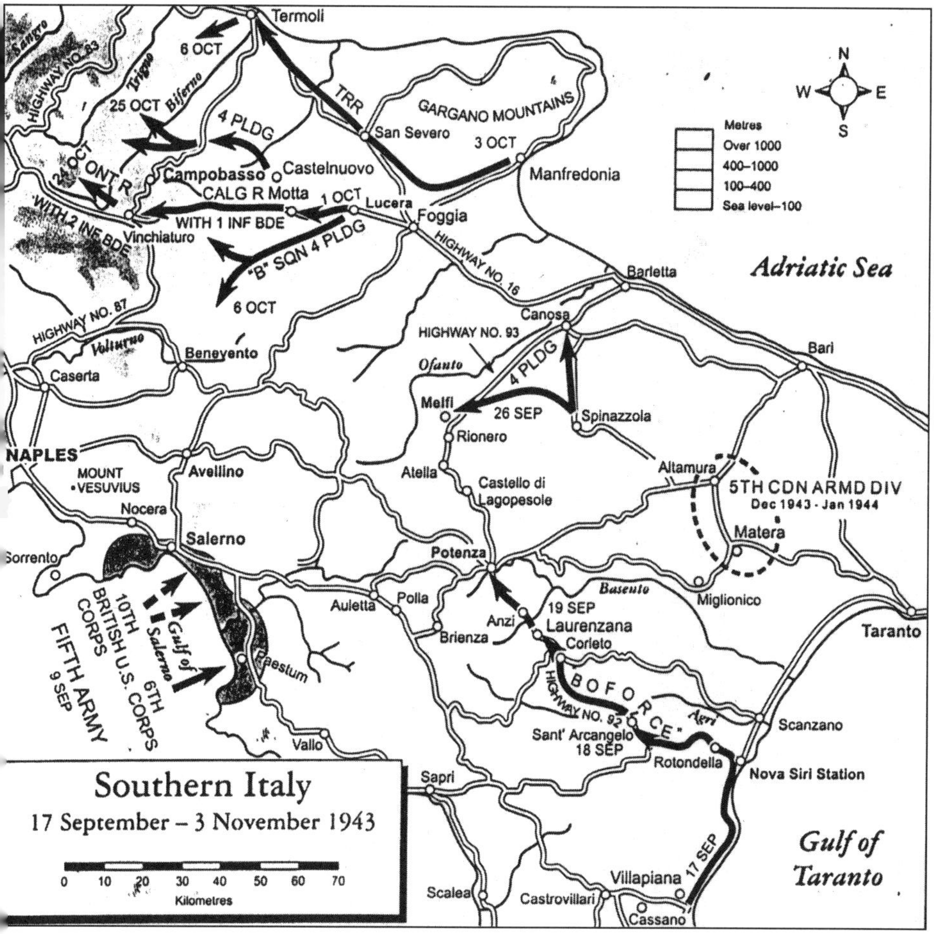

Southern Italy
17 September – 3 November 1943

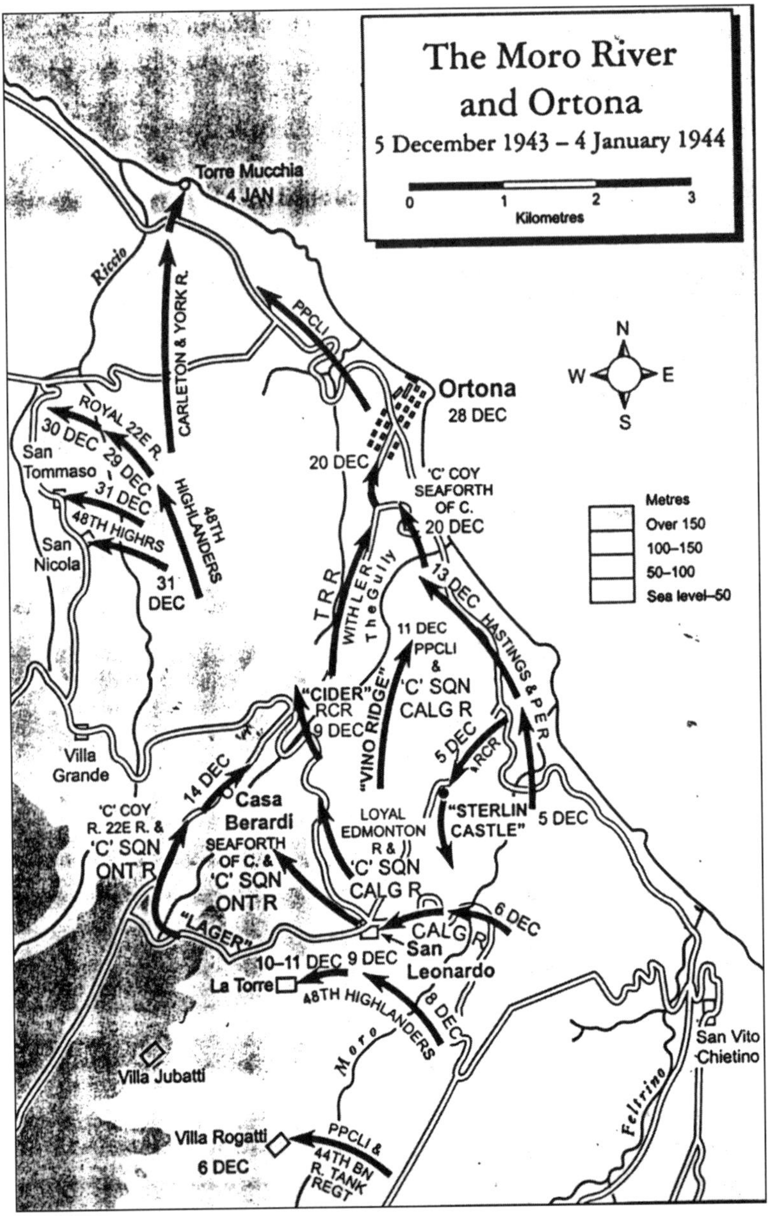
The Moro River
and Ortona
5 December 1943 – 4 January 1944
0
1
2
3
Kilometres
Torre Mucchia
4 JAN
Riccio
CARLETON & YORK R.
PPCLI
Ortona
28 DEC
N
W
E
S
ROYAL 22E R.
30 DEC
29 DEC
San
Tommaso
31 DEC
48TH HIGHRS
48TH
HIGHLANDERS
San
Nicola
31
DEC
20 DEC
'C' COY
SEAFORTH
OF C.
20 DEC
Metres
Over 150
100–150
50–100
Sea level–50
T R R
WITH L E R
The Gully
13 DEC
HASTINGS & P E R
11 DEC
PPCLI
&
'C' SQN
CALG R
"CIDER"
RCR
9 DEC
"VINO RIDGE"
5 DEC
RCR
Villa
Grande
14 DEC
Casa
Berardi
'C' COY
R. 22E R. &
'C' SQN
ONT R
SEAFORTH
OF C. &
'C' SQN
ONT R
LOYAL
EDMONTON
R &
'C' SQN
CALG R
"STERLIN
CASTLE"
5 DEC
"LAGER"
6 DEC
CALG R
San
Leonardo
10–11 DEC
9 DEC
La Torre
48TH HIGHLANDERS
8 DEC
Moro
Villa Jubatti
San Vito
Chietino
Feltrino
Villa Rogatti
6 DEC
PPCLI &
44TH BN
R. TANK
REGT

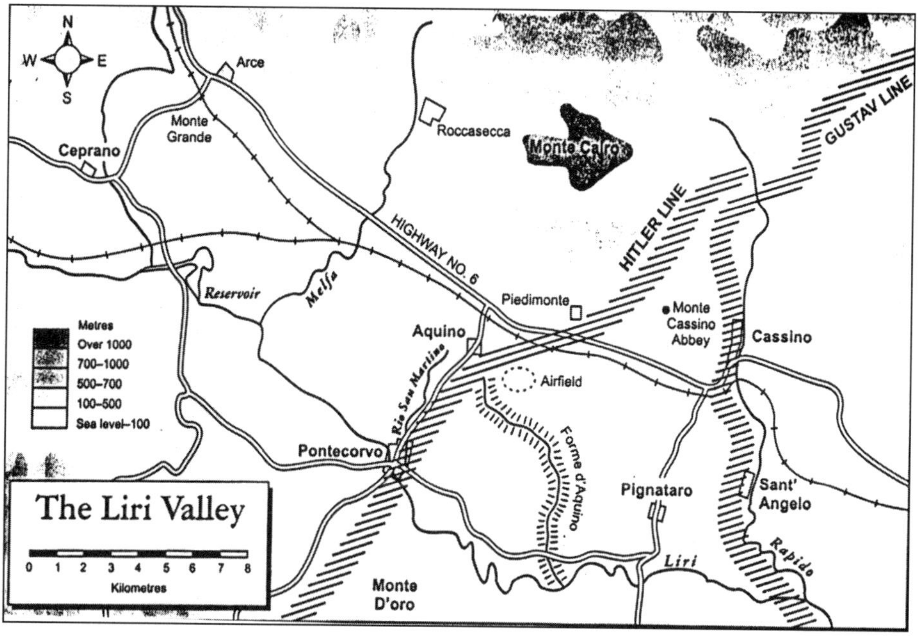
The Liri Valley
N
W
E
S
Arce
Monte Grande
Ceprano
Roccasecca
Monte Cairo
GUSTAV LINE
HITLER LINE
HIGHWAY NO. 6
Reservoir
Melfa
Piedimonte
Monte Cassino Abbey
Cassino
Aquino
Rio San Martino
Airfield
Metres
Over 1000
700–1000
500–700
100–500
Sea level–100
Pontecorvo
Forme d'Aquino
Pignataro
Sant' Angelo
Rapido
Liri
0 1 2 3 4 5 6 7 8
Kilometres
Monte D'oro

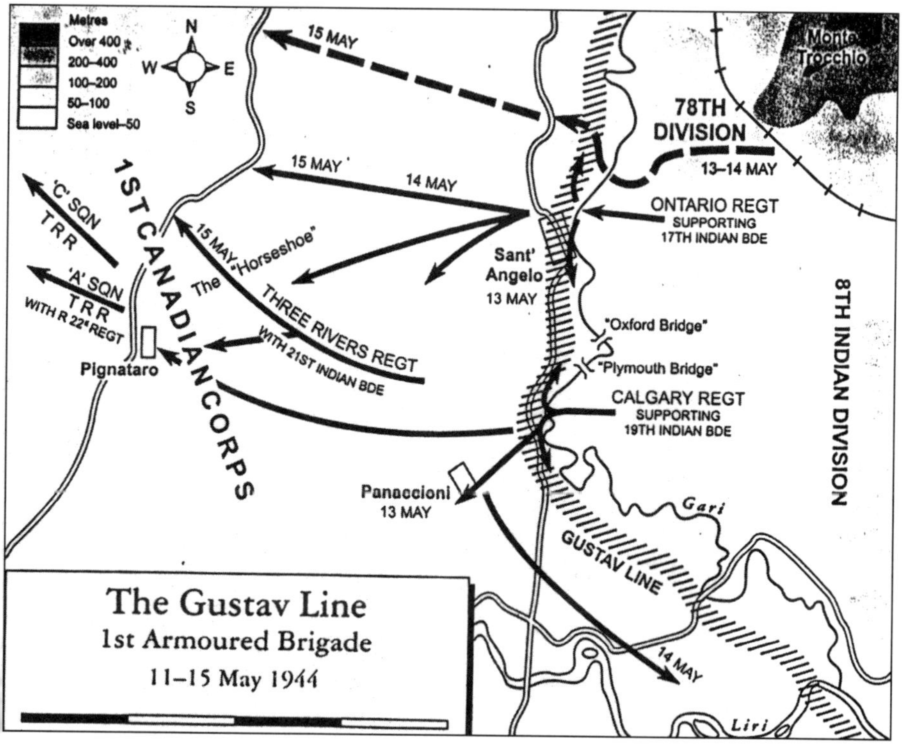
Metres
Over 400
200–400
100–200
50–100
Sea level–50
N
W
E
S
15 MAY
Monte Trocchio
78TH DIVISION
13–14 MAY
15 MAY
14 MAY
ONTARIO REGT
SUPPORTING
17TH INDIAN BDE
1ST CANADIAN CORPS
'C' SQN TRR
'A' SQN TRR
WITH R 22e REGT
15 MAY
The "Horseshoe"
THREE RIVERS REGT
WITH 21ST INDIAN BDE
Sant' Angelo
13 MAY
"Oxford Bridge"
"Plymouth Bridge"
8TH INDIAN DIVISION
Pignataro
CALGARY REGT
SUPPORTING
19TH INDIAN BDE
Panaccioni
13 MAY
Gari
GUSTAV LINE
14 MAY
Liri
The Gustav Line
1st Armoured Brigade
11–15 May 1944

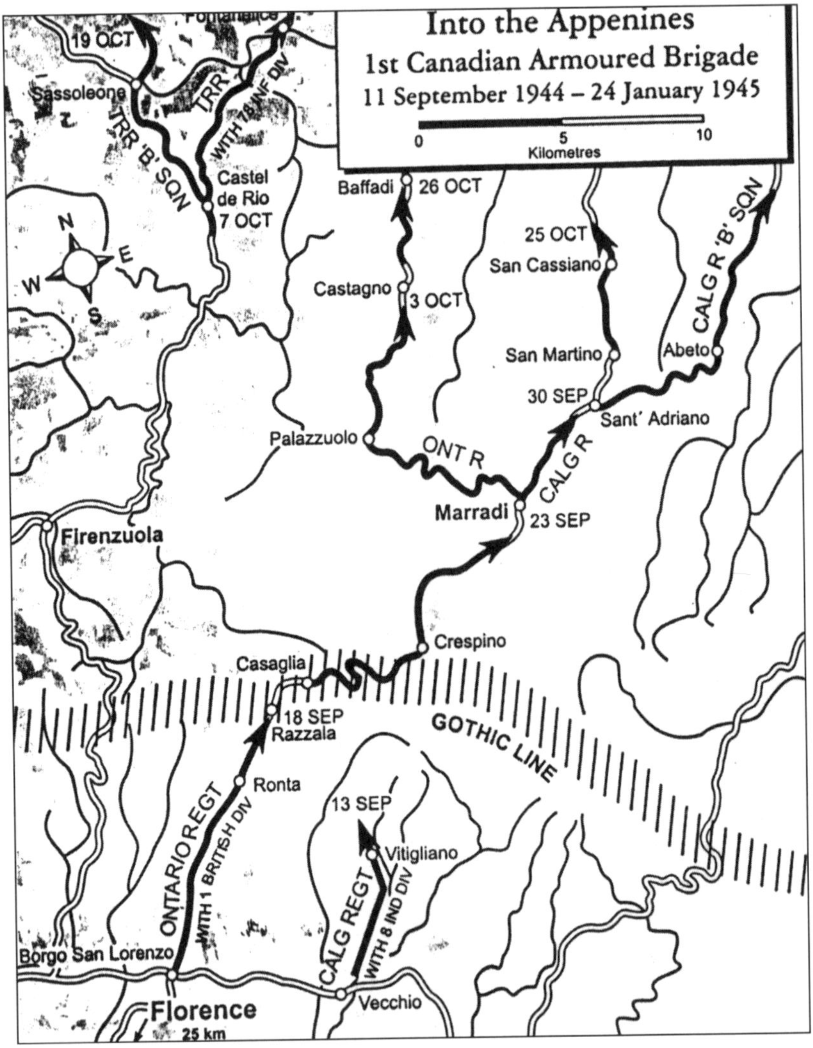

Into the Appenines
1st Canadian Armoured Brigade
11 September 1944 – 24 January 1945
0
5
10
Kilometres
N
E
S
W
19 OCT
Sassoleone
TRR 'B' SQN
TRR
WITH 78 INF DIV
Castel de Rio
7 OCT
Baffadi
26 OCT
Castagno
3 OCT
25 OCT
San Cassiano
San Martino
Abeto
CALG R 'B' SQN
30 SEP
Sant' Adriano
Palazzuolo
ONT R
CALG R
Marradi
23 SEP
Firenzuola
Crespino
Casaglia
18 SEP
Razzala
GOTHIC LINE
Ronta
ONTARIO REGT
WITH 1 BRITISH DIV
13 SEP
Vitigliano
CALG REGT
WITH 8 IND DIV
Borgo San Lorenzo
Florence
25 km
Vecchio

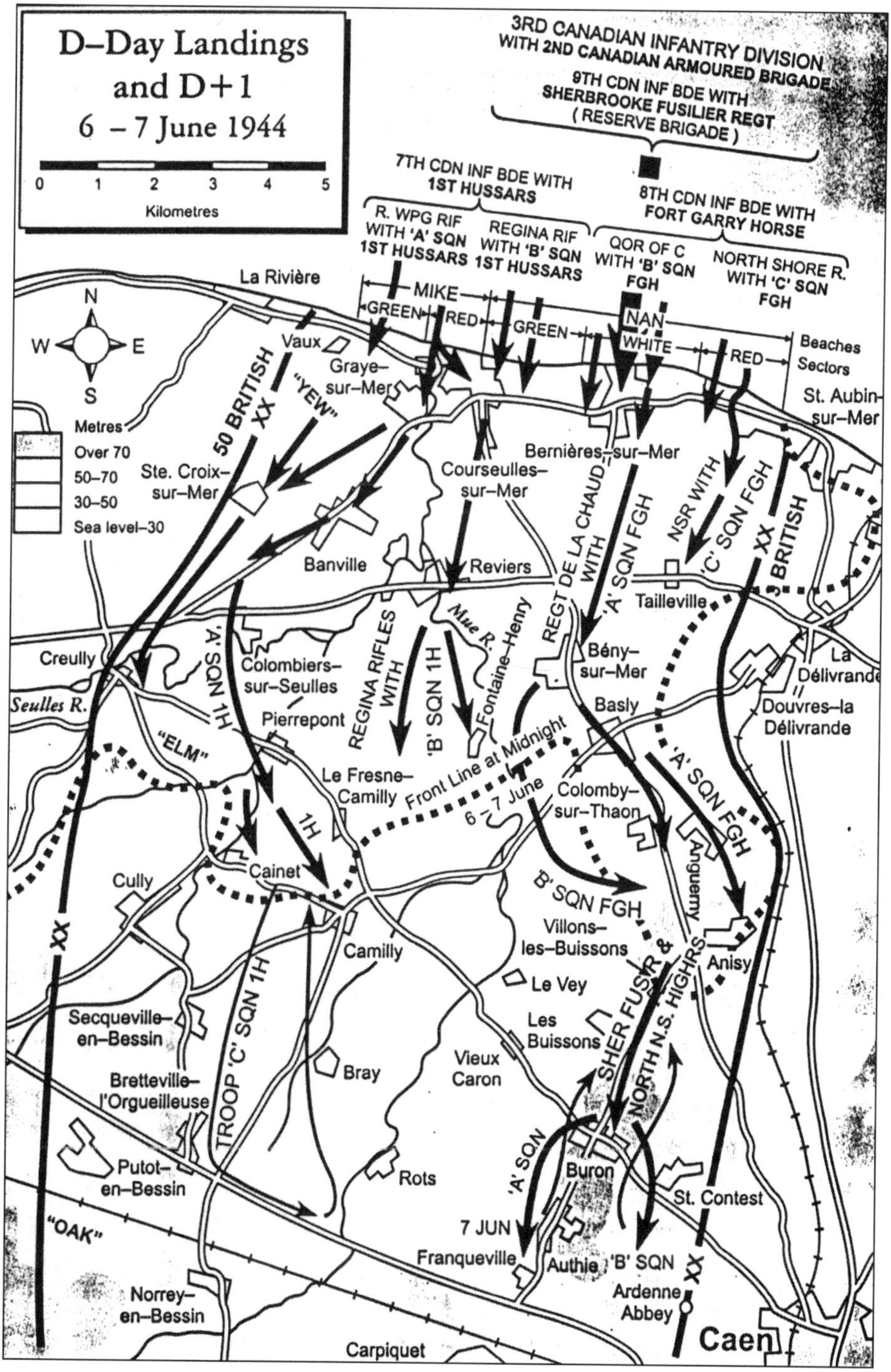
D–Day Landings
and D+1
6 – 7 June 1944
0 1 2 3 4 5
Kilometres
3RD CANADIAN INFANTRY DIVISION
WITH 2ND CANADIAN ARMOURED BRIGADE
9TH CDN INF BDE WITH
SHERBROOKE FUSILIER REGT
(RESERVE BRIGADE)
7TH CDN INF BDE WITH
1ST HUSSARS
8TH CDN INF BDE WITH
FORT GARRY HORSE
R. WPG RIF
WITH 'A' SQN
1ST HUSSARS
REGINA RIF
WITH 'B' SQN
1ST HUSSARS
QOR OF C
WITH 'B' SQN
FGH
NORTH SHORE R.
WITH 'C' SQN
FGH
La Rivière
MIKE
GREEN
RED
GREEN
NAN
WHITE
RED
Beaches
Sectors
N
W
E
S
Metres
Over 70
50–70
30–50
Sea level–30
Vaux
Graye-sur-Mer
50 BRITISH XX
"YEW"
Ste. Croix-sur-Mer
Courseulles-sur-Mer
Bernières-sur-Mer
St. Aubin-sur-Mer
Banville
Reviers
REGT DE LA CHAUD WITH 'A' SQN FGH
NSR WITH 'C' SQN FGH
3 BRITISH XX
Tailleville
Creully
Seulles R.
Colombiers-sur-Seulles
'A' SQN 1H
Mue R.
Fontaine-Henry
REGINA RIFLES WITH 'B' SQN 1H
Bény-sur-Mer
La Délivrande
Douvres-la Délivrande
Basly
Pierrepont
"ELM"
Le Fresne-Camilly
Front Line at Midnight 6 – 7 June
Colomby-sur-Thaon
'A' SQN FGH
1H
Cainet
Cully
Anguerny
'B' SQN FGH
Villons-les-Buissons
Camilly
Anisy
Le Vey
SHER FUS R & NORTH N.S. HIGHRS
Secqueville-en-Bessin
TROOP 'C' SQN 1H
Les Buissons
Bray
Vieux Caron
Bretteville-l'Orgueilleuse
'A' SQN
Buron
Putot-en-Bessin
Rots
St. Contest
"OAK"
7 JUN
Franqueville
Authie
'B' SQN
Ardenne Abbey
XX
Norrey-en-Bessin
Carpiquet
Caen

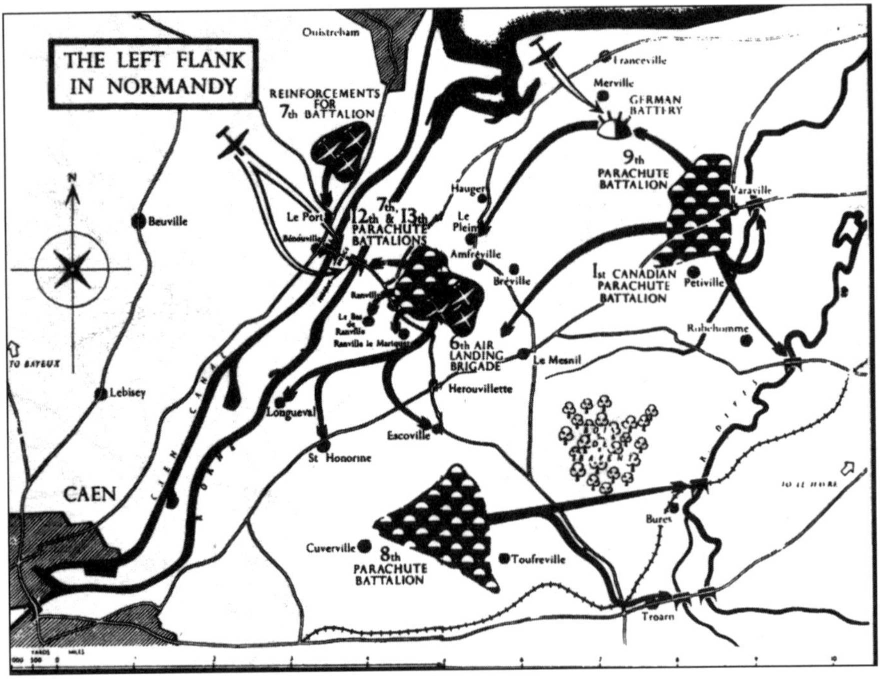
THE LEFT FLANK
IN NORMANDY
Ouistreham
REINFORCEMENTS FOR 7th BATTALION
Franceville
Merville
GERMAN BATTERY
9th PARACHUTE BATTALION
Varaville
Hauger
Le Plein
Amfréville
Bréville
7th, 12th & 13th PARACHUTE BATTALIONS
Le Port
Beuville
N
Ranville
Ranville le Mariquet
6th AIR LANDING BRIGADE
Le Mesnil
1st CANADIAN PARACHUTE BATTALION
Petiville
Robehomme
Lebisey
Herouvillette
Longueval
Escoville
St Honorine
CAEN
8th PARACHUTE BATTALION
Cuverville
Toufreville
Bures
Troarn

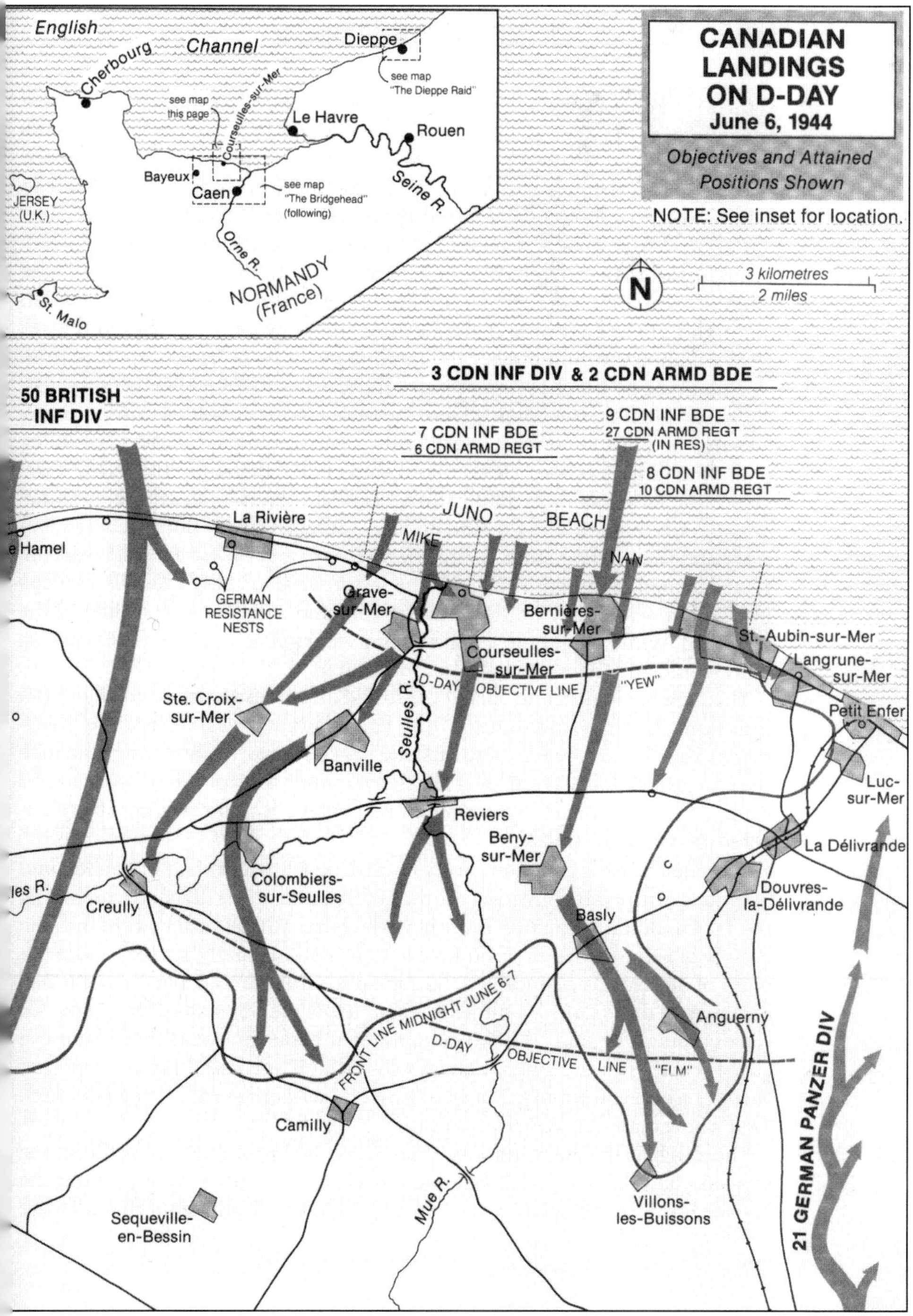
CANADIAN
LANDINGS
ON D-DAY
June 6, 1944
Objectives and Attained
Positions Shown
NOTE: See inset for location.
English
Channel
Cherbourg
Dieppe
see map
"The Dieppe Raid"
see map
this page
Courseulles-sur-Mer
Le Havre
Rouen
Seine R.
Bayeux
Caen
see map
"The Bridgehead"
(following)
JERSEY
(U.K.)
Orne R.
NORMANDY
(France)
St. Malo
N
3 kilometres
2 miles
3 CDN INF DIV & 2 CDN ARMD BDE
50 BRITISH
INF DIV
7 CDN INF BDE
6 CDN ARMD REGT
9 CDN INF BDE
27 CDN ARMD REGT
(IN RES)
8 CDN INF BDE
10 CDN ARMD REGT
JUNO
BEACH
MIKE
NAN
La Rivière
Hamel
GERMAN
RESISTANCE
NESTS
Grave-
sur-Mer
Bernières-
sur-Mer
St.-Aubin-sur-Mer
Langrune-
sur-Mer
Courseulles-
sur-Mer
D-DAY
OBJECTIVE LINE
"YEW"
Petit Enfer
Ste. Croix-
sur-Mer
Seulles R.
Banville
Luc-
sur-Mer
Reviers
Beny-
sur-Mer
La Délivrande
Colombiers-
sur-Seulles
Douvres-
la-Délivrande
Creully
Basly
FRONT LINE MIDNIGHT JUNE 6-7
D-DAY
OBJECTIVE
LINE
"ELM"
Anguerny
21 GERMAN PANZER DIV
Camilly
Mue R.
Sequeville-
en-Bessin
Villons-
les-Buissons

THE CAEN AREA

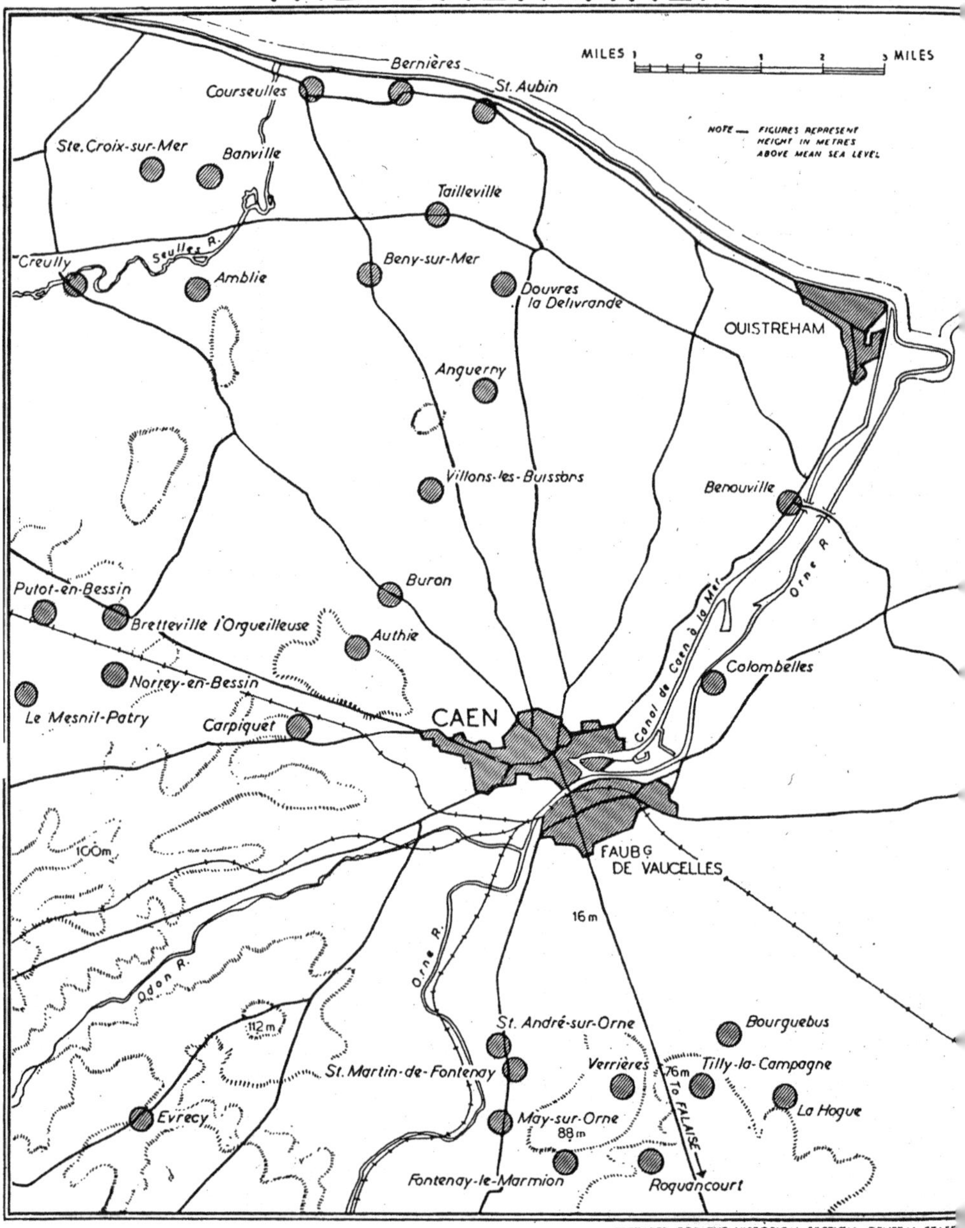

PREPARED FOR THE HISTORICAL SECTION, GENERAL STAFF

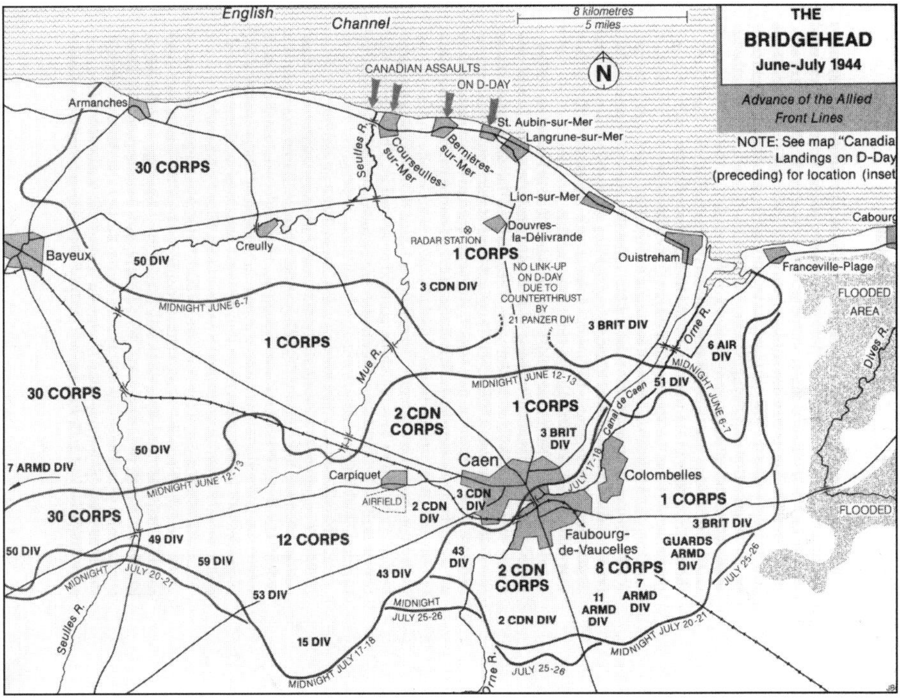
THE
BRIDGEHEAD
June-July 1944
Advance of the Allied Front Lines
NOTE: See map "Canadia
Landings on D-Day
(preceding) for location (inset
English Channel
8 kilometres
5 miles
N
CANADIAN ASSAULTS ON D-DAY
Armanches
Seulles R.
Courseulles-sur-Mer
Bernières-sur-Mer
St. Aubin-sur-Mer
Langrune-sur-Mer
Lion-sur-Mer
Cabourg
30 CORPS
Douvres-la-Délivrande
RADAR STATION
Creully
Bayeux
50 DIV
1 CORPS
NO LINK-UP ON D-DAY DUE TO COUNTERTHRUST BY 21 PANZER DIV
Ouistreham
Franceville-Plage
FLOODED AREA
3 CDN DIV
MIDNIGHT JUNE 6-7
3 BRIT DIV
Orne R.
6 AIR DIV
Dives R.
1 CORPS
Mue R.
MIDNIGHT JUNE 12-13
51 DIV
MIDNIGHT JUNE 6-7
30 CORPS
2 CDN CORPS
1 CORPS
Canal de Caen
3 BRIT DIV
50 DIV
7 ARMD DIV
MIDNIGHT JUNE 12-13
Caen
JULY 17-18
Colombelles
Carpiquet
AIRFIELD
2 CDN DIV
3 CDN DIV
1 CORPS
FLOODED
30 CORPS
3 BRIT DIV
49 DIV
12 CORPS
Faubourg-de-Vaucelles
GUARDS ARMD DIV
50 DIV
59 DIV
43 DIV
8 CORPS
MIDNIGHT JULY 20-21
43 DIV
2 CDN CORPS
JULY 25-26
7 ARMD DIV
53 DIV
MIDNIGHT JULY 25-26
11 ARMD DIV
Seulles R.
2 CDN DIV
15 DIV
MIDNIGHT JULY 20-21
MIDNIGHT JULY 17-18
Orne R.
JULY 25-26

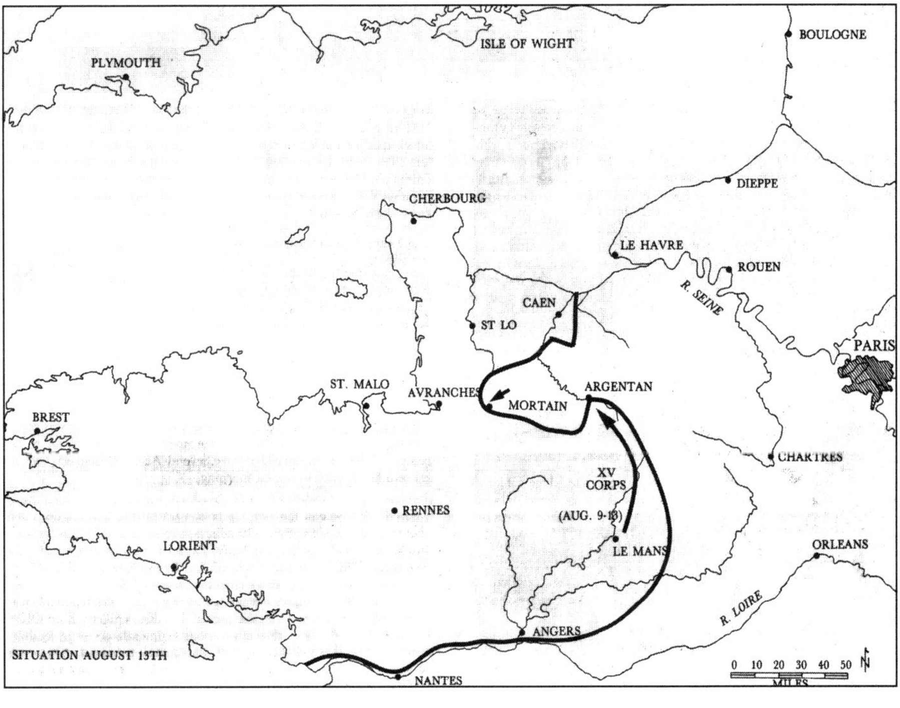
ISLE OF WIGHT
BOULOGNE
PLYMOUTH
DIEPPE
CHERBOURG
LE HAVRE
ROUEN
R. SEINE
CAEN
ST LO
PARIS
ST. MALO
AVRANCHES
ARGENTAN
MORTAIN
BREST
CHARTRES
XV CORPS
(AUG. 9-13)
RENNES
LORIENT
LE MANS
ORLEANS
R. LOIRE
ANGERS
SITUATION AUGUST 13TH
NANTES
0 10 20 30 40 50
MILES

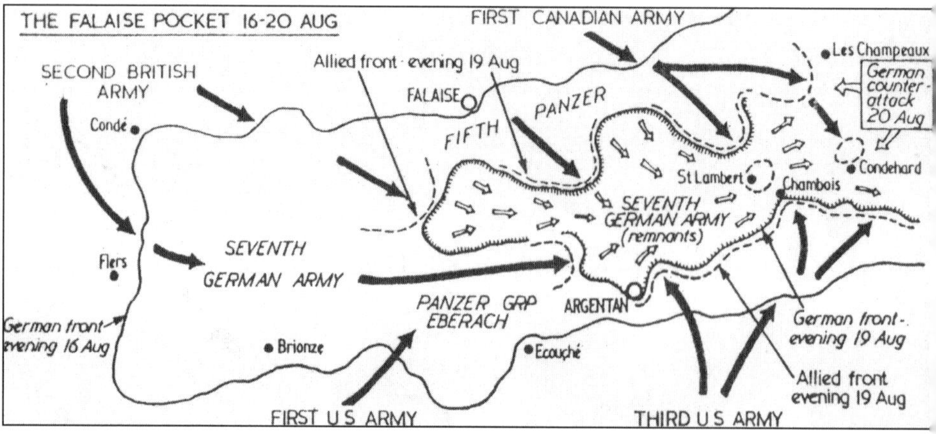
THE FALAISE POCKET 16-20 AUG
FIRST CANADIAN ARMY
SECOND BRITISH ARMY
Allied front evening 19 Aug
FALAISE
FIFTH PANZER
Les Champeaux
German counter-attack 20 Aug
Condé
St Lambert
Chambois
Condehard
SEVENTH GERMAN ARMY (remnants)
SEVENTH GERMAN ARMY
Flers
PANZER GRP EBERACH
ARGENTAN
German front evening 16 Aug
Brionze
Ecouché
German front evening 19 Aug
Allied front evening 19 Aug
FIRST U S ARMY
THIRD U S ARMY

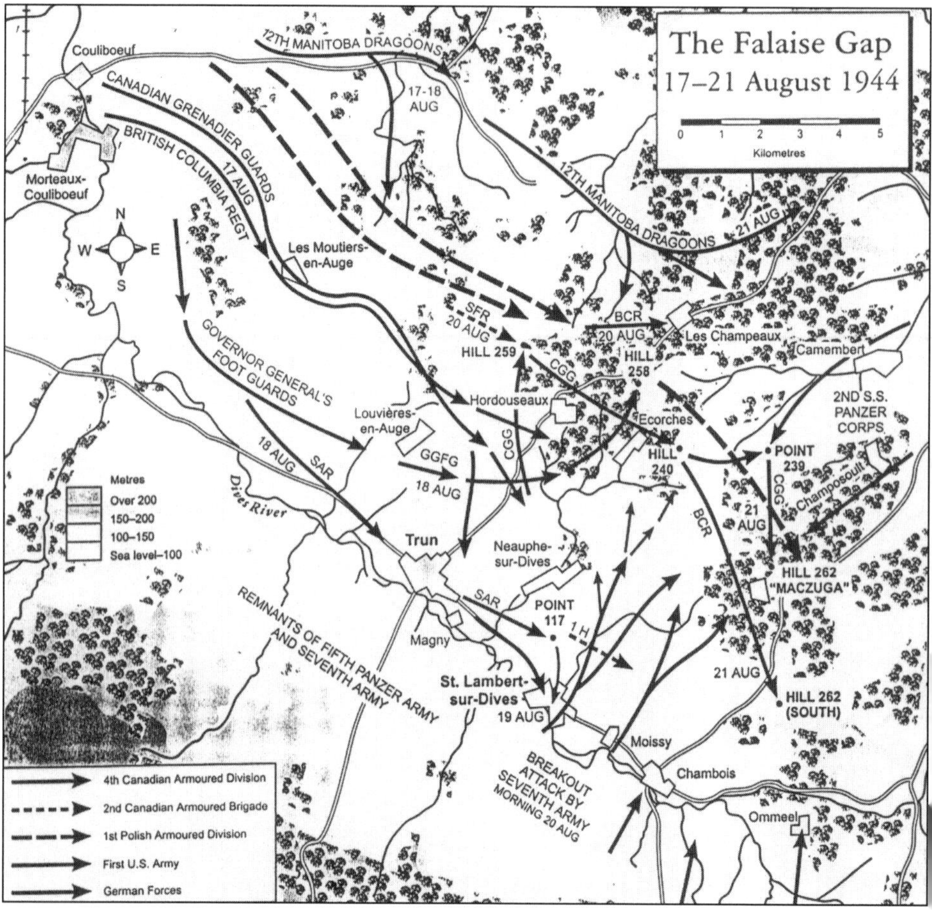
The Falaise Gap
17–21 August 1944
0 1 2 3 4 5
Kilometres
Couliboeuf
12TH MANITOBA DRAGOONS
17-18 AUG
CANADIAN GRENADIER GUARDS
17 AUG
BRITISH COLUMBIA REGT
Morteaux-Couliboeuf
N W E S
Les Moutiers-en-Auge
SFR 20 AUG
BCR 20 AUG
Les Champeaux
Camembert
HILL 259
HILL 258
CGG
GOVERNOR GENERAL'S FOOT GUARDS
Hordouseaux
Louvières-en-Auge
Ecorches
2ND S.S. PANZER CORPS
POINT 239
HILL 240
GGFG 18 AUG
18 AUG
SAR
Dives River
Metres
Over 200
150–200
100–150
Sea level–100
Trun
Neauphe-sur-Dives
BCR
21 AUG
Champosoult
HILL 262 "MACZUGA"
POINT 117
1 H
Magny
REMNANTS OF FIFTH PANZER ARMY AND SEVENTH ARMY
St. Lambert-sur-Dives
19 AUG
HILL 262 (SOUTH)
Moissy
Chambois
BREAKOUT ATTACK BY SEVENTH ARMY MORNING 20 AUG
Ommeel
4th Canadian Armoured Division
2nd Canadian Armoured Brigade
1st Polish Armoured Division
First U.S. Army
German Forces

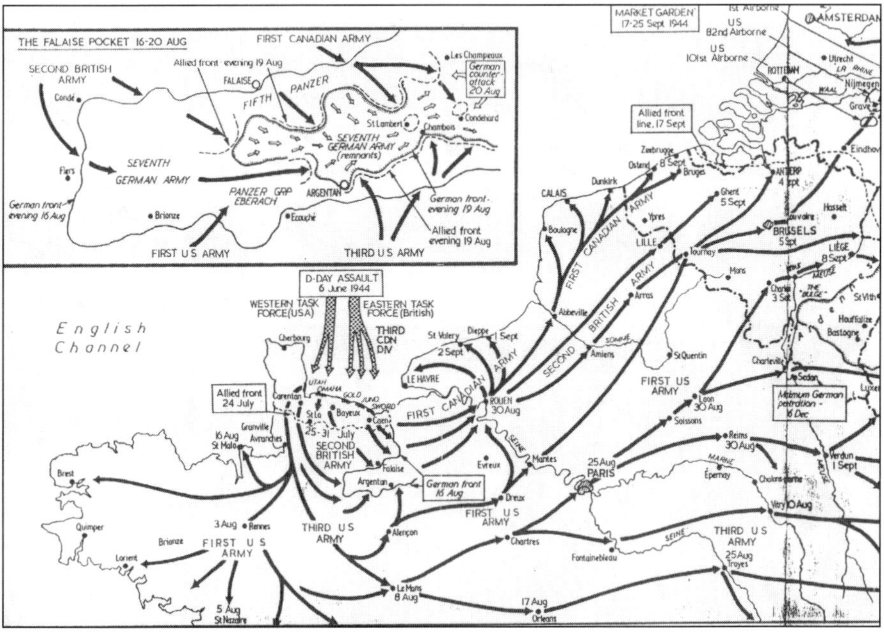

NORTH-WEST EUROPE
6 JUNE, 1944 - 7 MAY, 1945

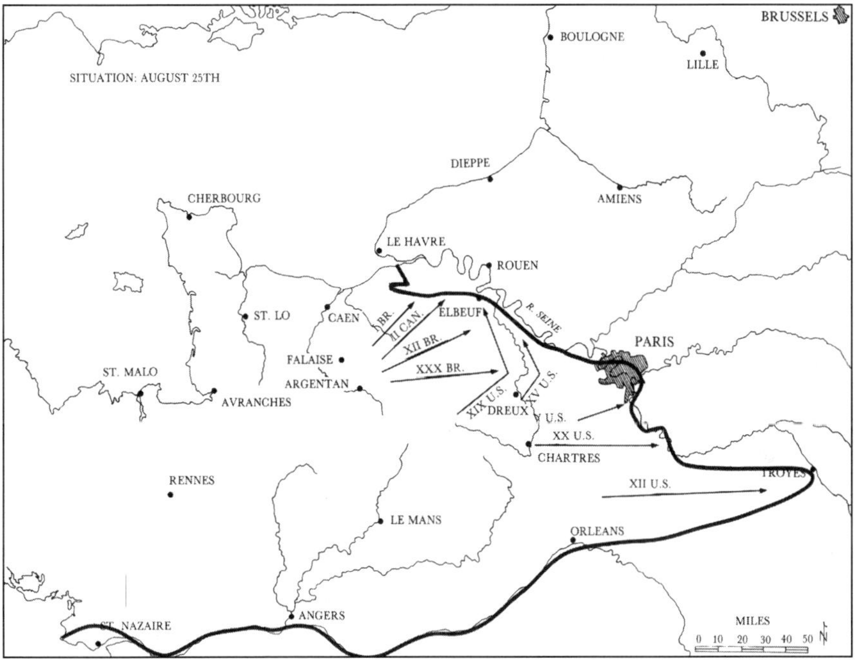

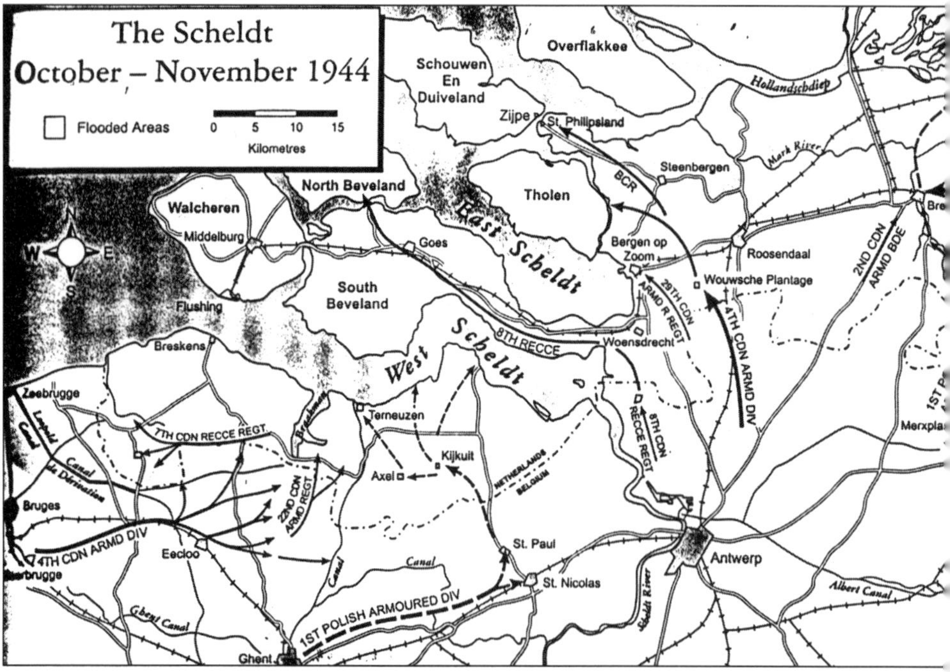
The Scheldt
October – November 1944
Flooded Areas
0 5 10 15
Kilometres
Overflakkee
Schouwen En Duiveland
Hollandschdiep
Zijpe
St. Philipsland
Steenbergen
Mark River
Tholen
North Beveland
Walcheren
Middelburg
Goes
East Scheldt
BCR
Bergen op Zoom
Roosendaal
2ND CDN ARMD BDE
Wouwsche Plantage
29TH CDN ARMD R REGT
4TH CDN ARMD DIV
South Beveland
Flushing
Breskens
8TH RECCE
Woensdrecht
West Scheldt
Zeebrugge
Leopold Canal
Terneuzen
8TH CDN RECCE REGT
Merxplas
7TH CDN RECCE REGT
Canal de Dérivation
Kijkuit
Axel
NETHERLANDS
BELGIUM
22ND CDN ARMD REGT
Bruges
4TH CDN ARMD DIV
Eecloo
St. Paul
Antwerp
Canal
St. Nicolas
Albert Canal
Scheldt River
Ghent Canal
1ST POLISH ARMOURED DIV
Ghent

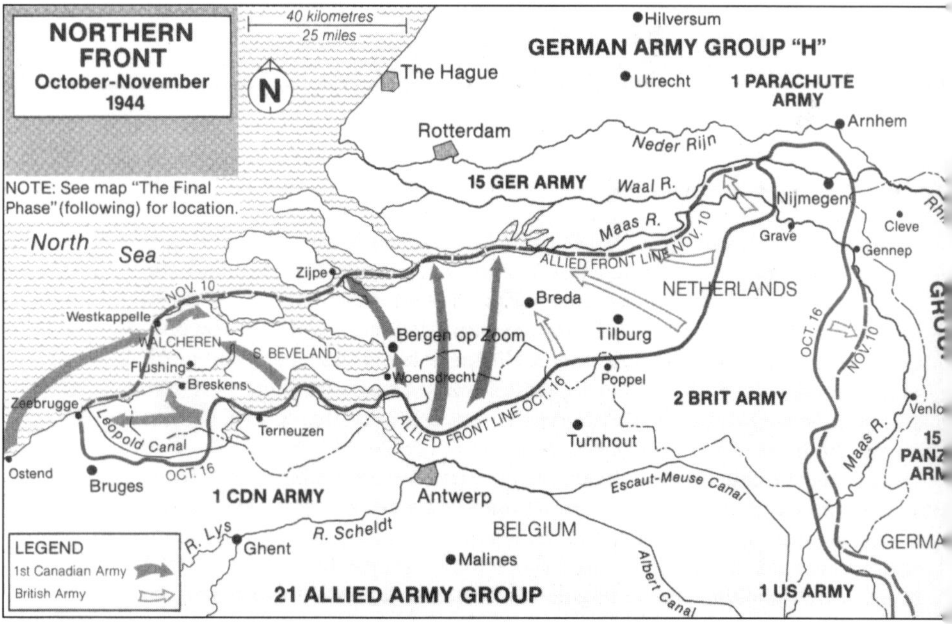
NORTHERN FRONT
October-November 1944
40 kilometres
25 miles
Hilversum
GERMAN ARMY GROUP "H"
The Hague
Utrecht
1 PARACHUTE ARMY
Arnhem
Rotterdam
Neder Rijn
15 GER ARMY
Waal R.
Nijmegen
NOTE: See map "The Final Phase" (following) for location.
North Sea
Maas R.
Grave
Cleve
Gennep
NOV. 10
ALLIED FRONT LINE NOV. 10
Zijpe
Breda
NETHERLANDS
Westkappelle
Bergen op Zoom
Tilburg
WALCHEREN
S. BEVELAND
OCT. 16
Flushing
Woensdrecht
Poppel
Breskens
2 BRIT ARMY
Zeebrugge
ALLIED FRONT LINE OCT. 16
Venlo
Terneuzen
Turnhout
Leopold Canal
Maas R.
Ostend
Bruges
OCT. 16
1 CDN ARMY
Antwerp
Escaut-Meuse Canal
R. Lys
R. Scheldt
BELGIUM
LEGEND
1st Canadian Army
British Army
Ghent
Malines
Albert Canal
21 ALLIED ARMY GROUP
1 US ARMY

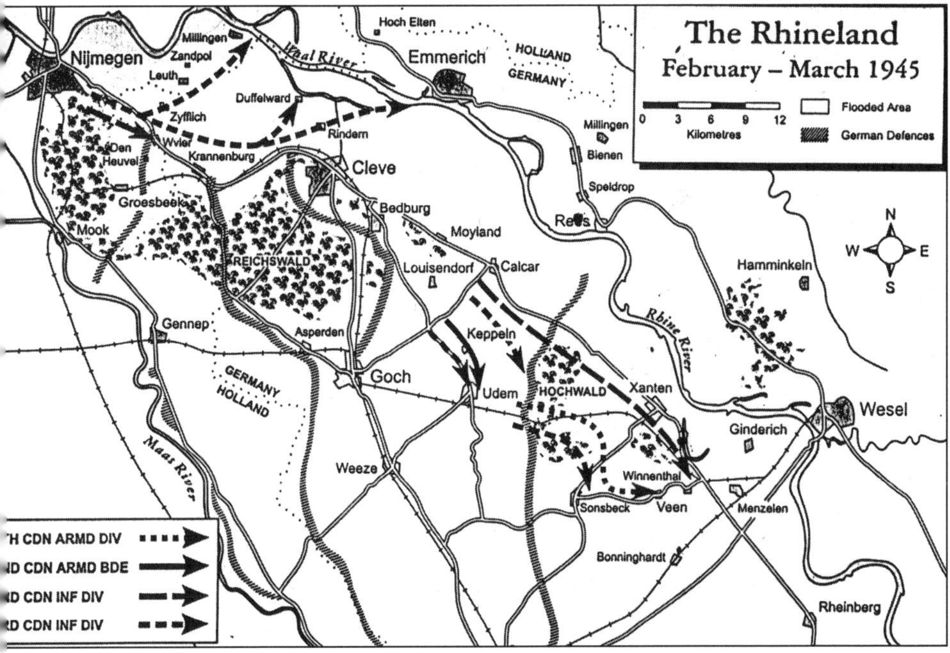
The Rhineland
February – March 1945
0 3 6 9 12
Kilometres
Flooded Area
German Defences
N
W
E
S
Nijmegen
Millingen
Zandpol
Leuth
Duffelward
Zyfflich
Wyler
Den Heuvel
Kranenburg
Rindern
Waal River
Hoch Elten
Emmerich
HOLLAND
GERMANY
Millingen
Bienen
Speldrop
Rees
Cleve
Bedburg
Moyland
Groesbeek
Mook
REICHSWALD
Louisendorf
Calcar
Hamminkeln
Gennep
Asperden
Keppeln
Rhine River
Goch
GERMANY
HOLLAND
Udem
HOCHWALD
Xanten
Wesel
Ginderich
Maas River
Weeze
Winnenthal
Sonsbeck
Veen
Menzelen
Bonninghardt
Rheinberg
TH CDN ARMD DIV
ND CDN ARMD BDE
ND CDN INF DIV
RD CDN INF DIV

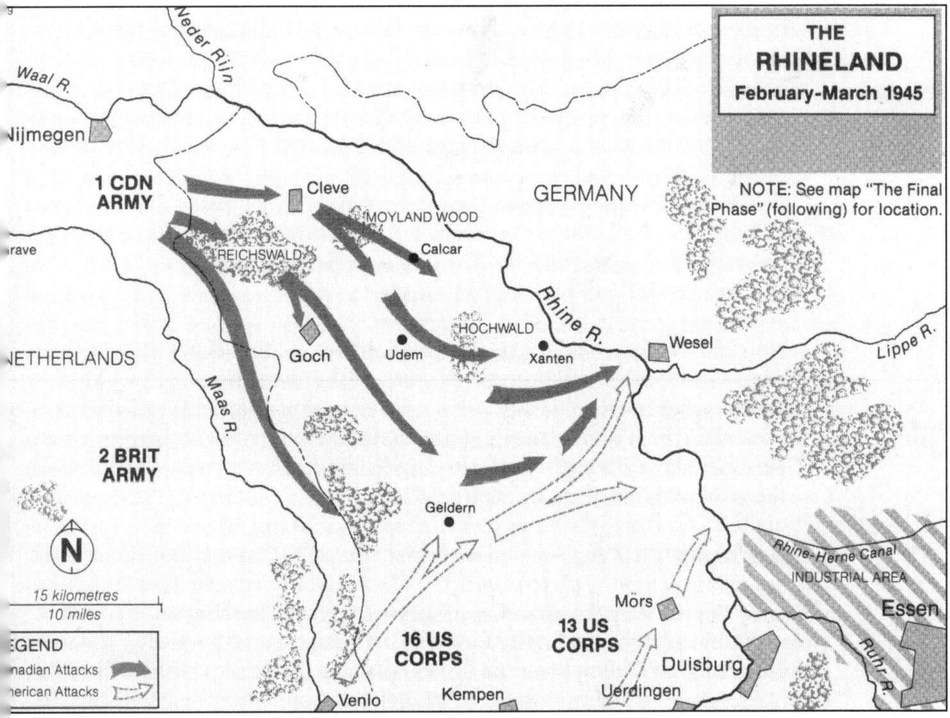
THE
RHINELAND
February-March 1945
NOTE: See map "The Final Phase" (following) for location.
Neder Rijn
Waal R.
Nijmegen
1 CDN
ARMY
Cleve
MOYLAND WOOD
Calcar
GERMANY
rave
REICHSWALD
Rhine R.
HOCHWALD
Udem
Xanten
Wesel
Goch
ETHERLANDS
Lippe R.
Maas R.
2 BRIT
ARMY
Geldern
Rhine-Herne Canal
INDUSTRIAL AREA
15 kilometres
10 miles
Mörs
Essen
EGEND
nadian Attacks
erican Attacks
16 US
CORPS
13 US
CORPS
Duisburg
Ruhr R.
Venlo
Kempen
Uerdingen

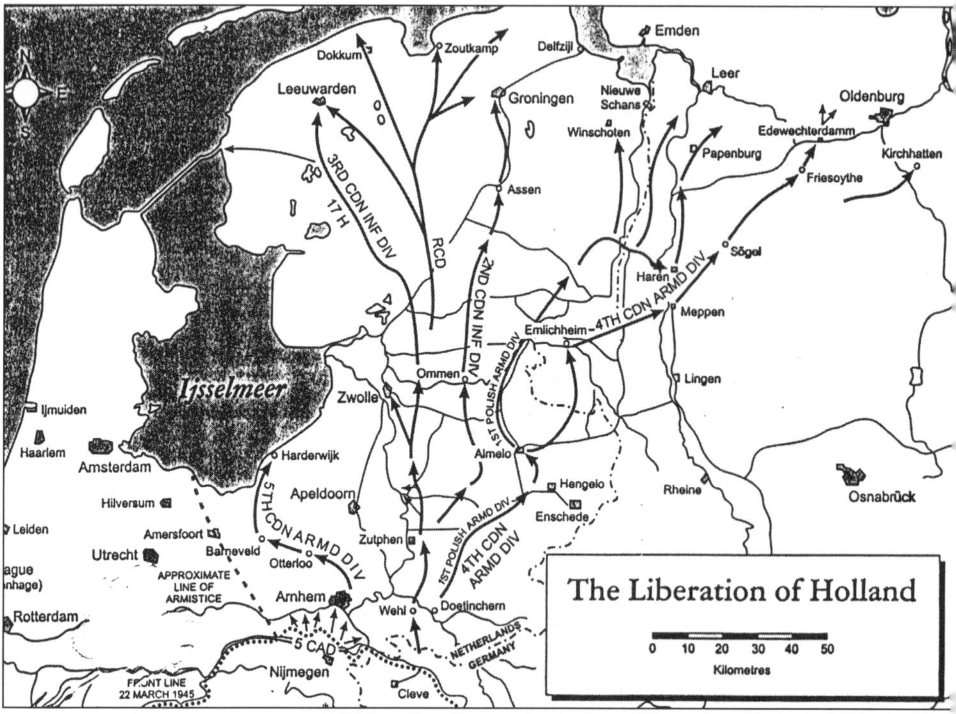
The Liberation of Holland
Emden
Leer
Oldenburg
Dokkum
Zoutkamp
Delfzijl
Leeuwarden
Groningen
Nieuwe Schans
Winschoten
Edewechterdamm
Papenburg
Kirchhatten
Friesoythe
Assen
3RD CDN INF DIV
17 H
RCD
2ND CDN INF DIV
Sögel
Haren
Meppen
Emlichheim
4TH CDN ARMD DIV
1ST POLISH ARMD DIV
Ommen
Lingen
Ijsselmeer
Zwolle
Ijmuiden
Haarlem
Amsterdam
Harderwijk
Almelo
Apeldoorn
Hengelo
Enschede
Rheine
Osnabrück
Hilversum
Leiden
Amersfoort
5TH CDN ARMD DIV
Zutphen
Utrecht
Barneveld
Otterloo
APPROXIMATE LINE OF ARMISTICE
Arnhem
Rotterdam
Wehl
Doetinchem
5 CAD
NETHERLANDS
GERMANY
Nijmegen
FRONT LINE 22 MARCH 1945
Cleve
0 10 20 30 40 50
Kilometres

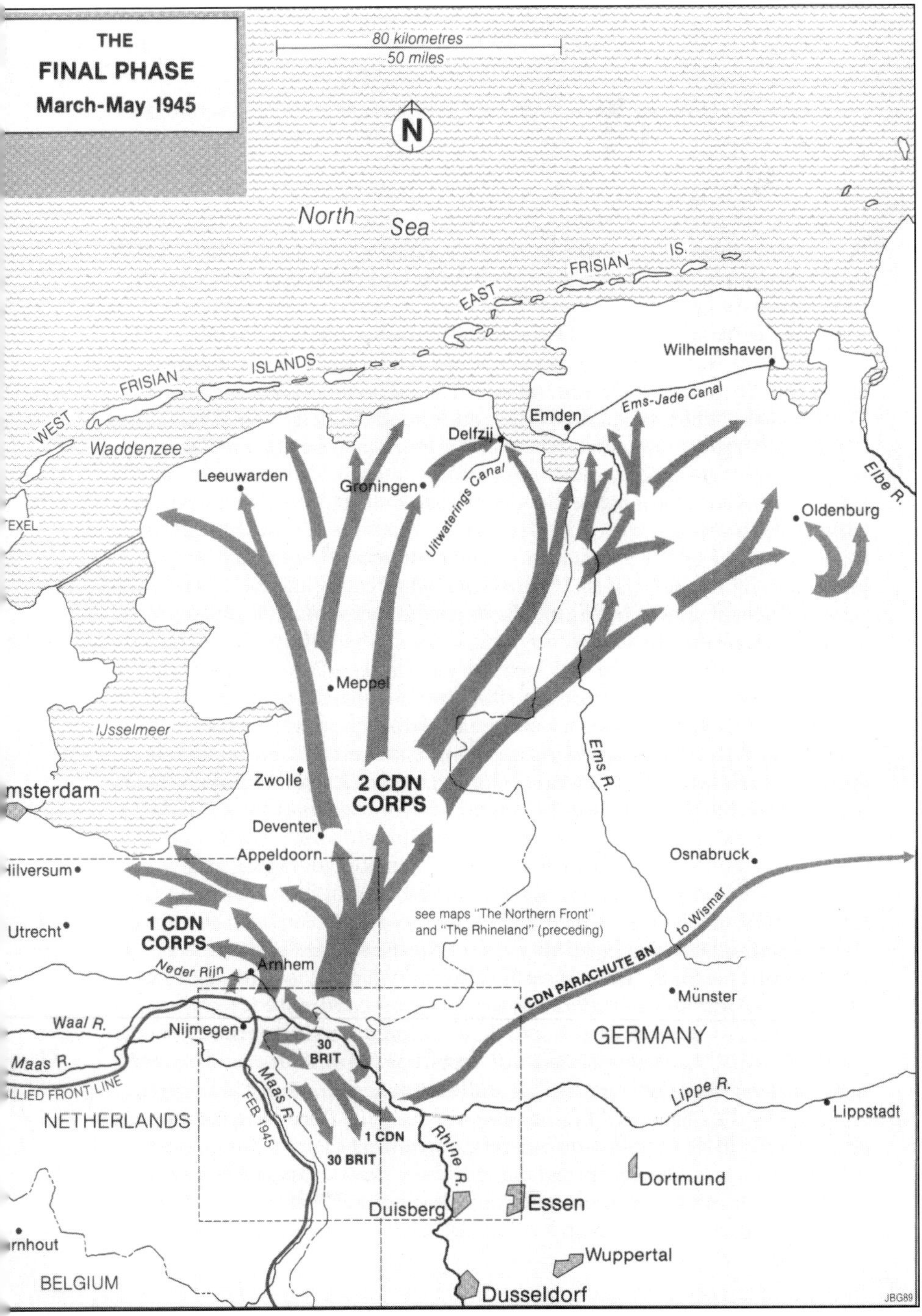
THE
FINAL PHASE
March-May 1945
80 kilometres
50 miles
N
North Sea
EAST FRISIAN IS.
WEST FRISIAN ISLANDS
Waddenzee
TEXEL
Wilhelmshaven
Ems-Jade Canal
Emden
Delfzij
Leeuwarden
Groningen
Uitwaterings Canal
Elbe R.
Oldenburg
Meppel
IJsselmeer
Ems R.
Zwolle
2 CDN CORPS
msterdam
Deventer
Appeldoorn
Osnabruck
Hilversum
Utrecht
1 CDN CORPS
see maps "The Northern Front" and "The Rhineland" (preceding)
to Wismar
1 CDN PARACHUTE BN
Neder Rijn
Arnhem
Münster
Waal R.
Nijmegen
GERMANY
Maas R.
30 BRIT
ALLIED FRONT LINE
Lippe R.
NETHERLANDS
FEB 1945
Maas R.
Lippstadt
1 CDN
30 BRIT
Rhine R.
Dortmund
Essen
Duisberg
Wuppertal
rnhout
BELGIUM
Dusseldorf
JBG89

CHINA
Chongjin
Yalu
N
W
E
S
Chosan
Chosin Reservoir
NORTH
Chongchon
Hungnam
Sea of Japan
KOREA
Tongjoson Bay
Sojoson Bay
Wonsan
Pyongyang
Imjin
Cease Fire Line July 1953
Sami-ch'on
Chorwon
38th Parallel
Kap'Yong
Seoul
Inchon
Han
Yellow Sea
SOUTH
Kum
Taejon
KOREA
Korea
1950 – 1954
0 40 80 120 160
Kilometres
Taegu
Pyongyong
Pusan
Mokpo

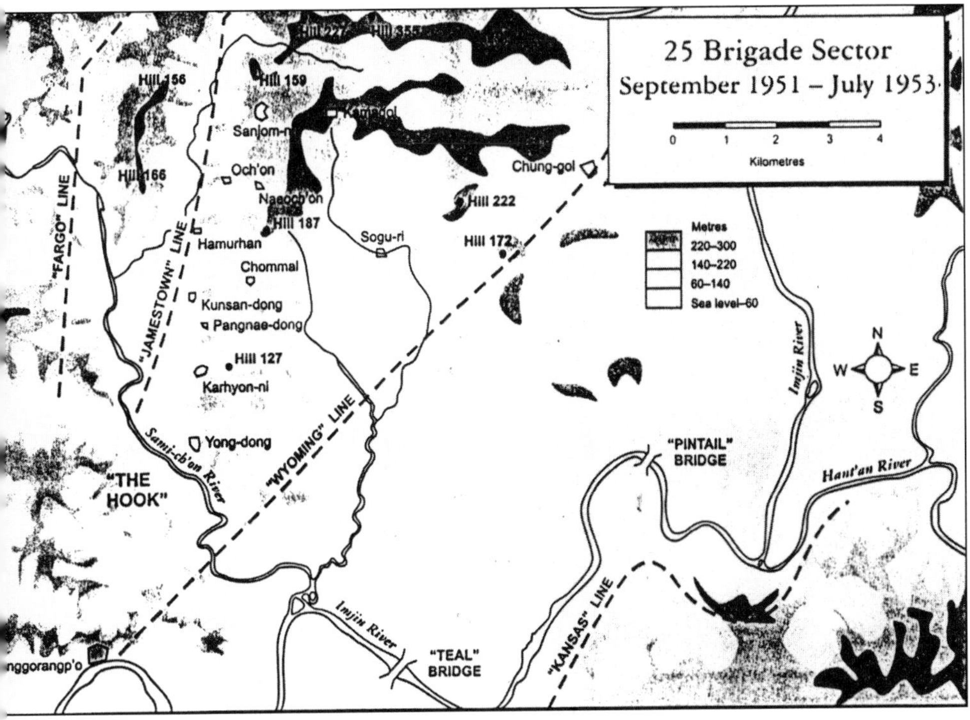
25 Brigade Sector
September 1951 – July 1953
0 1 2 3 4
Kilometres
Metres
220–300
140–220
60–140
Sea level–60
N
W
E
S
Hill 156
Hill 159
Hill 166
Sanjom-ni
Kamagol
Och'on
Chung-gol
Hill 222
Hill 187
Hamurhan
Sogu-ri
Hill 172
Chommal
Kunsan-dong
Pangnae-dong
Hill 127
Karhyon-ni
Yong-dong
"FARGO" LINE
"JAMESTOWN" LINE
"WYOMING" LINE
"KANSAS" LINE
Sami-ch'on River
"THE HOOK"
Imjin River
Hant'an River
"PINTAIL" BRIDGE
"TEAL" BRIDGE

Badges / Insignia

8th Reconnaissance Regiment

The Royal Canadian Army Service Corps

THE WHITE HORSE AT HANNOVER, 1945

Navigator's Wings

Observer's Wings

The Royal Canadian Ordnance Corps

Princess Patricia's Canadian Light Infantry

The Queen's Own Rifles of Canada

The Royal Canadian Regiment

The Three Rivers Regiment

The Royal Canadian Corps of Signals

The Royal Canadian Artillery

Battalion flag of the 1st Canadian Parachute Battalion, in which three members of Living History served.

Air Force Bombers / Fighter Escorts

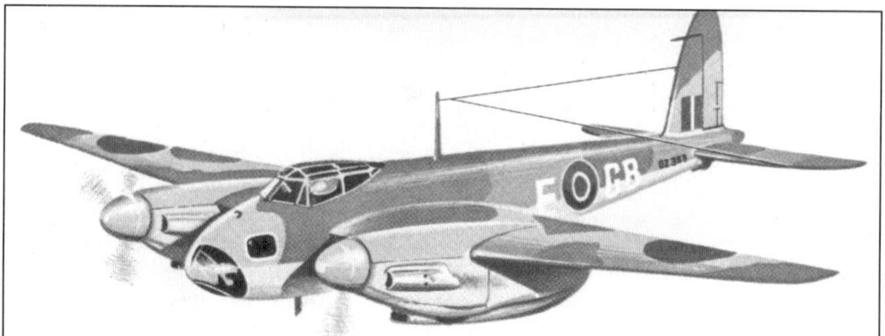

WW II, Navy Mural – HMCS Haida.

HMCS Uganda, Canada's largest naval craft, WW II.